GOD'S PASSION FOR HIS GLORY

GOD'S PASSION FOR HIS GLORY

Living the Vision of Jonathan Edwards

With the Complete Text of
The End for Which God Created the World

JOHN PIPER

CROSSWAY BOOKS

A PUBLISHING MINISTRY OF
GOOD NEWS PUBLISHERS
WHEATON, ILLINOIS

God's Passion for His Glory

Copyright © 1998 by John Piper

Published by Crossway Books
      A publishing ministry of Good News Publishers
      1300 Crescent Street
      Wheaton, Illinois 60187

Unless otherwise indicated, Bible quotations are taken from *The New American Standard Bible*, copyright © 1960, 1962, 1963, 1968, 1971, 1972, 1975, 1977, and 1995 by The Lockman Foundation, and are used by permission.

Cover design: D² DesignWorks

Cover Photo: Dale Sanders/Masterfile

First printing, 1998

First trade paper edition, 2006

Printed in the United States of America

Library of Congress Cataloging-in-Publication Data
Piper, John, 1946-
   God's passion for his glory : living the vision of Jonathan Edwards
with the complete text of "The end for which God created the world"
by Jonathan Edwards / John Piper.
     p.   cm.
   Includes bibliographical references and index.
   ISBN 13: 978-1-58134-745-6
   ISBN 10: 1-58134-745-6
   1. Edwards, Jonathan, 1703-1758. 2. Creation—History of
doctrines—18th century. 3. Glory of God—History of
doctrines—18th century. 4. Edwards, Jonathan, 1703-1758. End for
which God created the world. 5. Creation—Early works to 1800.
6. Glory of God—Early works to 1800.   I. Title.
BT695.P57   1998
231.7'65—dc21   98-19029

CH   15   14   13   12   11   10   09   08   07
14   13   12   11   10   9   8   7   6   5   4   3

The emanation or communication of the divine fullness, consisting in the knowledge of God, love to him, and joy in him, has relation indeed both to *God* and the *creature*: but it has relation to God as its *fountain*, as the thing communicated is something of its internal fullness. The water in the stream is something of the fountain; and the beams of the sun are something of the sun. And again, they have relation to God as their *object*: for the knowledge communicated is the knowledge of God; and the love communicated, is the love of God; and the happiness communicated, is joy in God. In the creature's knowing, esteeming, loving, rejoicing in, and praising God, the glory of God is both *exhibited* and *acknowledged*, his fullness is *received* and *returned*. Here is both an *emanation* and *remanation*. The refulgence shines upon and into the creature, and is reflected back to the luminary. The beams of glory come from God, are something of God, and are refunded back again to their original. So that the whole is *of* God, and *in* God, and *to* God; and he is the beginning, and the middle, and the end.

JONATHAN EDWARDS
The End for Which God Created the World

TABLE OF CONTENTS

OTHER BOOKS
BY THE AUTHOR

Love Your Enemies: Jesus' Love Command in the Synoptic Gospels and the Early Christian Paraenesis (Baker Book House, 1991, orig. 1979)

The Justification of God: An Exegetical and Theological Study of Romans 9:1-23; 2nd Edition (Baker Book House, 1993, orig. 1983)

The Supremacy of God in Preaching (Baker Book House, 1990)

The Pleasures of God: Meditations on God's Delight in Being God (Multnomah Press, 1991)

Recovering Biblical Manhood and Womanhood: A Response to Evangelical Feminism (edited with Wayne Grudem, Crossway Books, 1991)

What's the Difference: Manhood and Womanhood Defined According to the Bible (Crossway Books, 1991)

Let the Nations Be Glad: The Supremacy of God in Missions (Baker Book House, 1993)

The Purifying Power of Living by Faith in Future Grace (Multnomah Press, 1995)

Desiring God: Meditations of a Christian Hedonist (Multnomah Press, revised 1996)

A Hunger for God: Desiring God through Fasting and Prayer (Crossway Books, 1997)

A Godward Life: Savoring the Supremacy of God in All of Life (Multnomah Press, 1997)

PREFACE

The longer I live, the more clearly I see my dependence on those who have gone before. The more I know of what others have thought, the less original my thinking appears. I am content to have it so. For, at least in the realm of truth, the ancient Preacher does not overstate the case when he says: "There is nothing new under the sun" (Ecclesiastes 1:9).

This book is witness to my calling as a secondary teacher, not a primary one. Jonathan Edwards is a primary teacher in the Christian church; I am secondary. The difference was described by Mortimer Adler in 1939:

> [The secondary teacher] should regard himself as learning from the masters along with his [students]. He should not act as if he were a primary teacher, using a great book as if it were just another textbook of the sort one of his colleagues might write. He should not masquerade as one who knows and can teach by virtue of his original discoveries. . . . The primary sources of his own knowledge should be the primary sources of learning for his students, and such a teacher functions honestly only if he does not aggrandize himself by coming between the great books and their . . . readers. He should not "come between" as a nonconductor, but he should come between as a mediator—as one who helps the less competent make more effective contacts with the best minds.[1]

This is the role I want to play in relation to Jonathan Edwards and his book,[2] *The End for Which God Created the World*. Jonathan Edwards is in a class by himself in American history, perhaps in the history of Christendom. This will become plain in the pages that follow. Paul Ramsey, the editor of Edwards's *Ethical Writings*

---

[1] Mortimer Adler, *How to Read a Book* (New York: Simon and Schuster, 1940), p. 60.

[2] Strictly speaking, *The End for Which God Created the World* is half a book, since it was originally published in 1765 (seven years after Edwards's death) as the first of a pair of treatises entitled *Two Dissertations*. The other of the two was *The Nature of True Virtue*. Edwards saw the two as a pair and envisioned them published together. See Part One, Chapter One, footnote 3, p. 22 for why I believe publishing *The End for Which God Created the World* alone is warranted.

in the Yale critical edition, agrees: "One studies the time and back-
grounds of some men in order to understand them. Others have
such rare greatness that one studies them in order to understand
their times, or even to comprehend the deepest meaning of the
intellectual and other influences that were effectual upon them.
Jonathan Edwards was such an original."[3] It is not so much that
Edwards dealt with new reality but, as Vergilius Ferm said, he
"seemed to have had the powers and the drive to set his own stamp
upon anything which came to his purview."[4]

But even more important than making all things his own in
unique ways was his riveted focus on God, and his unwavering
passion to see all that could be seen of God in this life. "To live
with all my might, while I do live"[5] was his resolution. He applied
it mainly to the pursuit of God. Thus he resolved again, "When I
think of any theorem in divinity to be solved, immediately to do
what I can towards solving it, if circumstances do not hinder." The
channel where this passion for God flowed was the channel of
unremitting, prayerful thinking on the truths of Scripture. Hence
he resolved once more "to study the Scriptures so steadily, constantly, and frequently, as that I may find, and plainly perceive,
myself to grow in the knowledge of the same."

Which means in the end that Edwards too was a secondary
teacher—as are all honest Christian pastors and theologians. "He
was a man who put faithfulness to the Word of God before every
other consideration."[6] Seeing the unlimited expanse of divine
Reality that is really there in Scripture, not imagining new things,
was his passion. Over every vast field of divine knowledge
Edwards erected this banner: "I think the Word of God teaches us
more things concerning it . . . than has been generally believed, and
that it exhibits many things concerning it exceeding glorious and

---

[3] Paul Ramsey, "Editor's Introduction" to *The Ethical Writings*, *The Works of Jonathan Edwards*, vol. 8 (New Haven: Yale University Press, 1989), p. 12.

[4] Vergilius Ferm, *Puritan Sage* (New York: Library Publishers, 1953), p. xiv.

[5] The seventy resolutions of the young Edwards are found in Sereno Dwight, *Memoirs of Jonathan Edwards*, in: *The Works of Jonathan Edwards*, vol. 1 (Edinburgh: The Banner of Truth Trust, 1974), pp. xx-xxi.

[6] Iain Murray, *Jonathan Edwards, A New Biography* (Edinburgh: The Banner of Truth Trust, 1987) p. 471. If the reader desires a good starting point in the study of the life and ministry of Jonathan Edwards, I recommend this biography very highly.

wonderful than have been taken notice of."[7] In simple modern English: we have scarcely begun to see all of God that the Scriptures give us to see, and what we have not yet seen is exceedingly glorious.

Thus, in the most profound sense we are all secondary teachers and secondary beings. Only One is Primary. Why he created us, and how to join him in fulfilling that end, are the most important questions in the world. Only he can reveal the answer. That is why Jonathan Edwards gave himself to the Word of God and wrote *The End for Which God Created the World* (printed as Part Two of this book), and that is why I take my stand on his shoulders and write about *God's Passion for His Glory*.

For over thirty years I have been trying to see and savor this God-centered, soul-satisfying, sin-destroying vision of reality. Part One of this book is a focused glimpse into the roots of this vision as I have come to see it in the life and thought of Jonathan Edwards. In the vein of other concerned evangelicals in our day,[8] Chapter One argues that modern evangelicalism is being doctrinally hollowed out by its love affair with pragmatism and numerical success. Edwards's relentless God-centeredness and devotion to the Biblical contours of doctrine are profoundly needed in our day. In the second half of that chapter I offer fifteen summary statements of the implications of Edwards's vision for Christian thought and life.

In Chapter Two the reader is given a mini-biography of Edwards. It's a story that enables the reader to enjoy the man, and see his theology in the flow of his life and ministry. It puts flesh on the theological bones. Here you may meet "one of the most holy, humble and heavenly-minded men, that the world has seen, since the apostolic age" (Ashbel Green, President of the College of New

---

[7] Jonathan Edwards, *An Essay on the Trinity*, in: *Treatise on Grace and Other Posthumously Published Writings*, ed. by Paul Helm (Cambridge: James Clarke and Co. Ltd., 1971), pp. 127-128.

[8] For example, Os Guinness, *Fit Bodies Fat Minds: Why Evangelicals Don't Think and What to Do About It* (Grand Rapids: Baker Books, 1994); Os Guinness and John Seel, eds., *No God But God: Breaking with the Idols of Our Age* (Chicago: Moody Press, 1992); Mark Noll, *The Scandal of the Evangelical Mind* (Grand Rapids: William B. Eerdmans Publishing Co., 1994); David Wells, *No Place for Truth: or Whatever Happened to Evangelical Theology?* (Grand Rapids: William B. Eerdmans Publishing Co., 1993); *God in the Wasteland: The Reality of Truth in a World of Fading Dreams* (Grand Rapids, William B. Eerdmans Publishing Co., 1994); *Losing Our Virtue: Why the Church Must Recover Its Moral Vision* (Grand Rapids: William B. Eerdmans Publishing Co., 1998), p. 26.

Jersey, 1829), but also "the profoundest reasoner, and the greatest divine . . . that America ever produced" (Samuel Davies, 1759)—a man who was "greatest in his attribute of regnant permeating, irradiating spirituality" (John De Witt, 1912).[9]

In Chapter Three I take the reader on a personal tour along my thirty-year path of discovering the major writings of Jonathan Edwards. In this way I try to combine my own personal story with the life and writings of Edwards to show their meaning and relevance for at least one modern evangelical. My hope is that you will see at work in this chapter not just one, but two illustrations—one living and one dead—of "A Mind in Love with God."

Finally, in Chapter Four, I take up Edwards's radically God-centered view of virtue—which is, in fact, the end for which God created the world—and apply its scathing relevance to cultural transformation and world evangelization. The rediscovery of Edwards's God-centered moral vision in *The End for Which God Created the World* is my aim. And I pray that this endeavor will serve the purpose of God in our day to fill the hollow sounds of our God-neglect and its fatal successes. May the Lord restore a passion for truth and a passion for his glory, which has largely "disappeared from the modern evangelical world."[10]

---

[9] These quotes are taken from Iain Murray, *Jonathan Edwards, A New Biography* (Edinburgh: The Banner of Truth Trust, 1989), pp. vx-vxii.

[10] "It is this God, majestic and holy in his being, this God whose love knows no bounds because his holiness knows no limits, who has disappeared from the modern evangelical world" (David Wells, *No Place for Truth*, p. 300).

ACKNOWLEDGMENTS

God's gifts in this project have been many. Eric Johnson, Professor of Interdisciplinary Studies at Northwestern College (St. Paul, Minnesota), believed that Jonathan Edwards's *The End for Which God Created the World* was worthy of publication because of its God-centered vision of reality. He encouraged me all along the way and said he hoped to use the book as part of his curriculum in helping students grasp the supremacy of God in *all* of their studies. Not only that, he worked through the complex thought of Edwards's entire book twice, seeking the best way to handle its eighteenth-century features for the sake of modern readers. If more changes were not made to the original (see "Concerning the Text", pp. 121-123), chalk it up to my stubborn commitment to stay close to Edwards's own wording. Thank you, Eric, for your gentle and unwavering allegiance to the supremacy of God in all branches of learning and life.

The hard work of getting the actual words of Edwards from the Edward Hickman 1834 edition into electronic form for editing was done by Debra Lacher, whose work was as near to flawless as a human being this side of heaven can make it. I was simply amazed as I worked my way through it making comparisons with other editions. Thank you, Deb, for your love of the truth and the glory of God, and for channeling that love through the remarkable gifts God has given you for the sake of God's people.

The actual edition of Edwards's *The End for Which God Created the World* on which we leaned was The Banner of Truth republication of the Hickman edition (Edinburgh, 1974). Thanks to Mervyn T. Barter, General Manager of The Banner of Truth Trust, and the other members of the Trust for giving us permission to stand on your publishing shoulders. Your two-volume *Works of Jonathan Edwards* continues to serve the cause of Christ in extraordinary ways. I thank God that you keep it in print.

Thanks to Pedro Govantes, President of The Jonathan Edwards Institute, for inviting me to address the annual conference of the

Institute in the summer of 1997. Chapters Three and Four of this book are adapted from those two lectures. It was an honor to be associated with an Institute devoted to exalting the God of Jonathan Edwards. In addition, thanks to the former editors of *The Reformed Journal* (November, 1978, Vol. 28, Issue 11, pp. 13-17) where some of the material in Chapters Two and Three was first published.

The final preparation of this work was done during a four-week writing leave that I was generously given by my fellow elders of Bethlehem Baptist Church, Minneapolis, Minnesota. I do not take this for granted, because all the staff and elders bear a greater load when one of us is not there. Thanks to all of you for loving what this book is about enough to rejoice in my being away—and for wanting me back.

I have in my library a photocopy of *The End for Which God Created the World* from an old edition that I bought during seminary days. It is now triple-marked in different colors, with worshipful slashes, checks and asterisks scattered throughout. I owe the purchase of this copy, and my introduction to the theology of Jonathan Edwards, to Daniel Fuller, who led me into the truth, not through the door of the eighteenth century, but through the first-century door of Romans and Galatians and The Sermon on the Mount, and tied it all together in the final class called The Unity of the Bible.[1] The severe discipline of exegesis, proposition by proposition, sentence-diagram by sentence-diagram, and arc by arc, opened a window on a world of glory that has never been shut. Thank you again, Dan. The debt will never be repaid.

Rick Gamache tracked down obscure references for me and gave my four chapters such a careful reading that I was spared mistakes that three other readers did not catch. Carol Steinbach stands ever ready to help me make every book as useful as possible by creating indexes. I'm a stickler for indexes for one simple reason: I want to know where the things are that I have written. Where is that great quote by Mark Noll? Just look up Noll in the index, and I have it! Carol and I assume a few others might want to do the same. Hence the labor of indexing. Thanks again, Carol.

---

[1] See the published fruit of that class in Daniel Fuller, *The Unity of the Bible: Unfolding God's Plan for Humanity* (Grand Rapids: Zondervan Publishing House, 1992).

What I owe to Jonathan Edwards is expressed in part by the existence of this book. My "personal encounter" with him has been a thirty-year-long journey into some very high places. He may not have been the ideal pastor, since he studied too much and mingled too little. But for all that, he has been a pastor to many of us hungry shepherds. And because of that I am sure the disgruntled saints of Northampton have long since forgiven him.

The same thirty years have been spent in marriage to you, Noël. You have read and shaped every book I have written. I am thankful for every one of the ten thousand suggestions you have made—even the ones I declined. You have gotten your Edwards distilled (imperfectly, I am sure) through your husband's theological brewing. I do not doubt that, under God's incomparable grace, this is one reason that we have an "uncommon union."

PART ONE

A PERSONAL ENCOUNTER WITH JONATHAN EDWARDS

by John Piper

No man is more relevant to the present condition of Christianity than Jonathan Edwards.

D. MARTYN LLOYD-JONES
The Puritan Experiment in the New World

Edwards's *piety* continued on in the revivalist tradition, his *theology* continued on in academic Calvinism, but there were no successors to his God-entranced world-view or his profoundly theological philosophy. The disappearance of Edwards's perspective in American Christian history has been a tragedy.

MARK NOLL
"Jonathan Edwards's Moral Philosophy,
and the Secularization of American Christian Thought"
in *The Reformed Journal*

It is my belief that the prayers and work of those who love and obey Christ in our world may yet prevail as they keep the message of such a man as Jonathan Edwards.

CHARLES COLSON
"Introduction"
to Jonathan Edwards's *Religious Affections*

The happiness of the creature consists in rejoicing in God, by which also God is magnified and exalted.

JONATHAN EDWARDS
The End for Which God Created the World

The End for Which God Created the World [is] . . . unsurpassed in terms of its theological grandeur.

DAVID BRAND
Profile of the Last Puritan

THE END FOR WHICH GOD CREATED THE WORLD

WHY PUBLISH AN OLD BOOK?

A Personal and Public Concern

The message of Jonathan Edwards in *The End for Which God Created the World* is an intensely personal concern for me and a word of great public significance. In that book, a vision of God is displayed that took me captive thirty years ago and has put its stamp on every part of my life and ministry. But, more important than my own experience, is the immense significance of Edwards's vision of God for the wider public of our day.

<hr>

SECTION ONE

<hr>

An American Tragedy

Jonathan Edwards is one of the great fathers of evangelical Christianity in America. But it is a great tragedy, as Mark Noll observes, that "the theocentric emphasis of Edwards has played a remarkably small role in the history of evangelical Protestants."[1] There are reasons for this. Partly it is because our whole culture is

<hr>

[1] Mark Noll, "God at the Center: Jonathan Edwards on True Virtue," *Christian Century*, September 8-15, 1993, p. 857.

inhospitable to such a radically God-centered vision of life. Noll argues that since Edwards's day 250 years ago,

> evangelicals have not thought about life from the ground up as Christians, because their entire culture has ceased to do so. Edwards's *piety* continued on in the revivalist tradition, his *theology* continued on in academic Calvinism, but there were no successors to his God-entranced worldview or his profoundly theological philosophy. The disappearance of Edwards's perspective in American Christian history has been a tragedy.[2]

Unsurpassed in Theological Grandeur

This is why the publication of *The End for Which God Created the World* is a cultural, religious, and evangelical concern. Edwards's book (together with *True Virtue*[3]), Noll suggests, is "perhaps the best place to encounter both the breathtaking vision of divine glory and the human strain required to take in that vision."[4] I agree. So does David Brand in his book, *Profile of the Last Puritan. The End for Which God Created the World*, he says,

---

[2] Mark Noll, "Jonathan Edwards's Moral Philosophy, and the Secularization of American Christian Thought," *Reformed Journal*, February, 1983, p. 26. Noll, who teaches at Wheaton College, summarized Edwards's unusual juxtapositions in another place: "Although his biography presents many dramatic contrasts, these were in reality only different facets of a common allegiance to a sovereign God. Thus, Edwards both preached ferocious hell-fire sermons and expressed lyrical appreciations of nature because the God who created the world in all its beauty was also perfect in holiness. Edwards combined herculean intellectual labors with child-like piety because he perceived God as both infinitely complex and blissfully simple. In his Northampton church his consistent exaltation of divine majesty led to very different results—he was first lionized as a great leader and then dismissed from his pulpit. Edwards held that the omnipotent deity required repentance and faith from his human creatures so he proclaimed both the absolute sovereignty of God and the urgent responsibilities of men" (Caption under Edwards's portrait in *Christian History*, vol. iv, no. 4, p. 3).

[3] *The End for Which God Created the World* and *The Nature of True Virtue* were intended by Edwards to be published together. See Part Two, footnote 53, and Preface footnote 3. In spite of Edwards's intention that the *Two Dissertations* (the title given to the first edition in 1765) go together, there is little doubt that they *are* two and not one. Therefore I have felt free to publish *The End for Which God Created the World* on its own, especially in view of several other factors. For example, most criticism has been leveled against reading *True Virtue* without reading *The End* rather than vice versa, because *True Virtue* does not deal with Scripture, and some have argued that Edwards moved away from his Biblical base into a mere philosophical concern. The answer to this is that his Scripture argumentation was provided in Part Two of *The End for Which God Created the World* and is presupposed in *True Virtue*. Not only that, the main point of *True Virtue* is essentially contained in *The End for Which God Created the World*. Finally, *True Virtue* has already been published in a single volume, so that the need to make it accessible is not so great. *The Nature of True Virtue*, ed. by William Frankena (Ann Arbor, MI: The University of Michigan Press, 1960). Of course both treatises are available in the more expensive Banner of Truth edition (vol. 1) and Yale edition (vol. 8) of *The Works of Jonathan Edwards*.

[4] "God at the Center," p. 858.

is "a work which I have come to regard as unsurpassed in terms of its theological grandeur."[5]

My prayer is that the evangelical church today would stand in awe of the "breath-taking vision of divine glory" declared with "theological grandeur" in *The End for Which God Created the World*. This is one reason why I have undertaken to publish the book below on pages 115-251.

Hard and Helpful for Impatient Pragmatists

The difficulties that stand in the way of seeing this vision are daunting, but hopeful. They are daunting because, as Noll hinted, "the human strain required to take in that vision" is immense. The book is hard to read. It was hard to read in its own day[6] and it is harder today. Americans, as a whole (and evangelicals are little different in this), are not given to thinking much, let alone thinking at the level Edwards demands of us. This is especially true about doctrine. We are pragmatic. We demand quick solutions. We define success in measurable quantities. We have little patience with doctrinal precision. And we pastors who are infected with the pragmatic virus tend to justify our indifference to doctrine mainly by the fact that such reflection is not what the audience is looking for. Besides, it is stressful for relationships.

The recent lamentations[7] over the drift of evangelicalism into pragmatic, doctrinally vague, audience-driven, culturally uncritical Christianity are, in my judgment, warranted and needed, in spite of the fact that, at the level of professional scholarship, there have been remarkable advances in the last fifty years.[8] As a whole, and in the dominant shaping forces of evangelicalism, the criticism

---

[5] *Profile of the Last Puritan: Jonathan Edwards, Self-Love, and the Dawn of the Beatific* (Atlanta: Scholars Press, 1991), p. x.

[6] The original preface in the 1765 edition says, "Some readers may find the labor hard to keep pace with the writer, in the advances he makes, when the ascent is arduous." *Two Dissertations*, in *Ethical Writings*, ed. by Paul Ramsey, *The Works of Jonathan Edwards*, vol. 8 (New Haven: Yale University Press, 1989), p. 402.

[7] This view of the state of thinking in evangelicalism is laid out in Os Guinness, *Fit Bodies Fat Minds: Why Evangelicals Don't Think and What to Do about It* (Grand Rapids: Baker Books, 1994), Mark Noll, *The Scandal of the Evangelical Mind* (Grand Rapids: William B. Eerdmans Publishing Co., 1994), David Wells, *No Place for Truth: or Whatever Happened to Evangelical Theology?* (Grand Rapids: William B. Eerdmans Publishing Co., 1993).

[8] For a balancing, more positive, portrait of evangelicalism see Alister McGrath, *Evangelicalism and the Future of Christianity* (Downers Grove, IL: InterVarsity Press, 1995).

of Harry Blamires in 1963 is probably more true than ever: "There is no Christian Mind. . . . The Christian Mind has succumbed to the secular drift with a degree of weakness unmatched in Christian History."[9]

The increasing abandonment of truth and moral absolutes[10] in our culture, as militant diversity threatens all firm conviction, has dramatically influenced the evangelical mindset. The political spin doctors who specialize in deflecting attention away from truth onto feelings and relationships and styles have their counterpart in the evangelical tendency to avoid doctrinal disputes by casting issues in terms of demeanor and method rather than truth. Serious disagreements are covered over, while vague language and pragmatic concerns preserve hollow unity at the expense of theological substance and Biblical clarity and power.

A Voice of Lament from Sri Lanka

The lament over the pragmatic hollowing out of evangelical conviction may be felt with unusual poignancy when it comes, not just from the intellectual elite, but from a person like Ajith Fernando, who leads Youth for Christ in Sri Lanka. He not only delivers solid exposition around the world, but also works among the poor and has wept over the horrors of 50,000 casualties of insurgency in one year of Sri Lanka's unrest. That was 1989, and he says, simply, "I struggled much with despair that year."[11]

His strength, he says, came from the truth, and in that context he laments what he sees happening in the West: "A major shift . . . has taken place in western evangelicalism where truth has been replaced by pragmatism as the major influencer of thought and life. This path is suicidal." He is heartened that voices are being raised, but then he says, "However, I feel that many evangelical leaders are so caught up in and blinded by this bondage to pragmatism that even though they may heartily endorse pleas to return to

---

[9] Harry Blamires, *The Christian Mind* (London: SPCK, 1963), pp. vii, 3.

[10] David Wells records in 1998 that 67% of Americans do not believe in moral absolutes and 70% do not believe in absolute truth—truth that should be believed by all people in all places and all times. David Wells, *Losing Our Virtue: Why the Church Must Recover Its Moral Vision* (Grand Rapids: William B. Eerdmans Publishing Co., 1998), p. 26.

[11] Ajith Fernando, *The Supremacy of Christ* (Wheaton, IL: Crossway Books, 1995), p. 117.

greater dependence on truth, endorsements make minimal inroads into their ministry styles and strategies."[12] There is simply too little patience with the particularities of Biblical propositions that embody precious, life-sustaining doctrine.

So Much of Man, So Little of God

Jonathan Edwards had a profound insight into this very state of affairs, and it has to do directly with the absence of God-centeredness: "It is one great reason why speculative points [of doctrine] are thought to be of so little importance, that the modern religion consists so little in respect to the divine Being, and almost wholly in benevolence to men."[13] In other words, the sickness that needs healing is the main hindrance to the remedy.

This means that Jonathan Edwards's "grand style of feeling and thinking is not ours and is alien to our way of life."[14] Edwards's utter seriousness—his "blood-earnestness," as Thomas Chalmers called it—puts him out of sync with our chatty, humorous, entertainment-oriented, cartoon-illustrated spirituality.[15] Edwards's sense of the desperate condition of mankind without God is so weighty that it takes our breath away. H. Richard Niebuhr commented that Edwards's awareness of the precariousness of life put him in a rare class: "He recognized what Kierkegaard meant when he described life as treading water with ten thousand fathoms beneath us."[16]

---

[12] The Supremacy of Christ, pp. 112-113. From another standpoint, Henri Nouwen, the popular Catholic writer on spirituality, gave a similar critique of the wider religious scene. "Few ministers and priests think theologically. Most of them have been educated in a climate in which the behavioral sciences, such as psychology and sociology, so dominated the educational milieu that no true theology was being learned. Most Christian leaders today raise psychological and sociological questions even though they frame them in scriptural terms. Real theological thinking, which is thinking with the mind of Christ, is hard to find in the practice of ministry. Without solid theological reflection, future leaders will be little more than pseudo-psychologists, pseudo-sociologists, pseudo-social workers. They will think of themselves as enablers, facilitators, role models, father or mother figures, big brothers or big sisters, and so on, and thus join the countless men and women trying to help their fellow human beings to cope with the stresses and strains of everyday living. But that has little to do with Christian leadership." Henri Nouwen, In the Name of Jesus (New York: Crossroad, 1993), pp. 65-66.

[13] Quoted in Perry Miller, Jonathan Edwards (Westport, CT: Greenwood Press, Publishers, 1949), p.118.

[14] Joseph Haroutunian, "Preface" to The Philosophical Theology of Jonathan Edwards, by Douglas J. Elwood (New York: Columbia University Press, 1960), p. x.

[15] J. W. Alexander, Thoughts on Preaching (Edinburgh: The Banner of Truth Trust), p. 264.

[16] Quoted in Douglas J. Elwood, The Philosophical Theology of Jonathan Edwards (New York: Columbia University Press, 1960), p. 4.

We Need So Much More Than Benjamin Franklin

But at this very point the daunting difficulties in seeing Edwards's great vision of God may give way to hope. It may be that the theological impoverishment of the American church, and the precariousness of life, and the weariness with "successful" superficiality will make the voice of Jonathan Edwards more compelling than he has been for centuries.

Several others have held out this hope as they have contrasted the influence of Edwards and his contemporary Benjamin Franklin. Randall Stewart argues that

> Franklin started us on the road which has led to a gadgeteers' paradise. But now that it is becoming startlingly clear that gadgets can't save us, and may all too readily destroy us . . . now that Dr. Franklin's lightning rod begins to look, from one viewpoint, like a pathetic symbol of human pride and inadequacy, while Edwards's soul-probings seem more searching to this generation of readers perhaps than they have ever seemed before, it is possible that Edwards will yet emerge, is already emerging, as the more useful, the more truly helpful, of the two.[17]

Perry Miller, who professed no share in Edwards's faith, had a similar view of our condition: "[Edwards] is a reminder that, although our civilization has chosen to wander in the more genial meadows to which Franklin beckoned it, there come periods, either through disaster or through self-knowledge, when applied science and Benjamin Franklin's *The Way to Wealth* seem not a sufficient philosophy of national life."[18] That statement, made in 1949, seems to me like a thunderous understatement as the century closes. Franklin's pragmatism is theologically, morally, and spiritually bankrupt. That very cultural bankruptcy may awaken evangelicals from the folly of imitation.

Edwards vs. "Enlightened Human Intelligence"

In the heyday of nineteenth-century optimism, Oliver Wendell Holmes scoffed at Edwards's convictions as

---

[17] Randall Stewart, *American Literature and Christian Doctrine* (Baton Rouge: Louisiana State University Press, 1958), p. 34.

[18] Perry Miller, *Jonathan Edwards*, p. xiii.

not only false, not only absurd, but . . . *disorganizing forces* in the midst of the thinking apparatus. Edwards's system seems, in the light of today, to the last degree barbaric, mechanical, materialistic, pessimistic. If he had lived a hundred years later, and breathed the air of freedom, he could not have written with such old-world barbarism. . . . The truth is that [his] whole system of beliefs . . . is gently fading out of enlightened human intelligence, and we are hardly in a condition to realize what a tyranny it once exerted over many of the strongest minds.[19]

Edwards's vision has not faded. It is being recovered and reconsidered more extensively and with more vigor today, perhaps, than at any time since his own day.[20] The reason Oliver Wendell Holmes wrote him off, and the reason there is hope that we may not, is that our century has shown Holmes's "enlightened human intelligence" to be the factory of the greatest global evils ever perpetrated in human history. Mark Noll comments, "Since most of the 20th century has been such a [dark] period, we may be in a position to hear Edwards more clearly than was the progressive generation of Holmes."[21] In other words, in this case, the disease may make the remedy intelligible.

C. S. Lewis on the Necessity of Old Books

C. S. Lewis points to another reason we might see our darkening days as a hopeful opening to Edwards's *End for Which God Created the World*. Lewis was born in 1898 and died the same day as John F. Kennedy in 1963. His life was virtually coextensive with the twentieth century up to that point. From that perspective he

---

[19] Quoted in Mark Noll, "God at the Center," p. 856.

[20] "Interest in Edwards—and especially his theology—may be higher now than it ever has been, even in his own day. Edwards's biographer, M. X. Lesser, has estimated that the number of academic dissertations on Edwards has doubled every decade over the last forty years. The three-volume *Encyclopedia of the American Religious Experience*, published by Scribner's in 1988, contains far more references to Edwards than to any other single figure" (Mark Noll, "God at the Center," p. 857). How fickle history is in her judgments may be seen from the fact that when Samuel Hopkins, Edwards's friend, published the *Two Dissertations* in 1765, as well as some sermons and his own *Life of Edwards*, the response was so poor that he gave up publishing more of Edwards's works and his *Life of Edwards* was not sought out in America for another forty years. Murray comments: "Edwards was not regarded in his own age, in his own country, with the general esteem which he received at a later period" (Iain Murray, *Jonathan Edwards*, p. 449).

[21] "God at the Center," p. 856.

said, "I have lived nearly sixty years with myself and my own century and am not so enamoured of either as to desire no glimpse of a world beyond them."[22] Yes, and if he had lived to the end of the century, he would have been even less enamored of his own century than at the halfway mark.

From this Lewis goes on to stress that he wants and needs to read books from outside his own century. His reasons may open the wise to read Jonathan Edwards.

> There is a strange idea abroad that in every subject the ancient books should be read only by the professionals, and that the amateur should content himself with the modern books. . . . This mistaken preference for the modern books and this shyness of the old ones is nowhere more rampant than in theology. . . . Now this seems to me topsy-turvy. Naturally, since I myself am a writer, I do not wish the ordinary reader to read no modern books. But if he must read only the new or only the old, I would advise him to read the old. . . . It is a good rule, after reading a new book, never to allow yourself another new one till you have read an old one in between. If that is too much for you, you should at least read one old one to every three new ones. . . . We all . . . need the books that will correct the characteristic mistakes of our own period. And that means the old books. . . . We may be sure that the characteristic blindness of the twentieth century . . . lies where we have never suspected it. . . . None of us can fully escape this blindness. . . . The only palliative is to keep the clean sea breeze of the centuries blowing through our minds, and this can be done only by reading old books.[23]

If Lewis is right, the very foreignness of Edwards's greatness is a hope-filled reason to read him. Yes, his way of writing is elevated; ours tends to be mundane and conversational. His thought is complex; ours tends to be elementary. His vision of reality is steadily

---

[22] Quoted from *Studies in Medieval and Renaissance Literature*, in *The Quotable Lewis*, ed. by Wayne Martindale and Jerry Root (Wheaton, IL: Tyndale House Publishers, Inc., 1989), p. 509.

[23] C. S. Lewis, "On The Reading of Old Books," in *God in the Dock* (Grand Rapids: William B. Eerdmans Publishing Co., 1970), pp. 200-207. This essay was first published as the introduction to St. Athanasius' *The Incarnation of the Word of God*, trans. by A. Religious of C.S.M.V (London, 1944), pp. 200-202.

God-centered; ours tends to be man-centered with occasional attention to God. He is relentlessly serious; we incline to light-heartedness and comic relief. He is truth-focused and cherishes the contours of doctrine; we tend to be feeling-focused and suspicious of the claim that doctrine has contours. Yes, but in spite of all that—and Lewis would say, *because of all that*—the effort to read Edwards would be well spent.

Mortimer Adler on the Necessity of Hard Books

Mortimer Adler would use another argument to persuade us. In his classic, *How to Read a Book*, he makes a passionate case that the books that enlarge our grasp of truth and make us wiser must feel, at first, beyond us. They "must make demands on you. They must seem to you to be beyond your capacity."[24] If a book is easy and fits nicely into all your language conventions and thought forms, then you probably will not grow much from reading it. It may be entertaining, but not enlarging to your understanding. It's the hard books that count. Raking is easy, but all you get is leaves; digging is hard, but you might find diamonds.

Evangelical Christians, who believe God reveals himself primarily through a book, the Bible, should long to be the most able readers they can be. This means that we should want to become clear, penetrating, accurate, fair-minded thinkers, because all good reading involves asking questions and thinking.[25] This is one reason why the Bible teaches us, "Do not be children in your *thinking*; be babes in evil, but in *thinking* be mature" (1 Cor. 14:20 RSV). It's why Paul said to Timothy, "*Think over* what I say, for the Lord will grant you understanding in everything" (2 Tim. 2:7). God's gift of understanding is through thinking, not instead of thinking.[26]

Adler underlines his plea for the "major exertion" of reading

---

[24] Mortimer Adler and Charles Van Doren, *How to Read a Book* (New York: Simon and Schuster, 1972), p. 339.

[25] "Reading a book on any level beyond the elementary is essentially an effort on our part to ask it questions (and to answer them to the best of our ability). . . . That is why there is all the difference in the world between the demanding and the undemanding reader. The latter asks no questions—and gets no answers" (*How to Read a Book*, p. 47).

[26] For an expanded meditation on 2 Timothy 2:7, see John Piper, *A Godward Life: Savoring the Supremacy of God in All of Life* (Sisters, OR: Multnomah Press, 1997), pp. 122-123.

great books with the warning that such mental exercise may
lengthen your life, and television may be deadly.

> The mind can atrophy, like the muscles, if it is not used. . . . And
> this is a terrible penalty, for there is evidence that atrophy of the
> mind is a mortal disease. There seems to be no other explana-
> tion for the fact that so many busy people die so soon after
> retirement. . . .Television, radio, and all the sources of amuse-
> ment and information that surround us in our daily lives are . . .
> artificial props. They can give us the impression that our minds
> are active, because we are required to react to stimuli from out-
> side. But the power of those external stimuli to keep us going is
> limited. They are like drugs. We grow used to them, and we con-
> tinuously need more and more of them. Eventually, they have
> little or no effect.[27]

The Climb Will Be Worth It

Making the effort to read Jonathan Edwards merely for the sake
of living longer would be a great irony. His aim is not to help us
live long, nor even to live forever, but to help us live for God and
that forever. And since our media-intoxicated culture is neither
given to thinking, nor to straining Godward, the challenge and the
potential of reading Edwards is doubled. *The End for Which God
Created the World* may prove to be a life-giving fountain in more
ways than we know—all the better for its mountain-height, and
all the strain to climb worthwhile.

Attempting a Luther-like Copernican Revolution

In all this I long to persuade you to read and embrace Jonathan
Edwards's *The End for Which God Created the World*. The public significance of this vision of God, known and embraced, would
be epoch-making. Mark Noll compares Edwards's effort in this
book to the aim of Martin Luther, who turned the world upside-
down by restoring God to his rightful place. It "attempt[s] in the
18th century what Philip Watson once described as Martin
Luther's main concern in the 16th century—the promotion of a

---

[27] *How to Read a Book*, pp. 345-346.

theological 'Copernican Revolution' in which anthropocentric instincts are transformed into a theocentric picture of reality."[28]

Edwards is strongest where we are weakest. He knows God. He sees and savors the supremacy of God in all things. Our culture is dying for want of this vision and this food. And, therefore, the publication of *The End for Which God Created the World* is a matter of great public significance.

<hr />

SECTION TWO

A Personal Concern

Publishing *The End for Which God Created the World* is also an intensely personal concern for me. As I said at the beginning, the vision of God displayed in that book took me captive thirty years ago and has put its stamp on every part of my life and ministry. I believe and love its message. My personal reason for making the book more accessible is to join God in pursuing the invincible end for which he created the world. That end, Edwards says, is, first, that the glory of God might be magnified in the universe, and, second, that Christ's ransomed people from all times and all nations would rejoice in God above all things.

God's Glory Manifest in the Happiness of the Saints

But the depth and wonder and power of this book is the demonstration that these two ends are one. The *rejoicing* of all peoples in God, and the *magnifying* of God's glory are one end, not two. Why this is so, how it can be, and what difference it makes is what this book, and my life and Jonathan Edwards's theology, are about. The first biographer of Edwards describes *The End for Which God Created the World* like this: "From the purest principles of reason, as well as from the fountain of revealed truth, he demonstrates that the *chief* and *ultimate* end of the Supreme Being, in the works of creation and providence, was the manifestation of his own glory in the highest happiness of his creatures."[29]

<hr />

[28] "God at the Center," pp. 855. Noll makes this claim for the combined impact of *The End for Which God Created the World* along with *The Treatise on True Virtue*.

[29] Sereno Dwight, *Memoirs of Jonathan Edwards*, in *The Works of Jonathan Edwards*, vol. 1 (Edinburgh: The Banner of Truth Trust, 1974), p. clxiii.

"The manifestation of his own glory in the highest happiness of his creatures." Virtually everything I preach and write and do is shaped by this truth: that the exhibition of God's glory and the deepest joy of human souls are one thing. It has been a thirty-year quest, since I was first awakened to this vision through C. S. Lewis[30] and Daniel Fuller.[31] The quest goes on. But, over time, my most experienced and reliable guide in the Himalayas of Holy Scripture has been Jonathan Edwards. He said it like this: "The end of the creation is that the creation might glorify [God]. Now what is glorifying God, but a rejoicing at that glory he has displayed?"[32] "The happiness of the creature consists in rejoicing in God, by which also God is magnified and exalted."[33]

The implications of this vision are far-reaching. After spending thirty years pursuing the high paths of God's written revelation, I feel like I am just beginning to breathe the air of this lofty reality. Not to make you ferret out all the implications for yourself, I will mention in what follows fifteen of them. Keep in mind what I am illustrating. The further up you go in the revealed thoughts of God, the clearer you see that God's aim in creating the world was to display the value of his own glory, and that this aim is no other than the endless, ever-increasing joy of his people in that glory.

How Does Edwards Say It?

Let Edwards speak again for himself on this issue. How are God's glory and your joy related? He says it in many ways:

---

[30] I tell the story of the key encounters with C. S. Lewis in *Desiring God: Meditations of a Christian Hedonist* (Sisters, OR: Multnomah Press, 1996), pp. 16-19. One of the most awakening sentences of my life has proved to be, "I think we delight to praise what we enjoy because the praise not merely expresses but completes the enjoyment; it is its appointed consummation" (C. S. Lewis, *Reflections on the Psalms* [New York: Harcourt, Brace and World, 1958], p. 95).

[31] The importance of Fuller's impact is narrated in the foreword which I wrote to his book *Unity of the Bible: Unfolding God's Plan for Humanity* (Grand Rapids: Zondervan Publishing House, 1992), pp. x-xii. David Brand pays tribute to the same impact of Edwards through Daniel Fuller in his excellent book, *Profile of the Last Puritan*, p. x.

[32] Miscellany #3 in: Jonathan Edwards, *The Miscellanies,* ed. by Thomas Schafer, *The Works of Jonathan Edwards*, vol. 13 (New Haven: Yale University Press, 1994), p. 199. The Miscellanies are Edwards's private notebooks where he did his thinking, which later made its way into his sermons and books. The date for Miscellany #3 is estimated to be from Edwards's twentieth year. See Schafer's dating efforts in *The Miscellanies*, pp. 156-157.

[33] See below, *The End for Which God Created the World*, ¶ 72 and footnote 40.

God in seeking his glory seeks the good of his creatures, because the emanation of his glory . . . implies the . . . happiness of his creatures. And in communicating his fullness for them, he does it for himself, because their good, which he seeks, is so much in union and communion with himself. God is their good. Their excellency and happiness is nothing but the emanation and expression of God's glory. God, in seeking their glory and happiness, seeks himself, and in seeking himself, *i.e.* himself diffused . . . he seeks their glory and happiness.[34]

Thus it is easy to conceive how God should seek the good of the creature . . . even his happiness, from a supreme regard to *himself*; as his happiness arises from . . . the creature's exercising a supreme regard to God . . . in beholding God's glory, in esteeming and loving it, and rejoicing in it.[35]

God's respect to the creature's good, and his respect to himself, is not a divided respect; but both are united in one, as the happiness of the creature aimed at is happiness in union with himself.[36]

Thus the exhibition of God's glory and the deepest joy of human souls are one thing. The implications of this are breathtaking. I mention fifteen in acorn-form. Any one of them could become a great oak tree with book-length branches.

Two Great Passions Not at Odds

Implication #1. *God's passion for his own glory and his passion for my joy in him are not at odds.* God's righteousness[37] is not the enemy of his mercy. His commitment to uphold the worth of his name does not consign me to destruction, though I have besmeared

---

[34] *The End for Which God Created the World*, ¶ 114.

[35] *The End for Which God Created the World*, ¶ 277.

[36] *The End for Which God Created the World*, ¶ 278.

[37] God's righteousness is his unwavering commitment to uphold and display the infinite worth of his glory in all that he does, which would seem to require punishment for all who have "fallen short of the glory of God" (Rom. 3:23). But since God's righteousness (his commitment to his glory) and his mercy (his commitment to our joy) are not ultimately at odds, he made a way to "be both just and the justifier of him who has faith in Jesus" (Rom. 3:26). See footnote 21 in Jonathan Edwards, *The End for Which God Created the World*, p. 141.

his name by indifference and distrust. Rather, in the death of his Son, Jesus Christ, God conspired to vindicate his righteousness and justify sinners in one act. Which means that his zeal to be glorified and his zeal to save sinners are one.[38]

God Is Committed to the Joy of the Saints

Implication #2. *Therefore, God is as committed to my eternal and ever-increasing joy in him as he is to his own glory.* This gives us a glimpse into the massive theological substructure beneath some of the sweetest promises in the Bible—the ones that say God exerts omnipotent zeal to do us good. For example, 2 Chronicles 16:9, "For the eyes of the LORD run to and fro throughout the whole earth, to show his might in behalf of those whose heart is blameless toward him" (RSV). Psalm 23:6, "Surely goodness and mercy shall pursue[39] me all the days of my life" (author's translation). Zephaniah 3:17, "The LORD your God . . . will exult over you with joy, He will be quiet in His love, He will rejoice over you with shouts of joy." Luke 12:32, "Fear not, little flock, for it is your Father's good pleasure to give you the kingdom" (RSV).[40]

The Essence of God's Love for You

Implication #3. *The love of God for sinners is not his making much of them, but his graciously freeing and empowering them to enjoy*

---

[38] See especially Romans 3:25-26, "God displayed [Christ] publicly as a propitiation in His blood through faith. This was to demonstrate His righteousness, because in the forbearance of God He passed over the sins previously committed; for the demonstration, I say, of His righteousness at the present time, so that He would be just and the justifier of the one who has faith in Jesus." See my exposition of this text in the wider Biblical context of this truth in *The Pleasures of God: Meditations on God's Delight in Being God* (Sisters, OR: Multnomah Press, 1991), pp. 160-184.

[39] The traditional translation "follow" in Psalm 23:6 misses the uniform meaning of the Hebrew *radaph*, namely "pursue, chase or persecute." The verse does not mean that God's goodness and mercy follow us as though we were leaders and they were loyal subjects. It means they pursue us as though we were in constant need of omnipotent help—which we are. Daniel Fuller captures the force of this verse: "In that his goodness and mercy pursue after his people every day of their lives (see Ps. 23:6), God himself is modeling the benevolent love of 1 Corinthians 10:24: 'Nobody should seek his own good, but the good of others.' But this seeking the welfare of the creature does not contradict the oft-stated affirmation in Scripture that 'to [God] be the glory for ever! Amen' (e.g., Rom. 11:36), for the blessing of knowing God, enjoyed by believing people as his mercy and goodness pursue them daily, causes their hearts to well up constantly in praise to him" (*Unity of the Bible*, p. 136).

[40] See *The End for Which God Created the World*, Chapter Two, Section Five (¶¶ 226-240) for Edwards's collection of Biblical texts that show God created the world with a view to pursuing the creature's good.

making much of him. As Edwards says, "God is their good." Therefore if God would do us good, he must direct us to his worth, not ours. The truth that God's glory and our joy in God are one radically undermines modern views of self-centered love. God-centered grace nullifies the gospel of self-esteem. Today, people typically feel loved if you make much of them and help them feel valued. The bottom line in their happiness is that they are made much of.

Edwards observes, with stunning modern relevance, "True saints have their minds, in the first place, inexpressibly pleased and delighted with . . . the things of God. But the dependence of the affections of hypocrites is in a contrary order: they first rejoice . . . that they are made so much of by God; and then on that ground, he seems in a sort, lovely to them."[41] In other words, in his view, the bottom line of happiness is that we are granted to see the infinite beauty of God and make much of him forever. Human beings do, in fact, have more value than the birds (Matt. 6:26). But that is not the bottom line of our happiness. It simply means that we were created to magnify God's glory by enjoying him in a way birds never can.

What Is the Essence of True Virtue?

Implication #4. If the exhibition of God's glory and the deepest joy of human souls are one thing, then *all true virtue among human beings must aim at bringing people to rejoice in the glory of God.* No act is truly virtuous—that is, truly loving—that does not come from and aim at joy in the glory of God. The ground for this truth is laid in Edwards's *The End for Which God Created the World*, but the exposition of it was given in *The Nature of True Virtue* which Edwards wrote at the same time (1755) and intended to publish bound together with *The End* in one volume. There he said, "If there could be . . . a cause determining a person to benevolence towards the whole world of mankind . . . exclusive of . . . love to God, . . . it cannot be of the nature of true virtue."[42]

---

[41] Jonathan Edwards, *The Religious Affections*, ed. by John Smith, *The Works of Jonathan Edwards*, vol. 2 (New Haven: Yale University Press, 1959), pp. 249-250.

[42] Jonathan Edwards, *The Nature of True Virtue*, in *Ethical Writings*, *The Works of Jonathan Edwards*, vol. 8, ed. by Paul Ramsey (New Haven: Yale University Press, 1989), pp. 602-603.

The reason for this sweeping indictment of God-neglecting "virtue" is not hard to see in Edward's God-centered universe: "So far as a virtuous mind exercises true virtue in benevolence to created beings, it chiefly seeks the good of the creature, consisting in its knowledge or view of God's glory and beauty, its union with God, and conformity to him, love to him, and joy in him."[43] In other words, if God's glory is the only all-satisfying reality in the universe, then to try to do good for people, without aiming to show them the glory of God and ignite in them a delight in God, would be like treating fever with cold packs when you have penicillin. The apostle Paul warns that I can "give all my possessions to feed the poor, and . . . deliver my body to be burned," and still "not have love" (1 Cor. 13:3). The final reason for this is that man is not the center of true virtue, God is. So "whatever you do, do all to the glory of God" (1 Cor. 10:13).

Sin Is Sacrilege and Suicide

Implication #5. *It also follows that sin is the suicidal exchange of the glory of God for the broken cisterns of created things.* Paul said, "All have sinned and fall short of the glory of God" (Rom. 3:23). Sinning is a "falling short" of the glory of God. But the Greek word for "falling short" (*husterountai*) means "lack." The idea is not that you shot an arrow at God's glory and the arrow fell short, but that you could have had it as a treasure, but you don't. You have chosen something else instead. This is confirmed in Romans 1:23 where people "exchanged the glory of the incorruptible God for an image." That is the deepest problem with sin: it is a suicidal exchange of infinite value and beauty for some fleeting, inferior substitute. This is the great insult.

In the words of Jeremiah, God calls it appalling. "Be appalled, O heavens, at this, and shudder, be very desolate, declares the LORD. For My people have committed two evils: They have forsaken Me, the fountain of living waters, to hew for themselves cisterns, broken cisterns that can hold no water" (Jer. 2:12-13). What is the essence of evil? It is forsaking a living fountain for broken cisterns. God gets derision and we get death. They are one:

---

[43] *The Nature of True Virtue*, p. 559.

in choosing sugarcoated misery we mock the lifegiving God. It was meant to be another way: God's glory exalted in our ever-lasting joy.

Ever-increasing Joy in an Inexhaustible God

Implication #6. *Heaven will be a never-ending, ever-increasing discovery of more and more of God's glory with greater and ever-greater joy in him.* If God's glory and our joy in him are one, and yet we are not infinite as he is, then our union with him in the all-satisfying experience of his glory can never be complete, but must be increasing with intimacy and intensity forever and ever. The perfection of heaven is not static. Nor do we see at once all there is to see—for that would be a limit on God's glorious self-revelation, and therefore, his love. Yet we do not become God. Therefore, there will always be more, and the end of increased pleasure in God will never come.

Here is the way Edwards puts it: "I suppose it will not be denied by any, that God, in glorifying the saints in heaven with eternal felicity, aims to satisfy his infinite grace or benevolence, by the bestowment of a good [which is] infinitely valuable, because eternal: and yet there never will come the moment, when it can be said, that *now* this infinitely valuable good has been actually bestowed."[44] Moreover, he says, our eternal rising into more and more of God will be a "rising higher and higher through that infinite duration, and . . . not with constantly diminishing (but perhaps an increasing) celerity [that is, velocity] . . . [to an] infinite height; though there never will be any particular time when it can be said already to have come to such a height."[45] This is what we see through a glass darkly in Ephesians 2:7, "[God seats us in heaven with Christ] so that in the ages to come He might show the surpassing riches of His grace in kindness toward us in Christ Jesus." It will take an infinite number of ages for God to be done glorifying the wealth of his grace to us—which is to say he will never be done.

---

[44] *The End for Which God Created the World*, ¶ 285.

[45] *The End for Which God Created the World*, ¶ 279. See footnote 45 in *The End for Which God Created the World*, p. 160.

When Creatures Refuse to Be Happy in God

Implication #7. *Hell is unspeakably real, conscious, horrible and eternal—the experience in which God vindicates the worth of his glory in holy wrath on those who would not delight in what is infinitely glorious.* If infinitely valuable glory has been spurned, and the offer of eternal joy in God has been finally rejected, an indignity against God has been committed so despicable as to merit eternal suffering. Thus, Edwards says, "God aims at satisfying justice in the eternal damnation of sinners; which will be satisfied by their damnation, considered no otherwise than with regard to its eternal duration. But yet there never will come that particular moment, when it can be said, that now justice is satisfied."[46] Of the love of God and the wrath of God, Edwards says simply, "Both will be unspeakable."[47]

The words of Jesus and the words of his apostle confirm this: it will be unspeakable. Thus the Lord said, "Depart from Me, accursed ones, into the eternal fire which has been prepared for the devil and his angels. . . . These will go away into eternal punishment, but the righteous into eternal life" (Matt. 25:41, 46). And Saint Paul said that when Jesus returns, he will come "dealing out retribution to those who do not know God and to those who do not obey the gospel of our Lord Jesus [which means joyfully trusting the all-sufficient love of God in Christ]. These will pay the penalty of eternal destruction, away from the presence of the Lord and from the glory of His power" (2 Thess. 1:8-9).

Evangelism: Laboring to Waken a Taste for God

Implication #8. If the exhibition of God's glory and the deepest joy of human souls are one thing, then *evangelism means depicting the*

---

[46] *The End for Which God Created the World*, ¶ 285. For the Biblical evidence of hell's eternal conscious torment and the justice of it, see John Piper, *Let the Nations Be Glad: The Supremacy of God in Missions* (Grand Rapids: Baker Book House, 1993), pp. 115-128; and Jonathan Edwards, "The Justice of God in the Damnation of Sinners," in *The Works of Jonathan Edwards*, vol. 1 (Edinburgh: The Banner of Truth Trust, 1974), pp. 668-669; and Jonathan Edwards, "The Torments of Hell Are Exceeding Great," *Sermons and Discourses, 1723-1729*, ed. by Kenneth Minkema, in: *The Works of Jonathan Edwards*, vol. 14 (New Haven: Yale University Press, 1997), pp. 297-328.

[47] Unpublished sermon on Exodus 9:12, quoted in John Gerstner, *Jonathan Edwards on Heaven and Hell* (Grand Rapids: Baker Book House, 1980), p. 3. This entire book illustrates Edwards's capacity to show that heaven is unspeakably wonderful and hell is unspeakably horrible.

beauty of Christ and his saving work with a heartfelt urgency of love that labors to help people find their satisfaction in him. The most important common ground with unbelievers is not culture but creation, not momentary felt needs but massive real needs.[48] Augustine's famous prayer is all important: "You made us for yourself and our hearts find no peace till they rest in you."[49] If a person realizes that the *image of God* in man is man's ineffably profound fitness to image forth Christ's glory through everlasting joy in God, then he will not gut the great gospel of its inner life and power.

The gospel is not the good news that God makes much of me; it is "the gospel of *the glory of Christ*." And evangelism, St. Paul says, is the outshining of *"the light of the gospel* of the glory of Christ, who is the image of God" (2 Cor. 4:4). And when, by the agency of prayer and witness and the illuminating grace of the Holy Spirit, unbelievers suddenly see the glory of God in Christ and rejoice in hope, it is because the Creator of the universe "has shone in [their] hearts to give the Light of the knowledge of the glory of God in the face of Christ" (2 Cor. 4:6). Our evangelistic task is not to persuade people that the gospel was made for their felt needs, but that they were made for the soul-satisfying glory of God in the gospel.

Preaching: Luring out People to God

Implication #9. *Similarly, Christian preaching, as part of the corporate worship of Christ's church, is an expository exultation over the glories of God in his word, designed to lure God's people from the fleeting pleasures of sin into the sacrificial path of obedient satisfaction in him.* If preaching should aim to magnify God, and if God is magnified when his people prefer him over all "the riches and pleasures of life" (Luke 8:14), then preaching must aim to

---

[48] I owe this way of saying it to David Wells in personal conversation. Few people today are making wiser, more penetrating observations about this distinction than Wells in his three books, *No Place for Truth: Or Whatever Happened to Evangelical Theology?* (Grand Rapids: William B. Eerdmans Publishing Co., 1993); *God in the Wasteland: The Reality of Truth in a World of Fading Dreams* (Grand Rapids: William B. Eerdmans Publishing Co., 1994); *Losing Our Virtue: Why the Church Must Recover Its Moral Vision* (Grand Rapids: William B. Eerdmans Publishing Co., 1998).

[49] St. Augustine, *Confessions*, trans. by R. S. Pine-Coffin (New York: Penguin Books, 1961), p. 21, (I, 1).

expose the suicidal pleasures of sin and waken fullness of joy in God. The ever-present refrain will be,

> *Ho! Every one who thirsts, come to the waters;*
> *And you who have no money, come, buy and eat.*
> *Come, buy wine and milk*
> *Without money and without cost.*
> *Why do you spend money for what is not bread,*
> *And your wages for what does not satisfy?*
> *Listen carefully to Me, and eat what is good,*
> *And delight yourself in abundance.*
> *Incline your ear and come to Me.*
> *Listen, that you may live.*
> (Isaiah 55:1-3)

When Edwards pondered the aims of preaching for the glory of God he said, "I should think myself in the way of my duty to raise the affections of my hearers as high as possibly I can, provided that they are affected with nothing but truth, and with affections that are not disagreeable to the nature of what they are affected with."[50] High affections rooted in, and proportioned by, the truth—that is the goal of preaching. The truth is the manifold glory of God in his word; and the high affections are the delight of knowing God and the dread of not being happy in him. "Because you did not serve the LORD your God with joy and a glad heart . . . therefore you shall serve your enemies" (Deut. 28:47-48).

Corporate Worship: The Heart Hunger That Honors God

Implication #10. *The essence of authentic, corporate worship is the collective experience of heartfelt satisfaction in the glory of God, or a trembling that we do not have it and a great longing for it.* Worship is for the sake of magnifying God, not ourselves, and God is magnified in us when we are satisfied in him. Therefore, the unchanging essence of worship (not the outward forms which do change) is heartfelt satisfaction in the glory of God, the trembling when we do not have it and the longing for it.

---

[50] Jonathan Edwards, *Some Thoughts Concerning the Revival, The Great Awakening,* ed. by C. C. Goen, *The Works of Jonathan Edwards,* vol. 4 (New Haven: Yale University Press, 1972), p. 387.

The basic movement of worship on Sunday morning is not to come with our hands full to give to God, as though he needed anything (Acts 17:25), but to come with our hands empty, to receive from God. And what we receive in worship is the fullness of God, not the feelings of entertainment. We ought to come hungry for God. We should come saying, "As the deer pants for the water brooks, so my soul pants for You, O God. My soul thirsts for God, for the living God" (Ps. 42:1-2). God is mightily honored when a people know that they will die of hunger and thirst unless they have God.

Nothing makes God more supreme and more central in worship than when a people are utterly persuaded that nothing—not money or prestige or leisure or family or job or health or sports or toys or friends—nothing is going to bring satisfaction to their sinful, guilty, aching hearts besides God. This conviction breeds a people who go hard after God on Sunday morning. They are not confused about why they are in a worship service. They do not view songs and prayers and sermons as mere traditions or mere duties. They see them as means of getting to God or God getting to them for more of his fullness—no matter how painful that may be for sinners in the short run.

If the focus in corporate worship shifts onto our giving to God, one result I have seen again and again is that subtly it is not God that remains at the center but the quality of our giving. Are we singing worthily of the Lord? Do the instrumentalists play with a quality befitting a gift to the Lord? Is the preaching a suitable offering to the Lord? And little by little the focus shifts off the utter indispensability of the Lord himself onto the quality of our performances. And we even start to define excellence and power in worship in terms of the technical distinction of our artistic acts. Nothing keeps God at the center of worship like the Biblical conviction that the essence of worship is deep, heartfelt satisfaction in him, and the conviction that the trembling pursuit of that satisfaction is why we are together.

Furthermore, this vision of worship prevents the pragmatic hollowing out of this holy act. If the essence of worship is satisfaction in God, then worship can't be a means to anything else. We simply can't say to God, "I want to be satisfied in you so that I can have something else." For that would mean that we are not really satisfied in God but in that something else. And that would dishonor God, not worship him.

But, in fact, for thousands of people, and for many pastors, the event of "worship" on Sunday morning is conceived of as a means to accomplish something other than worship. We "worship" to raise money; we "worship" to attract crowds; we "worship" to heal human hurts; to recruit workers; to improve church morale; to give talented musicians an opportunity to fulfill their calling; to teach our children the way of righteousness; to help marriages stay together; to evangelize the lost; to motivate people for service projects; to give our churches a family feeling.

In all of this we bear witness that we do not know what true worship is. Genuine affections for God are an end in themselves. I cannot say to my wife: "I feel a strong delight in you so that you will make me a nice meal." That is not the way delight works. It terminates on her. It does not have a nice meal in view. I cannot say to my son, "I love playing ball with you—so that you will cut the grass." If your heart really delights in playing ball with him, that delight cannot be performed as a means to getting him to do something.

I do not deny that authentic corporate worship may have a hundred good effects on the life of the church. It will, just like true affection in marriage, make everything better. My point is that to the degree that we do "worship" for these reasons, to that degree it ceases to be authentic worship. Keeping satisfaction in God at the center guards us from that tragedy.

World Missions: A Passion for God's Glory in the Joy of All Peoples

Implication #11. If the exhibition of God's glory and the deepest joy of human souls are one thing, then *world missions is a declaration of the glories of God among all the unreached peoples, with a view to gathering worshippers who magnify God through the gladness of radically obedient lives.* "Tell of his *glory* among the nations," is one way to say the Great Commission (Ps. 96:3). "Let the nations be *glad* and sing for joy," is another way (Ps. 67:4).

They have one aim: the glory of God exalted in the gladness of the nations.

The apostle Paul combined the *glory* of God and the *gladness* of the nations by saying that the aim of the Incarnation was "to show God's truthfulness . . . in order that the Gentiles might *glorify God* for his mercy. As it is written . . . '*Rejoice*, O Gentiles, with his people'" (Rom. 15:8-10, RSV). In other words, rejoicing in God and glorifying God are one, and that one thing is the aim of world missions.

We Get the Help, He Gets the Glory

Implication #12. *Prayer is calling on God for help; so it is plain that he is gloriously resourceful and we are humbly and happily in need of grace.* The Giver gets the glory. We get help. That is the story of prayer. "Call upon me in the day of trouble; I will deliver you, and you shall glorify me" (Ps. 50:15, RSV). Jesus said to aim at two things in prayer: your joy and God's glory. "Ask and you will receive, so that *your joy* may be made full" (John 16:24). "Whatever you ask in My name, that will I do, so that *the Father may be glorified* in the Son" (John 14:13). These are not two aims, but one. When we delight ourselves in the Lord, the Lord is glorified in giving the desires of our heart (Ps. 37:4).

Scholarship: Seeing and Savoring God in Every Branch of Learning

Implication #13. *The task of Christian scholarship is to study reality as a manifestation of God's glory, to speak about it with accuracy, and to savor the beauty of God in it.* I think Edwards would regard it as a massive abdication of scholarship that so many Christians do academic work with so little reference to God. If all the universe and everything in it exists by the design of an infinite, personal God, to make his manifold glory known and loved, then to treat any subject without reference to God's glory is not scholarship but insurrection.

Moreover, the demand is even higher: Christian scholarship must be permeated by spiritual affections for the glory of God in all things. Most scholars know that without the support of truth, affections degenerate into groundless emotionalism. But not as many scholars recognize the converse: that without the awakening of true spiritual affections, seeing the fullness of truth in all things is impossible. Thus Edwards says, "Where there is a kind of light without heat, a head stored with notions and speculations, with a cold and unaffected heart, there can be nothing divine in that light, that knowledge is no true spiritual knowledge of divine things."[51]

One might object that the subject matter of psychology or sociology or anthropology or history or physics or chemistry or English or computer science is not "divine things" but "natural things." But that would miss the first point: to see reality in truth we must see it in relation to God, who created it, and sustains it, and gives it all the properties it has and all its relations and designs. To see all these things in each discipline is to see the "divine things"—and in the end, they are the main things. Therefore, Edwards says, we cannot see them, and therefore we cannot do Christian scholarship, if we have no spiritual sense or taste for God—no capacity to apprehend his beauty in the things he has made.

This sense, Edwards says, is given by God through supernatural new birth, effected by the Word of God. "The first effect of the power of God in the heart in regeneration, is to give the heart a divine taste or sense; to cause it to have a relish of the loveliness and sweetness of the supreme excellency of the divine nature."[52] Therefore, to do Christian scholarship, a person must be born again; that is, a person must not only *see* the effects of God's work, but also *savor* the beauty of God's nature.

It is not in vain to do rational work, Edwards says, even though everything hangs on God's free gift of spiritual life and sight. The reason is that "the more you have of a rational knowledge of divine things, the more opportunity will there be, when the Spirit shall be breathed into your heart, to see the excellency of these things, and to taste the sweetness of them."[53]

---

[51] *The Religious Affections*, p. 120.

[52] Jonathan Edwards, *Treatise on Grace*, in: *Treatise on Grace and Other Posthumously Published Writings*, ed. by Paul Helm (Cambridge: James Clarke and Co. Ltd., 1971), p. 49.

[53] "Christian Knowledge," in *The Works of Jonathan Edwards*, vol. 2 (Edinburgh: Banner of Truth Trust, 1974), p. 162.

It is evident here that what Edwards means by "rational knowledge" is not to be confused with modern *rationalism* that philosophically excludes "divine things." Even more relevant for the present issue of Christian scholarship is the fact that "rational knowledge" for Edwards would also exclude a Christian *methodological imitation* of rationalism in scholarly work. Edwards would, I think, find some contemporary Christian scholarship methodologically unintelligible because of the *de facto* exclusion of God and his word from the thought processes. The motive of such scholarship seems to be the obtaining of respect and acceptance in the relevant guild. But the price is high. And Edwards would, I think, question whether, in the long run, compromise will weaken God-exalting, Christian influence, because the concession to naturalism speaks more loudly than the goal of God's supremacy in all things. Not only that, the very nature of reality will be distorted by a scholarship that adopts a methodology that does not put a premium on the ground, the staying power, and the goal of reality, namely, God. Where God is methodologically neglected, faithful renderings of reality will be impossible.

How then is this view of Christian scholarship an outworking of the truth that the exhibition of God's glory and the deepest joy of human souls are one thing? God exhibits his glory in the created reality being studied by the scholar (Ps. 19:1; 104:31; Col. 1:16-17). Yet God's end in this exhibition is not realized if the scholar does not see it and savor it. Thus the savoring, relishing, and delighting of the scholar in the beauty of God's glory is an occasion when the exhibition of the glory is completed. In that moment, the two become one: the magnifying of God's glory is in and through the seeing and savoring of the scholar's mind and heart. When the echo of God's glory echoes in the affections of God's scholar and resounds through his speaking and writing, God's aim for Christian scholarship is achieved.

God Is Glorified When Death Is Gain

Implication #14. *The way to magnify God in death is by meeting death as gain.* Paul said his passion was that "Christ be exalted in [his] body, whether by life or by death." And then he added the words that show how Christ would be exalted in his death: "For to me, to live is Christ and to die is gain" (Phil. 1:20-21). Christ is shown as great, when death is seen as gain. The reason for this is plain: the glory of Christ is magnified when our hearts are more satisfied in him than in all that death takes from us. If we count death gain, because it brings us closer to Christ (which is what Phil. 1:23 says it does), then we show that Christ is more to be desired than all this world can offer.

The Great Duty: Be as Happy as You Can—in God Forever

Implication #15. Finally, if the exhibition of God's glory and the deepest joy of human souls are one thing, then, as C. S. Lewis said, *"It is a Christian duty, as you know, for everyone to be as happy as he can."*[54] Jonathan Edwards expressed this duty with tremendous forcefulness in one of his seventy resolutions before he was twenty years old: "Resolved, To endeavor to obtain for myself as much happiness in the other world as I possibly can, with all the power, might, vigor, and vehemence, yea violence, I am capable of, or can bring myself to exert, in any way that can be thought of."[55] And, of course, the duty is established by explicit commands of Scripture: "Delight yourself in the LORD" (Ps. 37:4); "Serve the LORD with gladness" (Ps. 100:2); "Rejoice in the Lord always; again I will say, rejoice!" (Phil. 4:4); and many more.

Sometimes people ask: should we pursue obedience to God or joy in God? Edwards would answer: The question involves a category confusion. It's like asking: should I pursue fruit or apples? Obedience is doing what we are told. And we are told to delight ourselves in the Lord. Therefore pursuing joy in God *is* obedience. In fact, when the psalm says, "Serve the Lord with gladness," it implies that the pursuit of joy must be part of *all* our obedience, which is what Implication #4 above already said. It could not be otherwise if joy in God is essential to magnifying the surpassing worth of God.

I hope it is evident now that this duty to be satisfied in God is not just a piece of good advice for the sake of our mental health.

---

[54] From a personal letter to Sheldon Vanauken in Vanauken's book, *A Severe Mercy* (New York: Harper and Row, 1977), p. 189.

[55] Resolution #22 in Edwards's *Memoirs*, in: *The Works of Jonathan Edwards*, vol. 1 (Edinburgh), p. xxi.

It is rooted in the very nature of God as one who overflows with the glory of his fullness, which is magnified in being known and loved and enjoyed by his creatures. Which is why I say again that this discovery has made all the difference in my life. What I owe Jonathan Edwards for guiding me in these things is incalculable. I love his words, "The happiness of the creature consists in rejoicing in God, by which also God is magnified and exalted."[56] But I also love to say it my way: God is most glorified in us when we are most satisfied in him.

A Final Plea and Prayer

Edwards's central insight—that God created the world to exhibit the fullness of his glory in the God-centered joy of his people—has made all the difference for me. Aside from all the other riches in Edwards's vision of God this alone would warrant Charles Colson's recommendation of Jonathan Edwards:

> The western church—much of it drifting, enculturated, and infected with cheap grace—desperately needs to hear Edwards's challenge. . . . It is my belief that the prayers and work of those who love and obey Christ in our world may yet prevail as they keep the message of such a man as Jonathan Edwards.[57]

O how I pray that these words, and all that I have written, will persuade many of you to read and embrace Edwards's great vision of God's passion for his glory in *The End for Which God Created the World*, printed as the second part of this book!

---

[56] *The End for Which God Created the World*, ¶ 72 and footnote 40.

[57] Charles Colson, "Introduction" to Jonathan Edwards, *Religious Affections* (Sisters, OR: Multnomah Press, 1984), pp. xxiii, xxxiv.

The man we so often call our greatest American Divine . . . was the greatest in his regnant, permeating, irradiating spirituality.

JOHN DE WITT
"Jonathan Edwards: A Study"

One of the most holy, humble and heavenly minded men, that the world has seen, since the apostolic age . . .

ASHBEL GREEN
Discourses Delivered in the College of New Jersey

As God delights in his own beauty, he must necessarily delight in the creature's holiness which is a conformity to and participation of it, as truly as [the] brightness of a jewel, held in the sun's beams, is a participation or derivation of the sun's brightness, though immensely less in degree.

JONATHAN EDWARDS
The End for Which God Created the World

JONATHAN EDWARDS,
THE MAN AND HIS LIFE

Learning from an Unmodern[1] Evangelical

Why Biography?

Besides the fact that reading biography is enjoyable, what other warrant for this chapter is there? Jonathan Edwards himself gives one, and the Bible gives one. Edwards published *The Life of David Brainerd* in 1749, and explained in his preface why he did so: "There are two ways of recommending true religion and virtue in the world, which God hath made use of: the one is by doctrine and precept; the other by instance and example."[2] What he said to justify telling Brainerd's life justifies the telling of his own.

---

[1] I am aware that Perry Miller, who is largely responsible for the revival of interest in Jonathan Edwards among scholars, said that he was "intellectually the most modern man of his age," and that "he speaks with an insight into science and psychology so much ahead of his time that our own can hardly be said to have caught up with him" (*Jonathan Edwards* [Westport, CT: Greenwood Press, Publishers, 1949], p. 305, xiii). Sang Lee goes even farther and says, "My contention . . . is that Edwards was actually more radically 'modern' than Miller himself might have realized. . . . Edwards departed from the traditional Western metaphysics of substance and form and replaced it with a strikingly modern conception of reality as a dynamic network of dispositional forces and habits. . . . It is this dispositional ontology that provides the key to the particular character of Edwards's modernity" (*The Philosophical Theology of Jonathan Edwards* [Princeton, NJ: Princeton University Press, 1988], pp. 3-4). But what I have in mind is Edwards's utter supernaturalism and Godwardness. If anything marks the modern period, it is the marginalizing of God. That is how Edwards is gloriously unmodern. The reality and supremacy of a personal, supernatural God is the center and the ground and the goal of all his thought and action.

[2] Jonathan Edwards, *An Account of the Life of the Reverend Mr. David Brainerd*, ed. by Norman Pettit, *The Works of Jonathan Edwards*, vol. 7 (New Haven: Yale University Press, 1985), p. 89.

The story of a good and holy life is a strong defense and confirmation of true Christianity and the beauty of goodness. Similarly, the Bible says, "Remember your leaders, those who spoke to you the word of God; consider the outcome of their life, and imitate their faith" (Heb. 13:7, RSV). So we are commanded to ponder the lives of faithful leaders, and trace out the issue of their lives to the end, and imitate the way faith shaped their conduct.

Edwards was a leader who spoke to us the word of God—and still speaks. What he spoke (and wrote) in *The End for Which God Created the World* would be enough to warrant the publication of this book. But his speaking and writing are what they are because of what he was. And we will be helped most if we see something of what John De Witt meant when he wrote, "[Edwards] was greatest in his attribute of regnant, permeating, irradiating spirituality."[3] Behind the greatness of his thought was the greatness of his soul. And his soul was great because it was filled with the fullness of God. In our day we need to see his God and to see the soul that saw this God.

How Not to Imitate the Great

Of course imitation across centuries and cultures is a delicate business. Slavish, external simulations of style or language will betray a failure to grasp what Edwards himself was pursuing in the creative adaptation of solid, ancient, Biblical truth to his own day. It takes wisdom to discern how the strengths of an old saint should appear in another time. As it is with proverbs, so it is with biography: "Like a thorn that goes up into the hand of a drunkard, is a proverb in the mouth of fools" (Prov. 26:9, RSV). "Like a lame man's legs, which hang useless, is a proverb in the mouth of fools" (Prov. 26:7, RSV). Therefore, let us beware lest we put on Edwards's waistcoat and wig and make ourselves fools. He has too much to give us that we desperately need.

Birth, Family, Youthful Intellect

Jonathan Edwards was born October 5, 1703, in Windsor, Connecticut. He was the only son among the eleven children of

---

[3] Quoted from "Jonathan Edwards: A Study," in *Biblical and Theological Studies* by Members of the Faculty of Princeton Theological Seminary, 1912, p. 136, in Iain Murray, *Jonathan Edwards: A New Biography* (Edinburgh: Banner of Truth Trust, 1987), p. xvii.

Timothy Edwards, the local Congregational pastor. Tradition has it that Timothy used to say God had blessed him with sixty feet of daughters. He taught Jonathan Latin when he was six and sent him off to Yale at twelve. The school was fifteen years old at the time and struggling to stay afloat. But it became a place of explosive intellectual excitement and growth for Jonathan Edwards.

As a student there at fifteen he read what was to be a seminal influence in his thought, John Locke's *Essay on Human Understanding*. He said later that he got more pleasure out of it "than the most greedy miser finds when gathering up handfuls of silver and gold from some newly discovered treasure."[4] Already at this early age he began a pattern of writing and thinking that would channel his great powers of mind and heart into extraordinary literary productivity.

Even while a boy, he began to study *with his pen in his hand*; not for the purpose of copying off the thoughts of others, but for the purpose of writing down, and preserving the thought suggested to his own mind, from the course of study that he was pursuing. This most useful practice he commenced in several branches of study very early; and he steadily pursued it in all his studies through life. His pen appears to have been in a sense always in his hand. From this practice steadily persevered in, he derived the very great advantages of thinking continually during each period of study; of thinking accurately; of thinking connectedly; of thinking habitually at all times.[5]

He graduated from Yale in 1720, gave the valedictory address in Latin, and then continued his studies there two more years preparing for the ministry. At nineteen he was licensed to preach and took a pastorate at the Scotch Presbyterian Church in New York for eight months from August, 1722 until April, 1723.

---

[4] Sereno Dwight, *Memoirs of Jonathan Edwards*, in: *The Works of Jonathan Edwards*, vol. 1 (Edinburgh: Banner of Truth Trust, 1974), p. xvii. Norman Fiering cautions us against assuming that this enthusiasm meant agreement. "It is not clear from [the above quote] what it was specifically that gave Edwards such pleasure. It was surely not Locke's empiricism or his tendencies toward skepticism and positivism, nor could it have been the materialist implications of his work. For if one thing is certain, it is that Edwards remained a philosophical rationalist, a supernaturalist, and a metaphysician all of his life." Thus "an understanding of Edwards's moral thought can be seriously skewed if the myth that Edwards began his career as a disciple of John Locke is not laid to rest" (*Jonathan Edwards's Moral Thought and Its British Context* [Chapel Hill: University of North Carolina Press, 1981], pp. 35-36).

[5] *Memoirs*, p. xviii.

The Intensity and Single-mindedness of His Inner Life

The intensity of his inner life in these early years was extraordinary. His famous "Resolutions" capture some of the remarkable passion of this season of his life. There was a single-mindedness that governed his life and enabled him to accomplish amazing things. For example, Resolution #44 says, "Resolved, That no other end but religion shall have any influence at all in any of my actions; and that no action shall be, in the least circumstance, any otherwise than the religious end will carry it."[6] And Resolution #61 says, "Resolved, That I will not give way to that listlessness which I find unbends and relaxes my mind from being fully and fixedly set on religion, whatever excuse I may have for it."[7]

This was a radical application of the Biblical dictum, "No soldier on service gets entangled in civilian pursuits, since his aim is to satisfy the one who enlisted him" (2 Tim. 2:4). It was precisely this single-minded focus on "religion" that yielded a lifetime of Godward study and writing. Religion, for Edwards, meant Christian living and thinking. And it was all rooted in a body of knowledge—a glorious "science" called divinity. He once preached a sermon on Hebrews 5:12 ("Ye ought to be teachers") in which he described what he was single-minded about, namely,

> God himself, the eternal Three in one, is the chief object of this science; and next Jesus Christ, as God-man and Mediator, and the glorious work of redemption, the most glorious work that ever was wrought: then the great things of the heavenly world, the glorious and eternal inheritance purchased by Christ, and promised in the gospel; the work of the Holy Spirit of God on the hearts of men; our duty to God, and the way in which we ourselves may become . . . like God himself in our measure. All these are objects of this science.[8]

O that this would be the central and all-pervasive focus of pastors and Christian leaders in our day! But there has been a great

---

[6] *Memoirs*, p. xxi.

[7] *Memoirs*, p. xxii.

[8] "Christian Knowledge: or The Importance and Advantage of a Thorough Knowledge of Divine Truth," in: *The Works of Jonathan Edwards*, vol. 2 (Edinburgh: The Banner of Truth Trust, 1974), p. 159.

loss of confidence that such a focus and devotion of energy will be "successful." This is one reason why Edwards's writings and his example is so needful in our time.

Falling in Love

In the summer of 1723, between his first short pastorate and his returning to Yale, he fell in love with Sarah Pierrepont. On the front page of his Greek grammar he wrote the only kind of love song his heart was capable of:

> They say there is a young lady in [New Haven] who is loved of that Great Being who made and rules the world and that there are certain seasons in which this Great Being, in some way or other invisible, comes to her and fills her mind with exceeding sweet delight; and that she hardly cares for anything except to meditate on him. . . . She is of a wonderful sweetness, calmness and universal benevolence of mind, especially after this great God has manifested himself to her. She will sometimes go about from place to place, singing sweetly, and seems to be always full of joy and pleasure; and no one knows for what. She loves to be alone walking in the fields and groves, and seems to have some-one invisible always conversing with her.[9]

Sarah was thirteen years old at the time! But four years later, five months after Edwards had been installed as pastor of the prestigious church of Northampton, Massachusetts, they were married on July 28, 1727. He was twenty-three and she was seventeen. In the next twenty-three years they had eleven children of their own, eight daughters and three sons.

Education and Settled Ministry

In September, 1723, Edwards returned to Yale for two more years of study. He earned his M.A. degree and became a tutor. But in September, 1726, he resigned his teaching post to accept a call to be the assistant to his grandfather, Solomon Stoddard, who had been the pastor at the prestigious Congregational Church of Northampton, Massachusetts, since 1672. In 1707, Stoddard had

---

[9] *Memoirs*, p. xxxix.

introduced a view of the Lord's Supper that treated it as a "converting ordinance" and people with no claim to regeneration were encouraged to join the church. This would prove ominous for Jonathan Edwards later when he came to a very different conclusion. In the meantime, one of the effects on the congregation was to produce a very lax and degenerate people at the time of Edwards's arrival.

The young became addicted to habits of dissipation and licentiousness; family government too generally failed; the Sabbath was extensively profaned; and the decorum of the sanctuary was not infrequently disturbed. There had also long prevailed in the town a spirit of contention between two parties, into which they had for many years been divided, which kept alive a mutual jealousy and prepared them to oppose one another in all public affairs. Such were the circumstances in which Mr. Edwards entered on his ministry at Northampton.[10]

Stoddard died on February 22, 1729, and Edwards became the pastor of the church for the next 23 years. It was a traditional Congregational church which in 1735 had 620 communicants.[11] During his ministry at this church Edwards delivered the usual two two-hour messages each week, catechized the children, and counseled people in his study. He did not visit regularly from house to house, though "he used to preach frequently at private meetings, in particular neighborhoods."[12] This meant that he could spend thirteen or fourteen hours a day in his study.[13] This may not have been pastorally wise. But Edwards thought pastors should "consult their own talents and circumstances, and visit more or less, according to the degree in which they could hope thereby to promote the great ends of the ministry. . . . It appeared to him, that he could do the greatest good to the souls of men, and most promote

---

[10] *Memoirs*, p. xxxviii.

[11] Jonathan Edwards, *A Narrative of Surprising Conversions*, in: *The Works of Jonathan Edwards*, vol. 1 Edinburgh: (Banner of Truth Trust, 1974), p. 350.

[12] *Memoirs*, p. xxxviii.

[13] *Memoirs*, p. xxxix. "He commonly spent thirteen hours every day in his study; and these hours were passed, not in perusing or treasuring up the thoughts of others, but in employments far more exhausting—in the investigation of difficult subjects, in the origination and arrangement of thoughts, in the invention of arguments, and in the discovery of truths and principles."

the cause of Christ, by preaching and writing, and conversing with persons under religious impressions in his study."[14]

The Assiduous, Pastoral Student of Scripture

Thus Edwards set for himself a course in ministry that would be preponderantly study and preaching. And most of that effort went into the direct study of the Scriptures. His great-grandson, Sereno Dwight, said that when Edwards came to the pastorate in Northampton, "he had studied theology, not chiefly in systems or commentaries, but in the Bible."[15] This was consistent with Edwards's counsel to all Christians, "Be assiduous in reading the Holy Scriptures. This is the fountain whence all knowledge in divinity must be derived. Therefore let not this treasure lie by you neglected."[16]

And he set an amazing example of his own counsel to study the Bible itself. I visited Yale's Beinecke Library where most of Edwards's unpublished works are stored. A friend took me down to the lower level into a little room where two or three men were working on old manuscripts with microscopes and special lighting. I was allowed to see some of Edwards's sermon manuscripts (including "Sinners in the Hands of an Angry God") and his catalogue of reading, and his interleaved Bible.

The interleaved Bible he had evidently made himself. He had taken a large Bible apart page by page and inserted a blank sheet of paper between each page and then resewn the book together. Then he drew a line down the center of each blank page in order to make two columns for notes. On page after page in even the remotest parts of Scripture there were extensive notes and reflections in his tiny, almost illegible, handwriting.

Thus there is good reason to believe that Edwards really did follow through on his 28th resolution: "Resolved: To study the Scriptures so steadily, constantly, and frequently, as that I may find, and plainly perceive, myself to grow in the knowledge of the same."[17] This was Edwards's personal application of 2 Peter 3:18, "Grow in

---

[14] *Memoirs*, p. xxxix.

[15] *Memoirs*, p.xxxvii.

[16] "Christian Knowledge," p. 162.

[17] *Memoirs*, p. xxi.

the . . . knowledge of our Lord and Savior Jesus Christ." He gave himself "assiduously" to study the very words of God, and would not allow them to lie by him neglected. This was the wellspring of his profoundly Biblical re-thinking of great theological questions.

Extraordinary Discipline for the Sake of Labor

Edwards's six-foot-one frame was not robust, and his health was always precarious. Nevertheless, "not at any time in his stormy career is there the slightest hint of either mental or emotional instability."[18] He maintained the rigor of his study schedule only with strict attention to diet and exercise. Everything was calculated to optimize his efficiency and power in study. Dwight tells us that he "carefully observed the effects of the different sorts of food, and selected those which best suited his constitution, and rendered him most fit for mental labor."[19] Thus he abstained from every quantity and kind of food that made him sick or sleepy. Edwards had set this pattern when he was 21 years old when he wrote in his diary, "By a sparingness in diet, and eating as much as may be what is light and easy of digestion, I shall doubtless be able to think more clearly, and shall gain time: 1. By lengthening out my life; 2. Shall need less time for digestion, after meals; 3. Shall be able to study more closely, without injury to my health; 4. Shall need less time for sleep; 5. Shall more seldom be troubled with the head-ache."[20] Hence he was "Resolved, To maintain the strictest temperance in eating and drinking."[21]

In addition to watching his diet so as to maximize his mental powers, he also took heed to his need for exercise. In the winter he would chop firewood a half-hour each day, and in the summer he would ride into the fields and walk alone in meditation. But there was more than mental efficiency in these trips to the woods.

A Lover of Nature and the God of Nature

For all his rationalism, Edwards had a healthy dose of the romantic and mystic in him. He wrote in his diary: "Sometimes

---

[18] Ola Winslow, *Jonathan Edwards* (New York: Octagon Books, 1973), p. 20.

[19] *Memoirs*, p. xxxviii.

[20] *Memoirs*, p. xxxv.

[21] *Memoirs*, p. xxi.

on fair days I find myself more particularly disposed to regard the glories of the world than to betake myself to the study of serious religion."[22] But romanticism is not at the bottom of such experiences in nature. Mark Noll comes closer to the explanation when he says, "Edwards both preached ferocious hell-fire sermons and expressed lyrical appreciation of nature because the God who created the world in all its beauty was also perfect in holiness."[23] Edwards really believed that "The heavens are telling the glory of God" (Ps. 19:1). He describes one of his experiences:

> Once as I rode out into the woods for my health in 1737, having alighted from my horse in a retired place, as my manner commonly has been, to walk for divine contemplation and prayer, I had a view, that for me was extraordinary, of the glory of the Son of God, as Mediator between God and man, and his wonderful, great, full, pure and sweet grace and love and meek, gentle condescension. This grace that appeared so calm and sweet appeared also great above the heavens. The person of Christ appeared ineffably excellent, with an excellency, great enough to swallow up all thought and conception—which continued, as near as I can judge, about an hour; which kept me the greater part of the time in a flood of tears, and weeping aloud.[24]

With such words in our ears it is not as difficult to believe the words of Elisabeth Dodds when she says, "The mythic picture of him is of the stern theologian. He was in fact a tender lover and a father whose children seemed genuinely fond of him."[25] It is not easy to know what his family life looked like under the kind of rigorous study schedule we have seen. We do know that he believed in filling every moment of life to the full and wasting none of them. His sixth resolution was simple and powerful: "Resolved: To live with all my might while I do live." And the fifth was similar:

---

[22] Quoted by Elisabeth Dodds, *Marriage to a Difficult Man* (Philadelphia: The Westminster Press, 1971), p. 22.

[23] Mark Noll, in a caption under Edwards's portrait in *Christian History*, vol. 4, no. 4, p. 3.

[24] *Memoirs*, p. xlvii.

[25] *Marriage to a Difficult Man*, p. 7.

"Resolved: Never to lose one moment of time, but to improve it in the most profitable way I possibly can."[26]

A Family Man

We have some reason to think that Edwards regarded his family as worthy of that kind of unwasted time. Sereno Dwight says, "In the evening, he usually allowed himself a season of relaxation, in the midst of his family."[27] But in another place Edwards himself says (in 1734, when he was thirty-one years old), "I judge that it is best, when I am in a good frame for divine contemplation, or engaged in reading the Scriptures, or any study of divine subjects, that, ordinarily, I will not be interrupted by going to dinner, but will forego my dinner, rather than be broke off."[28] One might think that Sarah Edwards would resent this and become disillusioned with her husband's theology. But it was not so. Her hospitality and piety are legendary.[29] I think it would be fair to say that the indispensable key to raising eleven believing children[30] in the Edwards's home was an "uncommon union" that Edwards enjoyed with his wife, rooted in a great theology of joy. Her great-grandson said, "Her religion had nothing gloomy or forbidding in its character. Unusual as it was in degree, it was eminently the religion of joy."[31] Sarah's story is well told in Elisabeth Dodds's *Marriage to a Difficult Man*, and given a historical-fictional rendering by Edna Gerstner in *Jonathan and Sarah Edwards: An Uncommon Union*.[32]

A Leader in the Great Awakening

About five years into Edwards's ministry as the pastor at Northampton, tremors of revival were felt. They were to continue

---

[26] *Memoirs*, p. xx.

[27] *Memoirs*, p. xxxviii.

[28] *Memoirs*, p. xxxvi.

[29] A short sketch of these strengths is found in the *Memoirs*, p. xlvi.

[30] One remarkable tribute to the grace of God through the lives and family of Jonathan and Sarah Edwards is the account by A. E. Winship of what became of their heirs over the next 150 years, in comparison with another family pseudonymously called the "Jukes." Of the Edwards came 13 college presidents, 65 professors, 100 lawyers, a dean of a law school, 30 judges, 66 physicians, 80 office holders, etc. See the whole comparison in Elisabeth Dodds, *Marriage to a Difficult Man*, pp. 37-39.

[31] *Memoirs*, p. xlvi.

[32] Elisabeth Dodds, *Marriage to a Difficult Man* (see footnote 22); Edna Gerstner, *Jonathan and Sarah Edwards: An Uncommon Union* (Morgan, PA: Soli Deo Gloria Publications, 1995).

on and off for about fifteen years, with the peak of the Great Awakening felt in Edwards's church in the mid-1730s and the early 1740s. Edwards was at the heart of this awakening, sparking it, defending it, analyzing it, and recounting it. He was known throughout New England as a leader in this awakening and was willing to take "missionary tours" to promote it. For example, on July 8, 1741, he preached "Sinners in the Hands of an Angry God" in Enfield, Connecticut, "which was the cause of an immediate revival of religion throughout the place."[33]

A series of sermons that he preached in 1742 and 1743, as the last crest of intense religious fervor was subsiding in Northampton, was published in 1746 under the title *Treatise Concerning the Religious Affections*. This book is the mature, seasoned reflection of Edwards, and the most profound analysis of the difference between true and false Christian experience that emerged from the season of the Great Awakening. In fact, it is probably one of the most penetrating and heart-searching Biblical treatments ever written of the way God works in saving and sanctifying the human heart. I often tell people that this would be a great place to start in their wider reading of Edwards.

The Lasting, Worldwide Fruit of a Young Man's Life and Death

What we owe to the unexpected and unplanned providences of life is incalculable.[34] In 1743, Jonathan Edwards met David Brainerd in New Haven. Brainerd was a young missionary to the Indians, whose life would have passed into the annals of heaven, but not earth, without this fortuitous encounter with Edwards. There was a bond established. In March, 1747, Brainerd was dying of tuberculosis and came to live with the Edwards family. He was cared for by Jerusha, Edwards's seventeen-year-old daughter. Brainerd died on October 9, 1747 at the age of twenty-nine. To her father's distress, Jerusha died five months later on February 14, 1748. Edwards lamented,

---

[33] *Memoirs*, p. li.

[34] "Providence" was Edwards's own designation of what is described here: "I have for the present, been diverted . . . by something . . . that Divine Providence unexpectedly laid in my way, and seemed to render unavoidable, viz. publishing Mr. Brainerd's Life." Quoted from a letter dated August 31, 1748, Jonathan Edwards, *Freedom of the Will*, ed. by Paul Ramsey, *The Works of Jonathan Edwards*, vol. 1 (New Haven: Yale University Press, 1957), pp. 3-4.

It has pleased a holy and sovereign God, to take away this my dear child by death, on the 14th of February, next following , after a short illness of five days, in the 18th year of her age. She was a person of much the same spirit with Brainerd. She had constantly taken care of and attended him in this sickness, for nineteen weeks before his death; devoting herself to it with great delight, because she looked on him as an eminent servant of Jesus Christ.[35]

Her father shared her estimate, so much so that he undertook to edit and publish Brainerd's journals—an act of devotion to Brainerd and to the great cause of world evangelization that his short life stood for. The reverberations for the sake of world missions in the following 250 years have been, as I said, incalculable. The book has never been out of print.

Almost immediately it challenged the spirit of God's great adventurers. Gideon Hawley, one of Edwards's missionary protégés, carried it in his saddlebag as the only other book besides his Bible, as he traveled among the Indians.[36] John Wesley put out a shortened version of Edwards's *Life of Brainerd* in 1768, ten years after Edwards's death. He disapproved of Edwards's and Brainerd's Calvinism,[37] but said that preachers of David Brainerd's spirit would be invincible.

The rise of the modern Protestant missionary movement took great inspiration from Edwards and Brainerd. For example, in the early 1800s in India, William Carey drew up a covenant for his missionary band that included the words, "Let us often look at Brainerd."[38] Andrew Fuller, the great "rope holder" back home in England, was dismayed several months before his death in 1815 to hear that people were belittling the influence of Jonathan Edwards on his colleague John Sutcliff and, by implication, on the

---

[35] *Memoirs*, p. xciv.

[36] Iain Murray, *Jonathan Edwards*, p. 470.

[37] Murray comments on this edition, "Wesley's judgment of priorities was right even if the liberties which he took in editing and abridging (with no leave from Edwards) are surprising by present-day standards. For besides popularizing Edwards, Wesley was also concerned 'to separate the rich ore of evangelical truth from the base alloy of . . . Calvinian error.'" *Jonathan Edwards, A New Biography* (Edinburgh: The Banner of Truth Trust, 1989), pp. 456-457.

[38] Quoted from S. Pearce Carey's biography of William Carey in Iain Murray, *Jonathan Edwards*, p. 470.

like-minded band who had gone to India. He wrote a letter to his friend John Ryland:

> We have some who have been giving out, of late, that "If Sutcliff and some other had preached more of Christ, and less of Jonathan Edwards, they would have been more useful." If those who talked thus preached Christ half as much as Jonathan Edwards did, and were half as useful as he was, their usefulness would be double what it is. It is very singular that the mission to the East should have originated with men of these principles and, without pretending to be a prophet, I may say, If ever it falls into the hands of men who talk in this strain, it will soon come to nothing.[39]

The list of missionaries who testify to the inspiration of Jonathan Edwards's influence through the labor of love he expended in writing *The Life of David Brainerd*[40] is longer than any of us knows: Francis Asbury, Thomas Coke, William Carey, Henry Martyn, Robert Morrison, Samuel Mills, Fredrick Schwartz, Robert M'Cheyne, David Livingstone, Andrew Murray. A few days before he died, Jim Elliot, who was martyred by the Aucas in 1956, entered in his diary, "Confession of pride—suggested by David Brainerd's *Diary* yesterday—must become an hourly thing with me."[41] For 250 years Edwards has been fueling the missionary movement with his biography of David Brainerd.

This impact on the modern missionary movement was not planned by Jonathan Edwards, as most of the turns of our lives are not planned by us. Brainerd came into his life, he died in Edwards's house, Edwards's daughter died soon after, and then there were all these journals to deal with in heartache and in longing for some good to come of it all.

---

[39] Andrew Fuller, *The Complete Works of the Rev. Andrew Fuller*, vol. 1 (Harrisonburg, VA: Sprinkle Publications, 1988, orig. 1845), p. 101.

[40] Jonathan Edwards, *An Account of the Life of the Reverend Mr. David Brainerd*, ed. by Norman Pettit, *The Works of Jonathan Edwards*, vol. 7. (Yale University Press, 1985).

[41] Elisabeth Elliot, ed., *The Journals of Jim Elliot* (Grand Rapids: Fleming H. Revell, 1978), p. 143.

The Inglorious Dismissal

Similarly Edwards did not plan the last chapter of his life in which he himself would be a missionary to the Indians, and in which he would write four of his most significant books. It all happened in a way that he would have never planned or wanted.

In 1750, Edwards was dismissed ingloriously from his pastorate after twenty-three years of ministry. Such things are always more convoluted and painful than anyone can know, but there are some reasons that we can point to. In 1744, some young people in Edwards's congregation were circulating "licentious books" and using obscene language. It came to Edwards's attention and he called a council with church approval, but then, unwisely it seems, read publicly the list of youths who were to report to his home without distinguishing in the list between the accused and the witnesses. So much resistance emerged among the people, Sereno Dwight says, that "it seemed in a great measure to put an end to his usefulness at Northampton and doubtless laid the foundation for his removal."[42]

But the decisive conflict emerged in the spring of 1749. It became generally known that Edwards had come to reject the former pastor's view on who should be admitted to the Lord's Supper. Solomon Stoddard had believed that the Lord's Supper could be a converting ordinance and that people could take communion in the hope of obtaining conversion by it. In August, Edwards wrote a detailed treatise to prove "that none ought to be admitted to the communion and privileges of members of the visible church of Christ in complete standing, but such as are in profession, and in the eye of the church's Christian judgment, godly or gracious persons."[43] The treatise was scarcely read, and there was a general outcry to have Edwards dismissed.

The Farewell Sermon

After almost a year of stressful controversy, the decision for dismissal was read to the people on June 22, 1750. Nine days later

---

[42] *Memoirs*, p. cxv.

[43] Jonathan Edwards, *A Humble Inquiry*, in : *The Works of Jonathan Edwards*, vol. 1 (Edinburgh: Banner of Truth Trust, 1974), p. 436.

on July 1, Edwards preached his famous Farewell Sermon, which is printed in the Banner of Truth edition of his *Works*.[44] It was a message, as were all his messages, utterly serious and without personal rancor. It closes with words of gracious yearning for the good of his people:

> I now take leave of you and bid you all, farewell; wishing and praying for your best prosperity. I would now commend your immortal souls to him, who formerly committed them to me, expecting the day when I must meet you again before him, who is the Judge of quick and dead. I desire that I may never forget this people, who have been so long my special charge, and that I may never cease fervently to pray for your prosperity. May God bless you with a faithful pastor, one that is well acquainted with his mind and will, thoroughly warning sinners, wisely and skillfully searching professors and conducting you in the way to eternal blessedness. May you have truly a burning and shining light set up in this candlestick; and may you, not only for a season, but during his whole life, that a long life, be willing to rejoice in his light.
>
> And let me be remembered in the prayers of all God's people that are of a calm spirit, and are peaceable and faithful in Israel, of whatever opinion they may be with respect to terms of church communion. And let us all remember, and never forget our future solemn meeting on that great day of the Lord; the day of infallible decision, and of the everlasting and unalterable sentence. Amen.[45]

Edwards was forty-six years old. He had nine children to support, the youngest, his son Pierrepont, having been born three months before his dismissal. Jerusha had died in 1747, and Sarah, the oldest, had married Elihu Parsons on June 11, just eleven days before Edwards was dismissed. We can feel some of the crisis in Edwards's own words from a letter written a week after his dismissal:

> I am now separated from the people between whom and me there was once the greatest union. Remarkable is the providence of God in this matter. In this event we have a striking instance of

---

[44] *Memoirs*, pp. cxcviii-ccvii.

[45] *Memoirs*, p. ccvii.

the instability and uncertainty of all things here below. The dispensation is indeed awful in many respects, calling for serious reflection and deep humiliation in me and my people. The enemy, far and near, will now triumph; but God can overrule all for his own glory. I have nothing visible to depend upon for my future usefulness, or the subsistence of my numerous family. But I hope we have an all-sufficient, faithful, covenant God, to depend upon. I desire that I may ever submit to him, walk humbly before him, and put my trust wholly in him. I desire, dear Sir, your prayers for us, under our present circumstances.[46]

The Move to Stockbridge

The church gave him support in the immediately following months, even asking him to preach at times. In early December of 1750, the church in Stockbridge, Massachusetts, about forty miles west of Northampton and very much a frontier village on the edge of settled New England, called Edwards to consider being their pastor. Simultaneously the Society in London for Propagating the Gospel in New England and the Parts Adjacent also called him to evangelize the Housatonnuck River Indians at Stockbridge. In January, 1751, Edwards went to visit Stockbridge and stayed the winter. In June he accepted the call and moved alone to the village to assume his responsibilities. His family moved to join him in August and on August 8, 1751, he was installed as the pastor of the little church made up of colonists and Indians.

In Northampton, Edwards had been financially well off, receiving (in his own words) "the largest salary of any country minister in New England."[47] But in Stockbridge he was so pressed for funds before selling his home in Northampton, that he lacked the necessary paper for writing. The mission and church in Stockbridge were beset with problems that demanded Edwards's attention. A house had to be built, sermons had to be prepared and preached (often through his Indian interpreter, John Wonwanonpequunnonnt),[48]

---

[46] *Memoirs*, p. cxxii.

[47] *Memoirs*, p. cxli.

[48] *Freedom of the Will*, p. 5.

special concerns of the Indian converts had to be addressed (e.g., the language issue and what sorts of schools to provide), parties had to be reconciled, misuse of mission funds had to be confronted. Edwards gave himself to these duties with faithfulness.

The Greater Purposes of God in Pain

But the greater purposes of God in this strange and painful providence of Edwards's removal to Stockbridge, I would venture, are in the thinking and writing that Edwards did in these seven years before he was called to be the president of Princeton. Four of Edwards's weightiest, most influential, books were written in the years 1752-1757. Paul Ramsey says that they "are not wholly undeserving of such high praise as 'four of the ablest and most valuable works which the Church of Christ has in its possession.'"[49] I describe my own personal encounter with these books in Chapter Three (pp. 77-97). That Edwards would interact with the dominant philosophical writings of his time and write theological-philosophical books in this out-of-the-way place under these primitive conditions is a wonder.

The Passion for Philosophical Engagement

There are few models for grasping the passion of Edwards to vindicate Christianity philosophically in the context of a pastoral and missionary life. Norman Fiering has argued that "his goal, if it can be put in one sentence, was to give seventeenth-century Puritan pietism a respectable philosophical structure, which would make it rationally credible and more enduring than it could be without the aid of philosophy."[50] A more sympathetic way of saying it would be that Edwards believed his Biblical theology was, in fact, a true rendering of reality, and therefore could stand confidently in the marketplace of philosophical ideas and give an account of itself—which in his hands it would do.

But Fiering is right that Edwards is not fully "comprehensible in terms of his New England Puritan background alone. He was

---

[49] *Freedom of the Will*, p. 8.

[50] *Jonathan Edwards's Moral Thought and Its British Context* (Chapel Hill: North Carolina University Press, 1981) p. 60.

too much of a philosopher for that context; his speculations carried him beyond the immediate concerns of the ministry to an engagement with metaphysics and ethics that was more than a collegiate exercise."[51] One of the reasons this dimension of Edwards's ministry is missed is that the middle, more well-known, part of his life was not spent mainly in philosophical pursuits but in the experience and analysis of the Great Awakening. But Fiering points out that "Edwards's strictly philosophical interests emerged in two phases. The first began in his earliest college days, extended through his tutorship at Yale, and lasted until he assumed pastoral duties in Northampton in 1727. The second phase began about 1746 and lasted until his death in 1758. The twenty years between 1727 and 1746 were in large part absorbed in working out the questions for the religious life posed by the Great Awakening, as well as by pastoral problems and responsibilities."[52]

So in this last part of Edwards's life, spent in Stockbridge far from the academic centers of philosophical learning, Edwards's mind turned again to the philosophical standing of his cherished Biblical vision of reality. Yet this was not a turning away from Biblical and theological foundations, as will be clear from *The End for Which God Created the World,* Part Two of this book. Fiering depicts Edwards's "method of utilizing moral philosophy in his arguments, but ultimately relying on moral theology for his conclusions."[53] Which meant, simply, for Edwards, that in the end he relied on the Bible.

As Iain Murray makes plain, even in Edwards's more philo-

---

[51] *Jonathan Edwards's Moral Thought and Its British Context,* p. 47.

[52] *Jonathan Edwards's Moral Thought and Its British Context,* p.106, note 2. One evidence for this division of Edwards's life is the remarkable fact that the concept of "consent" to being, which Edwards evidently hit upon early in his twenties, did not appear in print until thirty years later in his treatise on *True Virtue (Jonathan Edwards's Moral Thought and Its British Context,* p. 74). (The concept of "consent" to being is roughly equivalent to benevolence toward ultimate being, that is, God, or agreement and affirmation of being—willing that ultimate being be pleased and glorified.)

[53] *Jonathan Edwards's Moral Thought and Its British Context,* p. 55. Paul Ramsey is skeptical about Fiering's depiction of Edwards's ethics as "synthetic ethics" and "critical ethics" and warns that "to abstract moral philosophy from its theological context tends to obscure JE's extraordinary confidence that the truths of faith and of reason are *one*" (*Ethical Writings,* ed. by Paul Ramsey, *The Works of Jonathan Edwards,* vol. 8 [New Haven: Yale University Press, 1989], p. 6, note 5). David Brand makes the same point, perhaps even more forcefully, that "philosophy was useful to Edwards as a means of setting forth, synthesizing, and clarifying theological issues, it was subordinated to divine revelation." *Profile of the Last Puritan: Jonathan Edwards, Self-Love and the Dawn of the Beatific* (Atlanta: Scholars Press, 1991), p. 145.

sophical works, "The key to understanding Jonathan Edwards is that he was a man who put faithfulness to the Word of God before every other consideration."[54] Thus, "Edwards belongs properly in the company of Leibniz, Malebranche, and Pascal fifty years earlier, figures who like him philosophized freely, but did so *within* a dogmatic tradition."[55] Such people may have penetrated the deeper into reality because of their Biblically grounded theological insight, but they "confused and irritated opponents precisely because they loved God more than philosophy."[56]

The Freedom of the Will

The first of Edwards's four great works from this Stockbridge period was *Freedom of the Will*.[57] The editor of this book in the Yale critical edition, Paul Ramsey, says that this work "with ample reason has been called Edwards's greatest literary achievement."[58] It is all the more remarkable because of the condition of its composition, which is probably typical of the conditions for each of the four major works:

> Let it be remembered, that the Essay on the Freedom of the Will
> . . . was written within the space of four months and a half; and
> those not months of leisure, but demanding the additional duties
> of a parish, and of two distinct Indian missions; and presenting,
> also, all the cares, perplexities, and embarrassments of a furious
> controversy, the design of which was to deprive the author, and
> his family of their daily bread.[59]

The Fruit of a Lifetime of Redeeming the Time

The book was finished by April, 1753, and was published a year later after subscriptions came in from Scotland to the Boston publisher. The practical key to composing under such imperfect cir-

[54] *Jonathan Edwards: A New Biography*, p. 471.

[55] *Jonathan Edwards's Moral Thought and Its British Context*, p. 51.

[56] *Jonathan Edwards's Moral Thought and Its British Context*, p. 51.

[57] On the main content and argument of this book see my comments in Chapter Three, pp. 86-89.

[58] *Freedom of the Will*, p. 1.

[59] *Memoirs*, p. clx.

cumstances was to redeem every moment of time, which Edwards had learned to do through years of rigorous discipline. Even in his early resolutions he had steeled himself against the depleting power of procrastination. Resolution #11 says, "Resolved: When I think of any theorem in divinity to be solved, immediately to do what I can towards solving it, if circumstances do not hinder."[60]

Add to this that Edwards for over thirty years had not been a passive reader. He read with a view to solving problems and retaining his thoughts in writing. Most people have a lamentable penchant toward passive reading. They read the way people watch television. They don't ask questions, which Mortimer Adler says is the essence of active reading.[61] But we have seen already[62] that Edwards read with riveted focus and with a view to solving theological problems, ever writing and recording his thoughts. It has been said that "perhaps no person ever lived who so habitually and carefully committed his thoughts, on almost every subject, to writing, as the elder President Edwards. His ordinary studies were pursued pen in hand, and with his notebooks before him; and he not only often stopped in his daily rides by the wayside, but frequently rose even at midnight to commit to paper any important thought that had occurred to him."[63]

Even without book in hand, his mind was working. Edwards's great-grandson tells us how he used the many hours that it took on horseback to get from one town to another, thinking through an issue to some conclusion, and then pinning a piece of paper on his coat and charging his mind to remember the sequence of thought when he took the paper off at home.[64]

He maximized the opportunity for study also by rising early. In fact, he was probably entirely serious when he wrote in his diary in 1728, "I think Christ has recommended rising early in the morn-

---

[60] *Memoirs*, p. xx.

[61] "Reading a book . . . is essentially an effort on your part to ask it questions (and to answer them to the best of your ability)." Mortimer Adler and Charles Van Doren, *How to Read a Book* (New York: Simon and Schuster, 1972), p. 47.

[62] *Memoirs*, xviii. See above p. 51 footnote 5.

[63] From Tryon Edwards's Introduction to *Charity and Its Fruits, Ethical Writings*, ed. by Paul Ramsey, *The Works of Jonathan Edwards*, vol. 8 (New Haven: Yale University Press, 1989), p. 125.

[64] *Memoirs*, p. xxxviii.

ing, by his rising from the grave very early."[65] So he rose between 4:00 and 5:00 to study, always with pen in hand, thinking out every burst of insight as far as he could and recording it in his notebooks.[66] After a lifetime of this discipline, it is not as though he were starting any of his four great Stockbridge works from scratch. There were thousands of notes and thirty years of reflection ready to pour into these books.

Two More Books: What Is the End and What Is the Good?

This is especially true of the next two works that Edwards began to write, *The End for Which God Created the World* and *The Nature of True Virtue*, which Edwards intended to be published together (which we know because in *True Virtue* Edwards refers several times to *The End* as "the foregoing Treatise"). He began the composition in the spring of 1755 after the longest, most painful illness of his life. "I should have written long ago," he writes to a friend on April 15, 1755, "had I not been prevented by the longest and most tedious sickness that ever I had in my life: It being followed with fits of ague which came upon me about the middle of last July, and were for a long time very severe, and exceedingly wasted my flesh and strength, so that I became like a skeleton."[67] The *Two Dissertations* were not published until 1765, seven years after Edwards's death. This is probably owing to the fact that, even though they were basically complete, Edwards intended some additional work on them.[68]

We know from Edwards's *Miscellanies* that he had copious notes ready to pour into these works when the time came to write them. He had wrestled all his life, for example, with the issue of the end for which God created the world. Harvey Townsend lists a sampling of twenty-three entries in Edwards's notebooks that

---

[65] *Memoirs*, p. xxxvi.

[66] *Memoirs*, p. xviii.

[67] *Memoirs*, p. clxv.

[68] Samuel Hopkins, the first Editor of the *Dissertations*, wrote a Preface to go with both works in 1765 and commented that "'tis probable, that if his life had been spared, [Edwards] would have revised them and rendered them in some respects more complete. Some new sentiments, here and there, might probably have been added; and some passages brightened with farther illustrations. This may be conjectured from some brief hints or sentiments minuted down on loose papers, found in the manuscripts." *Ethical Writings*, p. 401.

deal with this question, some of them as long as nine pages, and some dating from his twenties.[69] In these two *Dissertations* it is true, as Iain Murray says, that Edwards, in essence, "is saying nothing more than he taught the Indian children on 'man's chief end' from the first question of the Shorter Catechism."[70] Nevertheless, much more than this was also going on. His mind "soars like an eagle towards the sun,"[71] and with a radically God-centered vision of creation and virtue "he responds to . . . the 'new moral philosophy' of the 18th century—that is, the sentimental ethics that was sweeping the English-speaking world in the works of the Earl of Shaftesbury (1671-1713), Francis Hutcheson (1694-1746) and Samuel Clarke (1675-1720)."[72]

The Last Work

Edwards's last literary labor was *The Great Christian Doctrine of Original Sin*,[73] which he finished in May, 1757. The book was not written in a vacuum, of course, but in direct response to a particular attack on the historic orthodox doctrine. This is evident from the rest of the title: "*Evidences of its Truth produced, and Arguments to the Contrary answered, Containing in particular, A Reply to the Objections and Arguings of Dr. John Taylor, in his Book, Intitled, 'The Scripture-Doctrine of Original Sin proposed to free and candid Examination, etc'.*"

Another Strange and Painful Providence

Four months after the completion of this last great work, Edwards's son-in-law and president of Princeton College, Aaron Burr, died on September 24, 1757. Two days later, the "corporation of the college" met and "made the choice of Mr. Edwards as

---

[69] Harvey Townsend, *The Philosophy of Jonathan Edwards* (Westport, CT: Greenwood Press, Publishers, 1955), pp. 126-153. On the dating of the Miscellanies, see Jonathan Edwards, *The Miscellanies*, ed. by Thomas Schafer, *The Works of Jonathan Edwards*, vol. 13 (New Haven: Yale University Press, 1994), p. 156.

[70] Iain Murray, *Jonathan Edwards*, p. 428.

[71] Iain Murray, *Jonathan Edwards*, p. 428.

[72] Mark Noll, "God at the Center: Jonathan Edwards on True Virtue," *Christian Century*, September 8-15, 1993, p. 855.

[73] The book is 435 pages in the Yale edition, Jonathan Edwards, *Original Sin*, ed. by Clyde A. Holbrook, *The Works of Jonathan Edwards*, vol. 3 (New Haven: Yale University Press, 1970).

his successor."[74] It is a tribute to Edwards's faith and fatherhood that his widowed daughter Esther, who had been married only five years, responded with such confidence in God's sovereign goodness. In a letter to her mother two weeks after the death of her husband she wrote,

> I would speak it to the glory of God's name, that I think he has, in an uncommon degree, discovered himself to be an all-sufficient God, a full fountain of all good. Although all streams were cut off, yet the fountain is left full. I think I have been enabled to cast my care upon him, and have found great peace and calmness in my mind, such as this world cannot give nor take. . . . Give me leave to entreat you both, to request earnestly of the Lord, that I may never despise his chastenings, nor faint under this his severe stroke.[75]

His Futile Resistance to the Princeton Call

Within seven months, her mother would write a similar letter to her daughter that the same "severe stroke" had struck her husband Jonathan. But none of that could be seen now, and Edwards was "not a little surprised" to receive word that he had been elected president of Princeton, if he would accept. He was not at all sure this was a wise choice. In a letter to the corporation on October 19, 1757, he outlined his hesitancies. Besides having "just begun to have our affairs in a comfortable situation," he deprecated his fitness for the role of president:

> I have a constitution, in many respects, peculiarly unhappy, attended with flaccid solids, vapid, sizy, and scarce fluids, and a low tide of spirits; often occasioning a kind of childish weakness and contemptibleness of speech, presence, and demeanor, with a disagreeable dullness and stiffness, much unfitting me for conversation, but more especially for the government of a college. . . . I am also deficient in some parts of learning, particularly in algebra, and the high parts of mathematics, and the Greek classics; my Greek learning having been chiefly in the New Testament.[76]

---

[74] *Memoirs*, p. clxxiii.

[75] *Memoirs*, p. clxxiii-clxxiv.

[76] *Memoirs*, p. clxxiv.

Besides this personal unfitness, as he saw it, he had writing projects in view that would consume the rest of his life and he
described them in some detail in the letter. Then he said, "I think
I can write better than I can speak. My heart is so much in these
studies, that I cannot find it in my heart to be willing to put myself
into an incapacity to pursue them any more in the future part of
my life."[77] But he closed the letter with the promise to seek counsel and take the matter seriously.

The advisory council was held January 4, 1758, in Stockbridge
and decided it was Edwards's duty to accept the call. When he was
told of the decision he "fell into tears on the occasion, which was
very unusual for him in the presence of others."[78] He remonstrated
that they too easily overlooked his arguments, but in the end he
acquiesced. The missionary society with whom he served gave their
permission, and he left for Princeton in January, planning to move
his family in the spring.

Great Faith Before the Fatal Defense of Life

On February 13, 1758, one month after he had assumed the pres-
idency of Princeton, Edwards was inoculated for smallpox. It had
the opposite effect from that intended. The pustules in his throat
became so large that he could take no fluids to fight the fever. When
he knew that there was no doubt he was dying, he called his daughter Lucy—the only one of his family in Princeton—and gave her
his last words. There was no grumbling over being taken in the
prime of his life with his great writing dreams unfulfilled, but
instead, with confidence in God's good sovereignty, he spoke
words of consolation to his family:

> Dear Lucy, it seems to me to be the will of God that I must shortly
> leave you; therefore give my kindest love to my dear wife, and tell
> her, that the uncommon union, which has so long subsisted between
> us, has been of such a nature as I trust is spiritual and therefore will
> continue for ever: and I hope she will be supported under so great
> a trial, and submit cheerfully to the will of God. And as to my chil-

[77] *Memoirs*, p. clxxv.

[78] *Memoirs*, p. clxxvii.

dren you are now to be left fatherless, which I hope will be an inducement to you all to seek a father who will never fail you.[79]

He died on March 22. His physician wrote the hard letter to his wife, who was still in Stockbridge. She was quite sick when the letter arrived, but the God who held her life was the God whom Jonathan Edwards preached. So on April 3 she wrote to her daughter Esther:

> What shall I say: A holy and good God has covered us with a dark cloud. O that we may kiss the rod, and lay our hands on our mouths! The Lord has done it, he has made me adore his goodness that we had him so long. But my God lives; and he has my heart. O what a legacy my husband, and your father, has left to us! We are all given to God: and there I am and love to be.
>
> Your ever affectionate mother,
> *Sarah Edwards*[80]

The Quest for Spiritual Sight

Thus ended the earthly life of one whose passion for the supremacy of God was perhaps unsurpassed in the history of the church. The pursuit was with vehemence because he knew what was at stake, and he knew that no mere speculative or rational knowledge of God would save his soul or bless the church. All his energy was bent on serving the true end of all things, namely, the manifestation of the glory of God in a spiritual sight and enjoyment of that glory.

> A true sense of the glory of God is that which can never be obtained by speculative [reasoning]; and if men convince themselves by argument that God is holy, that never will give a sense of his amiable [i.e., pleasing, admirable] and glorious holiness. If they argue that he is very merciful, that will not give a sense of his glorious grace and mercy. It must be a more immediate, sensible discovery that must give the mind a real sense of the excellency and beauty of God.[81]

---

[79] *Memoirs*, p. clxxviii.

[80] *Memoirs*, p. clxxxix.

[81] Sermon on Matthew 5:8 ("Blessed are the pure in heart; for they shall see God.") in: *The Works of Jonathan Edwards*, vol. 2 (Edinburgh: Banner of Truth Trust, 1974), p. 906.

In other words, it is to no avail merely to believe *that* God is holy and merciful. For that belief to be of any saving value, we must "sense" God's holiness and mercy. That is, we must have a true taste for it and delight in it for what it is in itself. Otherwise the knowledge is no different than what the devils have.

The Aim of Life in the Labor of Thought

Does this mean that all his rational study and thinking was in vain? No. Because he says, "The more you have of a rational knowledge of divine things, the more opportunity will there be, when the Spirit shall be breathed into your heart, to see the excellency of these things, and to taste the sweetness of them."[82] But the goal of all his study was this spiritual taste, not just knowing God but delighting in him, savoring him, relishing him. And so for all his intellectual might, Edwards was the farthest thing from a cool, detached, neutral, disinterested academician.

He said in his 64th Resolution, "Resolved, When I find those 'groanings which cannot be uttered,' of which the apostle speaks, and those 'breathings of soul for the longing it hath,' of which the psalmist speaks . . . I will not be weary of earnestly endeavoring to vent my desires, nor of the repetitions of such earnestness."[83]

In other words, he was as intent on cultivating his passion for God as he was of cultivating his knowledge of God. He strained forward in the harness of his flesh not only for truth, but also for more grace. The 30th Resolution says, "Resolved, To strive every week to be brought higher in religion, and to a higher exercise of grace, than I was the week before."[84]

And that advancement was for Edwards intensely practical. He said to his people what he sought for himself,

> Seek not to grow in knowledge chiefly for the sake of applause,
> and to enable you to dispute with others; but seek it for the ben-

---

[82] "Christian Knowledge," p. 162.

[83] *Memoirs*, p. xxii.

[84] *Memoirs*, p. xxi.

efit of your souls, and in order to practice. . . . Practice according to what knowledge you have. This will be the way to know more. . . . [According to Ps. 119:100] "I understand more than the ancients, because I keep thy precepts."[85]

The great end of all study—all theology—is a heart for God and a life of holiness. The great goal of all Edwards's work was the glory of God. And the greatest thing I have ever learned from Edwards, and the driving vision of this book, is that God is glorified most not merely by being known, nor by merely being dutifully obeyed, but by being enjoyed in the knowing and the obeying.

> God made the world that he might communicate, and the creature receive, his glory; but that it might [be] received both by the mind and heart. He that testifies his having an idea of God's glory [doesn't] glorify God so much as he that testifies also his approbation of it and his delight in it.[86]

And so the final and most important exhortation to us from the life and work of Jonathan Edwards is this: in all our life and all our study and all our ministry let us seek to glorify God by being satisfied in him above all things. Let us press on to know in the depth of our being that "the steadfast love of the Lord is better than life" (Ps. 63:3). And so let us find the God-exalting freedom from this world that will make us the most radical, sacrificial servants of good on earth—that men may see our good works and join us in glorifying God by enjoying him forever.

> The enjoyment of [God] is the only happiness with which our souls can be satisfied. To go to heaven, fully to enjoy God, is infinitely better than the most pleasant accommodations here. Fathers and mothers, husbands, wives, or children, or the company of earthly friends, are but shadows; but God is the substance. These are but scattered beams, but God is the sun. These are but streams. But God is the ocean.[87]

---

[85] "Christian Knowledge," p. 162-163.

[86] Miscellany #448, The "Miscellanies," ed. by Thomas Schafer, The Works of Jonathan Edwards, vol. 13 (New Haven: Yale University Press, 1994), p. 495.

[87] Jonathan Edwards, "The Christian Pilgrim," The Works of Jonathan Edwards, vol. 2 (Banner of Truth Trust, 1974), p. 244.

God is glorified not only by His glory's being seen, but by its being rejoiced in. When those that see it delight in it, God is more glorified than if they only see it. His glory is then received by the whole soul, both by the understanding and by the heart. God made the world that He might communicate, and the creature receive, His glory; and that it might [be] received both by the mind and heart. He that testifies his idea of God's glory [doesn't] glorify God so much as he that testifies also his approbation of it and his delight in it.

JONATHAN EDWARDS
Miscellanies

Even while a boy, he began to study with his pen in his hand; not for the purpose of copying off the thoughts of others, but for the purpose of writing down, and preserving the thought suggested to his own mind, from the course of study which he was pursuing. This most useful practice he commenced in several branches of study very early; and he steadily pursued it in all his studies through life. His pen appears to have been in a sense always in his hand. From this practice steadily persevered in, he derived the very great advantages of thinking continually during each period of study; of thinking accurately; of thinking connectedly; of thinking habitually at all times.

Perhaps no person ever lived who so habitually and carefully committed his thoughts, on almost every subject, to writing, as the elder President Edwards. His ordinary studies were pursued pen in hand, and with his notebooks before him; and he not only often stopped in his daily rides by the wayside, but frequently rose even at midnight to commit to paper any important thought that had occurred to him.

SERENO DWIGHT
Memoirs of Jonathan Edwards

CHAPTER THREE

JONATHAN EDWARDS,
A MIND IN LOVE WITH GOD

The Private Life of a Modern Evangelical

My approach in this present chapter will be to take you on a guided tour of my own personal encounter with Edwards over the last thirty years. I hope I can introduce you to his writings and thought, as it became powerful in my own life. In this way, perhaps I can mingle enough biblical theology, biography, and autobiography so that you not only have a fresh meeting with Edwards, but also see how his life and thought have shaped one modern evangelical. The point of the title is to say that the life and thought of Jonathan Edwards is relevant for the way modern evangelicals think and feel about God in relation to our own devotion, study, and worship.

The Doctrinal Weakening of Evangelicalism

I resonate with the lament of Os Guinness and David Wells that evangelicalism today is basking briefly in the sunlight of hollow success. Evangelical industries of television and radio and publishing and music recordings, as well as hundreds of growing mega-churches and some highly visible public figures and political movements, give outward impressions of vitality and strength. But both Wells and Guinness, in their own ways, have called attention to the hollowing out of evangelicalism from within.[1]

In other words, the strong timber of the tree of evangelicalism has historically been the great doctrines of the Bible—God's glorious perfections, man's fallen nature, the wonders of redemptive history, the magnificent work of redemption in Christ, the saving and sanctifying work of grace in the soul, the great mission of the church in conflict with the world and the flesh and the devil, and the greatness of our hope of everlasting joy at God's right hand. These things once defined us and were the strong fiber and timber beneath the fragile leaves and fruit of our religious experiences. But this is the case less and less. And that is why the waving leaves of success and the sweet fruit of prosperity are not as auspicious to David Wells and Os Guinness as they are to many. It is a hollow triumph, and the tree is getting weaker and weaker while the branches are waving in the sun.

Edwards: Beware of Pragmatic Criticisms of Pragmatism

But right at this point Jonathan Edwards comes to our aid. And the first thing he would say is this: Beware lest even in your description of the problem your diagnosis falls prey to the very categories of pragmatism that constitute the problem. In other words, don't bemoan the condition of evangelicalism because it is hollow and therefore weakening—as if the real goal is *lasting* prominence

---

[1] "In one generation the evangelical movement has experienced a sea of change: It has moved from being, in large part, confessionally defined to being a fraternity of institutions to being virtually a coalition of causes to being a movement in plain disarray. Worst of all, there is neither an agreed defining character of 'evangelical' around which reformation and regrouping can occur nor any evident leadership willing or able to assert it. . . . The truth is, for those who think, the present state of American evangelicalism is appalling. As a spiritually and theologically defined community of faith, evangelicalism is weak or next to nonexistent; as a subculture, it is stronger but often embarrassing and downright offensive" (Os Guinness, *Fit Bodies Fat Minds: Why Evangelicals Don't Think and What to Do About It* [Grand Rapids: Baker Books, 1994], p.15). In his recent book, *Losing Our Virtue*, David Wells continues the lament: "Twenty-five years ago, I am quite certain, I could have cheerfully used the word *theology* without having to reach for the smelling salts. . . . It was a time when evangelical beliefs were more certain than they are now, theology was a more honorable word, and there was a sense of mission that was infectious. That was the day when the trees that stood tall in this world were usually made so by their theological conviction and not simply by their money, the size of their church, or the expansiveness of their organization. . . . [To be sure there has been growth, but] along with this astounding growth—indeed, we might even say, conquest—there has nevertheless come a hollowing out of evangelical conviction, a loss of the biblical Word in its authoritative function, and an erosion of character to the point that today, no discernible ethical differences are evident in behavior when those claiming to have been reborn and secularists are compared" (*Losing Our Virtue: Why the Church Must Recover Its Moral Vision* [Grand Rapids: William B. Eerdmans Publishing Co., 1998], pp. 2-3).

rather than *temporary* prominence. Instead, bemoan the condition of evangelicalism because it contradicts the truth of God and belittles his worth.

What would he mean? He would mean something implied in the title of this chapter—"Jonathan Edwards, A Mind in Love with God." Here you have two words orienting on God: *Mind* and *Love*. These two words correspond to one of the deepest lessons Edwards ever taught. *Mind* (or understanding) and *love* (or affection) correspond to two great acts of the Godhead, and two ways that humans in his image reflect back to God his own glory. Here's the way he put it in his notebooks called the *Miscellanies*, many of which formed the basis of *The End for Which God Created the World* (Part Two of this book):

> God is glorified within Himself these two ways: 1. By appearing . . . to Himself in His own perfect idea [of Himself], or in His Son, who is the brightness of His glory. 2. By enjoying and delighting in Himself, by flowing forth in infinite love and delight towards Himself, or in his Holy Spirit. . . . So God glorifies Himself toward the creatures also in two ways: 1. By appearing to . . . their understanding. 2. In communicating Himself to their hearts, and in their rejoicing and delighting in, and enjoying, the manifestations which He makes of Himself. . . . *God is glorified not only by His glory's being seen, but by its being rejoiced in.* When those that see it delight in it, God is more glorified than if they only see it. His glory is then received by the whole soul, both by the understanding and by the heart. God made the world that He might communicate, and the creature receive, His glory; and that it might [be] received both by the mind and heart. He that testifies his idea of God's glory [doesn't] glorify God so much as he that testifies also his approbation of it and his delight in it.[2]

Glorifying God by Enjoying Him Forever

This is the same vision of God that we saw in Chapter One. And as I said there, I can scarcely overstate what it has meant in my

---

[2] Jonathan Edwards, *The Miscellanies*, ed. by Thomas Schafer, *The Works of Jonathan Edwards*, vol. 13 (New Haven: Yale University Press, 1994), p. 495. Miscellany #448; see also #87, pp. 251-252; #332, p. 410. Emphasis added.

life and theology and preaching. Virtually everything I write is
an effort to explain and illustrate that truth. In Chapter One I
paraphrased Edwards with the words, "God is most glorified in
us when we are most satisfied in him." Here my paraphrase is:
"The chief end of man is to glorify God *by* enjoying him forever."
This is the essence of what I call "Christian hedonism."[3] There
is no final conflict between God's passion to be glorified and
man's passion to be satisfied. Here is another way that Edwards
says it:

> Because [God] infinitely values his own glory, consisting in the
> knowledge of himself, love to himself, [that is,] complacence[4] and
> joy in himself; he therefore valued the image, communication or
> participation of these, in the creature. And it is because he val-
> ues himself, that he delights in the knowledge, and love, and joy
> of the creature; as being himself the object of this knowledge,
> love and complacence [i.e., satisfaction, delight]. . . . [Thus]
> *God's respect to the creature's good [that is, our passion to be
> satisfied], and his respect to himself [that is, his passion to be glo-
> rified], is not a divided respect; but both are united in one, as the
> happiness of the creature aimed at, is happiness in union with
> himself.*[5]

You Can't Love Your Own Happiness Too Much

It follows from all this that it is impossible that anyone can pursue joy or satisfaction with too much passion and zeal and intensity. Edwards said, "I do not suppose it can be said of any, that
their love to their own happiness . . . can be in too high a degree."[6]
It can be misdirected to wrong objects, but not too strong. It's the

[3] The concept of Christian Hedonism and the vision of God and life behind it are unfolded in
Desiring God: Meditations of a Christian Hedonist (Sisters, OR: Multnomah Press, 1996).

[4] The term "complacence" in Edwards's writings has none of the negative connotations of indifference or apathy that we give the word. It was a positive and strong sense of satisfaction or
delight or contentment in something because of its worth or beauty. He distinguished between
a love of complacence (taking delight in what something is) and a love of benevolence (willing
that good come to a person).

[5] *The End for Which God Created the World*, ¶ 278. Emphasis added.

[6] Jonathan Edwards, *Charity and Its Fruits*, in: *Ethical Writings, The Works of Jonathan
Edwards*, vol. 8, ed. by Paul Ramsey (New Haven: Yale University Press, 1989), p. 255.

same thing C. S. Lewis said in that fateful passage that began to turn my world upside-down in 1968:

> If we consider the unblushing promises of reward and the staggering nature of the rewards promised in the Gospels, it would seem that our Lord finds our desires not too strong, but too weak. We are half-hearted creatures, fooling about with drink and sex and ambition when infinite joy is offered us, like an ignorant child who wants to go on making mud pies in a slum because he cannot imagine what is meant by the offer of a holiday at the sea. We are far too easily pleased.[7]

Sin Is the Suicidal Abandonment of Joy

In other words, the pursuit of our soul's satisfaction—our joy and delight and happiness—is not sin. Sin is the exact opposite: pursuing happiness where no lasting happiness can be found. "My people have committed two evils: they have forsaken me, the fountain of living waters, and hewed out cisterns for themselves, broken cisterns, that can hold no water" (Jer. 2:13, RSV). Sin is trying to quench our unquenchable soul-thirst anywhere but in God. Or, more subtly, sin is pursuing satisfaction in the *right* direction, but with lukewarm, halfhearted affections (Rev. 3:16).

"To Live with All My Might"

Virtue, on the other hand, is to pursue the enjoyment of God with all our might. No halfhearted, polite, dutiful religiosity here! One of Edwards's resolutions that he recorded in his notebooks early in life and seems to have kept all his days was #6: "Resolved: To live with all my might, while I do live."[8] Pursuing delight in God is not something one may do halfheartedly, if he realizes who he is pursuing and what is at stake. The cultivation of spiritual appetite is a great duty for all the saints. So Edwards says in a sermon on the Song of Solomon, "Men . . . ought to indulge those

---

[7] C. S. Lewis, *The Weight of Glory, and Other Addresses* (Grand Rapids: Eerdmans Publishing Company, 1965), p. 2.

[8] Jonathan Edwards's "Resolution #6," in: *The Works of Jonathan Edwards*, vol. I (Edinburgh: The Banner of Truth Trust), p. xx.

appetites. To obtain as much of those spiritual satisfactions as lies in their power."[9]

Doctrine to Be Seen and Glory to Be Savored

Now connect all this with the title of this chapter and those two words that I said correspond to two great acts of the Godhead—and two ways that humans in God's image reflect back to God his own glory: "Jonathan Edwards, A Mind in Love with God." *Mind* corresponds to the understanding of the truth of God's perfections. *Love* corresponds to the delight in the worth and beauty of those perfections. God is glorified both by being understood and by being delighted in. He is not glorified so much by one brand of evangelicals who divorce delight from understanding. And he is not glorified so much by another branch of evangelicals who divorce understanding from delight. There is truth to be known aright, and there is beauty to be cherished aright. There is doctrine to be seen, and there is glory to be savored.

At Stake Is the Loss of God

What is at stake in the doctrinal hollowing out of contemporary evangelicalism is the loss of God. And with him the loss of his truth and beauty. And with the loss of divine truth and beauty, the loss of truly seeing God and savoring God. Soon we may wake up and discover the evangelical king has no clothes on. The successes are hollow. And worst of all, our very reason for being may be lost—the capacity to know and love the glory of God. And if we lose the true knowledge of God and the true love of God—the seeing and savoring of God—then we lose our ability to reflect his truth and beauty in the world. And the world loses God. That is finally what is at stake.

I turn now to the story of my personal encounter with Edwards, and the pilgrimage of the last thirty years of friendship with him. The point here is to whet your appetite for his

---

[9] I owe this quote to Professor Don Westblade of Hillsdale College, who transcribed the unpublished sermon of Edwards (from the Jonathan Edwards Project at Yale University) on Canticles 5:1, with the doctrine stated: "That persons need not and ought not to set any bounds to their spiritual and gracious appetites."

works—especially the one in Part Two of this book—and to supplement the account of Edwards's life in Chapter Two by giving the gist of his main writings. My conviction is that if I can infect you with Edwards, you will have a very powerful inoculation against the hollowing disease of our times.

Sinking One Deep Shaft

When I was in seminary, a wise professor told me that besides the Bible I ought to choose one great theologian and apply myself throughout life to understanding and mastering his thought, to sink at least one shaft deep into reality rather than always dabbling on the surface of things. I might in time become this man's peer and know at least one system with which to bring other ideas into fruitful dialogue. It was good advice.

The theologian I have devoted myself to more than any other is Jonathan Edwards. All I knew of Edwards when I went to seminary was that he had preached a sermon called "Sinners in the Hands of an Angry God," in which he said something about hanging over hell by a slender thread.[10] This is typical of the caricature of Edwards portrayed in literature and history classes. Identifying Jonathan Edwards with "Sinners in the Hands of an Angry God" is like identifying Jesus with the woes against Chorazin and Bethsaida. This is a fraction of the whole, and it is not the main achievement.

I was unaware of assessments like those of Samuel Davies (in 1759), that Edwards "was the profoundest reasoner, and the greatest divine . . . that America ever produced"; or of Ashbel Green (in

---

[10] "The God that holds you over the pit of hell, much as one holds a spider, or some loathsome insect, over the fire, abhors you, and is dreadfully provoked: his wrath towards you burns like fire; he looks upon you as worthy of nothing else, but to be cast into the fire; he is of purer eyes than to bear to have you in his sight; you are ten thousand times more abominable in his eyes, than the most hateful venomous serpent is in ours" (Jonathan Edwards, "Sinners in the Hands of an Angry God," a sermon on Deuteronomy 32:35, "Their foot shall slide in due time," in: *The Works of Jonathan Edwards*, vol. 2 [Edinburgh: The Banner of Truth Trust, 1974], p. 10). Edwards believes that the words of Scripture on hell "are exceeding terrible," which they certainly are: "the winepress of the fierceness and wrath of Almighty God" (Rev. 19:15); "the furnace of fire . . . weeping and gnashing of teeth" (Matt. 13:42); "this place of torment" (Luke 16:28), "their worm does not die and their fire is not quenched" (Mark 9:48). Thus his own words are also "exceedingly terrible." When the horror has been seen the offer of mercy comes in the sermon: "Now God stands ready to pity you; this is a day of mercy; you may cry now with some encouragement of obtaining mercy. . . . You have an extraordinary opportunity, a day wherein Christ has thrown the door of mercy wide open, and stands in calling, and crying with a loud voice to poor sinners" (pp. 10-11).

1822), that "He was . . . one of the most holy, humble and heavenly minded men, that the world has seen, since the apostolic age"; or of Thomas Chalmers, that "Never was there a happier combination of great power with great piety"; or Benjamin Warfield, that "Jonathan Edwards, saint and metaphysician, revivalist and theologian, stands out as the one figure of real greatness in the intellectual life of colonial America."[11] Now I know this from the inside out and don't need witnesses anymore. But I would become a witness for others. And to that I now turn.

Encountering the Trinity

My first real encounter with Edwards was in a church history course with Geoffrey Bromiley when I chose to write a paper on Edwards's "Essay on the Trinity." It was one of those defining moments when my view of God's being was forever stamped. The Son of God is the eternal idea or image that God has of himself. And the image that he has of himself is so perfect and so complete and so full as to *be* the living, personal reproduction (or begetting) of God the Father. And this living, personal image or radiance or form of God *is* God, namely, God the Son. And therefore God the Son is coeternal with God the Father and equal in essence and glory.

And between the Son and the Father there arises eternally an infinitely holy personal communion of love. "The divine essence itself flows out and is, as it were, breathed forth in love and joy. So that the Godhead therein stands forth in yet another manner of subsistence, and there proceeds the third person in the Trinity, the Holy Spirit."[12] He sums up his vision of the Trinity with these words:

> This I suppose to be that blessed Trinity that we read of in the holy Scriptures. The Father is the deity subsisting in the prime, unoriginated and most absolute manner, or the deity in its direct existence. The Son is the deity generated by God's understand-

---

[11] These are all quoted in Iain Murray, *Jonathan Edwards, A New Biography* (Edinburgh: The Banner of Truth Trust, 1987), pp. xv-xvii.

[12] Jonathan Edwards, "An Essay on the Trinity," in *Treatise on Grace and Other Posthumously Published Writings*, ed. by Paul Helm (Cambridge: James Clarke and Co. Ltd., 1971), p. 108.

ing, or having an idea of Himself and subsisting in that idea. The Holy Ghost is the deity subsisting in act, or the divine essence flowing out and breathed forth in God's infinite love to and delight in Himself. And I believe the whole Divine essence does truly and distinctly subsist both in the Divine idea and Divine love, and that each of them are properly distinct persons.[13]

You can see how this understanding of the Trinity coheres with what Edwards says about the conception of God glorifying himself in two ways: by being known and being loved or enjoyed.[14] That corresponds to the very way the Godhead exists: the Son is the standing forth of God *knowing* himself perfectly, and the Spirit is the standing forth of God *loving* himself perfectly. You can perhaps feel the fire that began to burn in my bones as I saw a more profound unity in the nature of things than I had ever imagined.

The Mystery Is Greater for Knowing More

Nevertheless Edwards was not simplistic and did not leave me with naïve notions that I now had the Trinity in my back pocket. Far from it. Those who have climbed highest see more clearly than those in the cloudy regions below how much higher the reaches of the mountains of God really are. Below we talk about mystery because we cannot see above the clouds. Above the clouds Edwards talks of mystery because the peaks of divinity stretch out into space without end. Here is the way he cautioned and sobered me.

> I am far from affording this as any explication of this mystery, that unfolds and renews the mysteriousness and incomprehensibleness of it, for I am sensible that however by what has been said some difficulties are lessened, others that are new appear, and the number of those things that appear mysterious, wonderful and incomprehensible, is increased by it. I offer it only as a farther manifestation of what of divine truth the Word of God exhibits to the view of our minds concerning this great mystery. I think the Word of God teaches us more things concerning it to be believed by us than have been generally believed, and that it

---

[13] "Essay on the Trinity," p. 118.

[14] See above, footnote 2.

exhibits many things concerning it exceeding glorious and wonderful than have been taken notice of.[15]

This encounter with Edwards and his vision of the Trinity happened in 1969, and I knew that the Edwards I had met in high
school was a caricature.

The Greatest Work: Freedom of the Will

The next work of Edwards that I read was *The Freedom of the
Will*. I found it to be in harmony with my exegetical efforts in
classes on Romans and Galatians, and I found it compelling philosophically. Thus Saint Paul and Jonathan Edwards conspired to
demolish my previous notions about freedom. The book was a
defense of Calvinistic theology, but Edwards says in the preface,
"I should not take it at all amiss, to be called a Calvinist, for distinction's sake: though I utterly disclaim a dependence on Calvin,
or believing the doctrines which I hold, because he believed and
taught them, and cannot justly be charged with believing in everything just as he taught."[16]

In a capsule, the book argues that "God's moral government
over mankind, his treating them as moral agents, making them the
objects of his commands, counsels, calls [and] warnings . . . is not
inconsistent with a *determining disposal* of all events, of every kind
throughout the universe, *in his providence;* either by positive efficiency or permission."[17] There is no such thing as freedom of the
will in the Arminian sense of a will that ultimately determines
itself. The will rather is determined by "that motive which, as it
stands in the view of the mind, is the strongest."[18] But motives are
given, not ultimately controllable by the will.

For Augustine It Is the Delight That Guides the Will

Here Edwards found himself squarely in the great Reformed-
Augustinian tradition. Augustine, the African Bishop of Hippo,

---

[15] "Essay on the Trinity," pp. 127-128.

[16] Jonathan Edwards, *The Freedom of the Will*, in: *The Works of Jonathan Edwards*, vol. 1, ed.
by Paul Ramsey (Yale University Press, 1957), p. 131.

[17] *The Freedom of the Will*, p. 431.

[18] *The Freedom of the Will*, p. 141.

had analyzed his own motives down to this root: Everything springs from delight. He saw this as a universal: "Every man, whatsoever his condition, desires to be happy. There is no man who does not desire this, and each one desires it with such earnestness that he prefers it to all other things; whoever, in fact, desires other things, desires them for this end alone."[19] This is what guides and governs the will, namely, what we consider to be our delight. But the catch that made Pelagius, Augustine's antagonist, so angry was that it is not in our power to determine what this delight will be. Thus Augustine asks,

> Who has it in his power to have such a motive present to his mind that his will shall be influenced to believe? Who can welcome in his mind something which does not give him delight? But who has it in his power to ensure that something that will delight him will turn up? Or that he will take delight in what turns up? If those things delight us which serve our advancement towards God, that is due not to our own whim or industry or meritorious works, but to the inspiration of God and to the grace which he bestows.[20]

So saving grace, converting grace, for Augustine is *God's giving us a sovereign joy in God* that triumphs over all other joys and therefore sways the will. The will is free to move toward whatever it delights in most fully, but it is not within the power of our will to determine what that *sovereign joy* will be.

Therefore Augustine concludes, "A man's free-will, indeed, avails for nothing except to sin, if he knows not the way of truth; and even after his duty and his proper aim shall begin to become known to him, unless he also take delight in and feel a love for it, he neither does his duty, nor sets about it, nor lives rightly. Now, in order that such a course may engage our affections, God's 'love is shed abroad in our hearts' not through the free-will which arises

---

[19] Thomas A. Hand, *Augustine On Prayer* (New York: Catholic Book Publishing Co., 1986), p. 13 (Sermon 306). See Aurelius Augustine, *Confessions*, p. 228 (x, 21): "Without exception we all long for happiness. . . . All agree that they want to be happy. . . . They may all search for it in different ways, but all try their hardest to reach the same goal, that is, joy."

[20] Quote from Augustine's *To Simplician* (ii, 21) in T. Kermit Scott, *Augustine: His Thought in Context* (New York: Paulist Press, 1995), p. 203.

from ourselves, but 'through the Holy Ghost, which is given to us' (Romans 5:5)."[21]

An Inability That Leaves Responsibility in Place

In this tradition, Jonathan Edwards explained that all people are enslaved, as Saint Paul says, either to sin or to righteousness (Rom. 6:16-23; see also John 8:34; 1 John 3:9); but slavery to sin, inability to love and trust God (see Rom. 8:8), does not excuse the sinner, for this inability is moral, not physical. It is not an inability that prevents a man from believing when he would like to believe; rather, it is a moral corruption of the heart that renders motives to believe ineffectual. The person thus enslaved to sin cannot believe without the miracle of regeneration, but is nevertheless accountable because of the evil of his heart, which disposes him to be unmoved by reasonable motives in the gospel.

In this way Edwards tried to show that the Arminian notion of the will's ability to determine itself is *not* a prerequisite of moral accountability. Rather, in Edwards's words, "All inability that excuses may be resolved into one thing, namely, want of natural capacity or strength; either capacity of understanding, or external strength."[22]

A pastor and missionary all his life, Jonathan Edwards wrote what is probably the greatest defense and explanation of the Augustinian-Reformed view of the will. It is primarily due to this book, *The Freedom of the Will*, that many subsequent scholars have called Edwards the greatest American philosopher-theologian. Paul Ramsey, who edited the book for the Yale edition of the collected works, agrees that it is "Edwards's greatest literary achievement."[23] Aside from its intrinsic power, the clearest witness to its merit is its enduring impact in theology and philosophy.

Finney's Fury

When evangelist Charles G. Finney a hundred years later wanted to level his guns against the Calvinistic view of the will, he did not

---

[21] T. Kermit Scott, *Augustine: His Thought in Context*, p. 208 (*Spirit and Letter*, v).

[22] *The Freedom of the Will*, p. 310.

[23] *The Freedom of the Will*, p. 1.

see any of his own contemporaries or even Calvin himself as the chief adversary. There was one great opponent among the Calvinists that had to be defeated: Jonathan Edwards's *Freedom of the Will*. Finney's assessment of the book in a word: "Ridiculous! Edwards I revere; his blunders I deplore. I speak thus of this Treatise on the Will, because while it abounds with unwarrantable assumption, distinctions without difference, and metaphysical subtleties, it has been adopted as the textbook of a multitude of what are called Calvinistic divines for scores of years."[24]

But for all its vehemence, Finney's shot missed the mark, and Edwards's great vision of God's sovereignty over the fallen human will endures today, relentlessly exerting its power in theology and philosophy alike. In 1949, Perry Miller would chastise academics for their prejudice against Edwards and their frequent caricatures of him as an antiquarian specimen of hell-fire preaching from the long-lost times of the Great Awakening. Miller's own assessment: "He speaks with an insight into science and psychology so much ahead of his time that our own can hardly be said to have caught up with him."[25]

Cementing the Truth of God's Supremacy in All Things

Beginning in 1957, Yale University Press began to publish a new critical edition of Edwards's works, which is scheduled for completion in 2003, the tercentennial of Edwards's birth. It is not surprising that the first work they chose to publish was *The Freedom of the Will*. It is simply without peer. We would live in a different and better world of evangelicalism if Christians would read it and embrace its truth. Nothing cements the truth of God's supremacy in all things for the joy of all peoples like an unshakable Biblical confidence in the sovereignty of God over the will of man.

Georgia Woods and The Nature of True Virtue

That was all of Edwards that I read in seminary. After graduation in 1971, before graduate work in Germany, my wife and I

---

[24] Charles Finney, *Finney's Systematic Theology* (Minneapolis: Bethany Fellowship, Inc., 1976), p. 269.

[25] Perry Miller, *Jonathan Edwards* (Westport, CT: Greenwood Press, Publishers, 1973, orig. 1949), p. xiii.

spent some restful days at her folks' place in rural Georgia. Here I had my third encounter with Edwards. Sitting on one of those old-fashioned two-seater swings in the backyard under a big hickory tree, with pen in hand, I read *The Nature of True Virtue*. This is Edwards's only purely non-polemical work. If you have ever felt a sense of aesthetic awe at beholding a pure idea given lucid expression, you may understand what I mean when I say that this book aroused in me a deeply pleasurable aesthetic experience. But more importantly it gave me a brand-new awareness that the categories of morality resolve ultimately into categories of spiritual aesthetics, and one of the last things you can say about virtue is that it is "a kind of beautiful nature, form or quality."[26]

Perry Miller said that "the book is not a reasoning about virtue but a beholding it." Edwards gazes on the conception of virtue "until it yields up meaning beyond meaning, and the simulacra fall away. The book approaches, as nearly as any creation in our literature, a naked idea."[27] I think it was perfectly in accord with Edwards's intention that when I finished that book I not only had a deep longing to be a good man, but I also wrote a poem called "Georgia Woods," because nothing looked the same when I put the book down.

Clothing the Naked Idea of Virtue with Love

Noël and I left for Germany in the fall of 1971 to study at the University of Munich for three years. The field was New Testament, not systematic theology. But I would venture to say that Edwards was as inspiring and helpful in my studies as any New Testament scholar I read. During those years I read three more works by Edwards and biographies by Samuel Hopkins and Henry Pamford Parkes. For our family time in the evenings Noël and I read to each other a collection of his sermons called *Charity and Its Fruits*,[28] a 360-page exposition (in our old edition) of 1 Corinthians 13. We agreed that it was verbose and repetitive, but

---

[26] Jonathan Edwards, *The Nature of True Virtue*, in: *The Works of Jonathan Edwards*, vol. 8 (New Haven: Yale University Press, 1989), p. 619.

[27] *Jonathan Edwards*, p. 286.

[28] *Charity and Its Fruits*, in: *Ethical Writings*, ed. by Paul Ramsey, *The Works of Jonathan Edwards*, vol. 8 (New Haven: Yale University Press, 1989), pp. 123-398.

it did help me clothe with nitty-gritty experience that "naked idea" in *The Nature of True Virtue*.

Is Love Allowed to "Seek Its Own" Joy?

Perhaps the most important insight we saw related to my emerging Christian Hedonism. Is 1 Corinthians 13:5 ("Love seeks not its own") contrary to the conviction—which I learned from Edwards—that we should glorify God by *seeking our holy joy* in all that we do? Is that pursuit of our own joy contrary to the truth, "Love seeks not its own"? Here is Edwards's answer:

> Some, although they love their own happiness, do not place that happiness in their own confined good, or in that good which is limited to themselves, but more in the common good, in that which is the good of others as well as their own, in good to be enjoyed *in* others and to be enjoyed *by* others. And man's love of his own happiness which runs in this channel is not what is called selfishness, but is quite opposite to it. . . . This is the thing most directly intended by that self-love which the Scripture condemns. When it is said that charity seeketh not her own, we are to understand it of her own private good, good limited to herself.[29]

In other words, if what makes a person happy is the extension of his joy in God into the lives of others, then it is not wrong to seek that happiness, because it magnifies God and blesses people. Love is the labor of Christian Hedonism, not its opposite.[30]

Turning a German Pantry into a Vestibule of Heaven

Just off the kitchen in our little apartment in Munich was a pantry about 8 by 5 feet, a most unlikely place to read a *Dissertation Concerning the End for Which God Created the World*. From my perspective now, I would say that if one book captures the essence or wellspring of Edwards's theology it is this. That is why I have

---

[29] Jonathan Edwards, *Charity and Its Fruits*, in: *The Works of Jonathan Edwards*, vol. 8 (Yale University Press, 1989), p. 257-258.

[30] "The Labor of Christian Hedonism" is the name of the chapter on love in *Desiring God: Meditations of a Christian Hedonist* (Sisters, OR: Multnomah Press, 1996) and is my fuller effort to give an account for the "true virtue" of pursuing our joy in loving others.

wanted for a long time to make the book more accessible for serious Christian readers on their own quest for more of God. You can read it for yourself in Part Two of this book.

Edwards's answer to why God created the world was that God has a disposition to emanate the fullness of his glory for his people to know, praise, and enjoy. Here is the heart of his theology in his own words:

> It appears that all that is ever spoken of in the Scripture as an ultimate end of God's works is included in that one phrase, *the glory of God*. . . . In the creature's knowing, esteeming, loving, rejoicing in, and praising God, the glory of God is both *exhibited* and *acknowledged*; his fullness is *received* and *returned*. Here is both an *emanation* and *remanation*. The refulgence shines upon and into the creature, and is reflected back to the luminary. The beams of glory come from God, are something of God, and are refunded back again to their original. So that the whole is *of* God, and *in* God, and *to* God; and he is the beginning, and the middle, and the end.[31]

That is the heart and center of Jonathan Edwards and, I believe, of the Bible too. That kind of reading can turn a pantry into a vestibule of heaven. And it is the essence of what is needed today to overcome the hollowing out of evangelical life and the collapsing of our private meditations into self-centered musings.

Sunday Evening Fire

The last work of Edwards's I read in Germany was his *Treatise Concerning Religious Affections*. For several months it was the meat of my Sunday evening meditations. I can remember writing letters week after week to former teachers, to friends, and to my parents about the effect this book was having on me. Far more than *The Nature of True Virtue*, this book convicted me of sinful lukewarmness in my affections toward God and inspired in me a passion to know and love God as I ought.

The thesis of the book is very simple: "True religion, in great

---

[31] See below, *The End for Which God Created the World*, ¶ 272.

part, consists in the Affections."[32] Perhaps the reason the book moved me so deeply is because it was Edwards's effort to save the best of two worlds—the very worlds in which I grew up and now live, and the two worlds implied in the title of this chapter: "A *Mind* in *Love* with God."

Saving the Best of Two Worlds—My Worlds

On the one hand, Edwards wanted to defend the genuine and necessary place of the affections[33] in religious experience. On the other hand, he was ruthlessly devoted to objective truth and wanted all emotion to be rooted in a true apprehension of reality and shaped by that reality. He had been more responsible than any man for the revival fervor that deluged New England in the fifteen years following 1734. Charles Chauncy of Boston led the opposition to this Great Awakening with its "swooning away and falling to the Ground . . . bitter Shriekings and Screamings; Convulsion-like Tremblings and Agitations, Strugglings and Tumblings."[34] He charged that it was "a plain stubborn Fact that, the Passions have, generally, in these Times, been applied to as though the main Thing in Religion was to throw them into Disturbance."[35] He insisted, "The plain truth is that an *enlightened Mind* and not *raised Affections* ought always to be the Guide of those who call themselves Men. . . ."[36]

Edwards took the other side: "I should think myself in the way of my duty to raise the affections of my hearers as high as possibly I can, provided that they are affected with nothing but truth, and with affections that are not disagreeable to the nature of what they are affected with."[37] That sentence shows that Edwards did

---

[32] Jonathan Edwards, *Treatise Concerning the Religious Affections*, ed. by John Smith, *The Works of Jonathan Edwards*, vol. 2 (New Haven: Yale University Press, 1959), p. 95.

[33] On the meaning of Edwards's term "affections" see Part Two, *The End for Which God Created the World*, footnote 27.

[34] Charles Chauncy, *Seasonable Thoughts on the State of Religion in New England*, quoted in *Jonathan Edwards: Selections*, ed. by Clarence Faust and Thomas Johnson (New York: Hill and Wang, 1962), p. xviii.

[35] *Seasonable Thoughts*, p. xx.

[36] *Seasonable Thoughts*, p. xx.

[37] Jonathan Edwards, *Some Thoughts Concerning the Revival*, in: *The Works of Jonathan Edwards*, vol. 4, ed. by C. Goen (New Haven: Yale University Press, 1972), p. 387.

not condone the enthusiastic excesses of the Great Awakening. Yet, it took time for him to sort out the true, spiritual affections from the false, merely human ones. *The Treatise Concerning Religious Affections,* published in 1746 (preached in 1742), was his mature effort to describe the signs of truly gracious and holy affections. It amounts to a Yes and a No to revivalistic religion: *yes* to the place of appropriate emotions springing from perceptions of truth, but *no* to the frenzies, private revelations, irrational swoonings, and false assurances of godliness.

Revival fervor and the reasonable apprehension of truth—these were the two worlds Edwards struggled to bring together. They are my worlds too. My father is an evangelist. He conducted evangelistic crusades for over fifty years, and I respect him very highly. I wish I had some of his gifts. I will probably never attain the fruitfulness of his soul-winning life. Rather, I am a theologically oriented pastor. I love my people and cherish our life together in worship and ministry. But I am fairly analytic and given to study. The ministry of the Word is my (protecting and guiding and encouraging) shepherd's staff. It is not surprising, then, that the *Religious Affections* should seem to me a very contemporary and helpful message. It brought together more of my personal history and personal makeup than any other of Edwards's books.

I said it was my food for many weeks. I give just one sampling that still feeds me. Edwards describes the person with truly gracious affections like this:

> As he has more holy boldness, so he has less of self-confidence . . . and more modesty. As he is more sure than others of deliverance from hell, so he has more of a sense of the desert of it. He is less apt than others to be shaken in faith, but more apt than others to be moved with solemn warnings, and with God's frowns, and with the calamities of others. He has the firmest comfort, but the softest heart: richer than others, but poorest of all in spirit; the tallest and strongest saint, but the least and tenderest child among them.[38]

---

[38] *Religious Affections,* p. 364.

That litany of unusual juxtapositions is what Jonathan Edwards embodied in himself. He kept together so many things that we are prone to separate. This is one of the reasons, as we saw in Chapter One, why he is so important for our day.[39]

Fifteen Minutes a Day Will Go a Long Way

Since those heady days of discovery and profound transformation from 1968 to 1974, I have tried to stay on the quest for "all the fullness of God" both intellectually and emotionally. And over the years Edwards has remained a faithful guide. When I left Germany and took up my teaching post at Bethel College in St. Paul, Minnesota, I continued to converse with Edwards regularly. I recall resolving one year to read Edwards fifteen minutes a day. That was the way I plodded through *Humble Inquiry*[40] and *The Great Christian Doctrine of Original Sin.*[41] This latter book gives evidence of what Mark Noll, in another place, called Edwards's "herculean intellectual labors."[42]

One Stunning Insight on Original Sin

One stunning insight stands out from the 335 pages of Edwards's massive exegetical and theological effort to understand original sin. Edwards asks how one man (like me) can be morally implicated in the sin of another (like Adam). He answers by asking why the "I" that exists today is responsible for the moral acts I did or didn't do yesterday. The answer, evidently, is that there is a union between the me of today and the me of yesterday. But why is there? he asks. He answers that "God's upholding created substance, or causing its existence in each successive moment, is altogether equivalent to *an immediate production out of nothing*, at each moment, because its existence at this moment is not merely in part

---

[39] See Chapter One, footnote 2.

[40] Jonathan Edwards, *An Humble Inquiry into the Rules of the Word of God, Concerning the Qualifications Requisite to a Complete Standing and Full Communion in the Visible Christian Church, The Works of Jonathan Edwards*, vol. 1 (Edinburgh: The Banner of Truth Trust, 1974), pp. 431-484.

[41] Jonathan Edwards, *The Great Christian Doctrine of Original Sin*, ed. by Clyde Holbrook, *The Works of Jonathan Edwards*, vol. 3 (New Haven: Yale University Press, 1970).

[42] *Christian History*, vol. 4, No. 4, p. 3.

from God, but wholly from him; and not in any part, or degree, from its antecedent existence."[43]

This implies, then, that the all-important union between the me of today and the me of yesterday is wholly dependent on God's "arbitrary constitution." "There is no identity or oneness . . . but what depends on the *arbitrary* constitution of the Creator; who by his wise sovereign establishment so unites these successive new effects, that he treats them as one, by communicating to them like properties, relations, and circumstances."[44] This means that ultimately the reason the me of today is morally responsible for the actions of the me of yesterday is that God has arbitrarily willed that it be so.

A Divine Constitution Makes Truth in Affairs of This Nature

Now you can see where Edwards is going with this in relation to original sin. Why are Adam's posterity so responsible for Adam's sin that they die as part of Adam's condemnation (Rom. 5:18)? How can there be a true union between us and Adam such that we are implicated in Adam's sin? Edwards's answer is that, just as God arbitrarily establishes a union between the moral consciousness of a person from one day to the next, so he can and does establish a union between Adam and his posterity on the analogy of the oneness of a tree including its root and branch. To the objection that this is not consistent with truth, he answers, "The objection we are upon, made against a supposed divine constitution, whereby Adam and his posterity are viewed and treated as one, in the manner and for the purposes supposed, as if it were not consistent with truth, because no constitution can make those to be one, which are not one, I say, it appears that this objection is built on a false hypothesis: for it appears, that a *divine constitution* is the thing which *makes truth*, in affairs of this nature."[45]

Whether or not this helps you to grasp the reality of original sin, which Saint Paul teaches in Romans 5:12-21, it certainly helped me, not by making it all simple and clear, but by showing me that there are possibilities of conceptuality and reality that I have not yet begun

---

[43] Jonathan Edwards, *Original Sin*, p. 402.

[44] *Original Sin*, p. 403.

[45] *Original Sin*, p. 404.

to think of. Which means it behooves me to keep my mouth shut rather than question a hard Biblical teaching. That is a humbling work, which Edwards has performed for me more than once.

Love for Truth and Love for God Are Inseparable

I could go on and tell of my encounters with the *Narrative of Surprising Conversions*, the *Treatise On Grace*, the unfinished *History of Redemption*, *The Memoirs of David Brainerd*, *Thoughts on the Revival of Religion in New England*, *Qualification for Communion*, *An Humble Attempt to Promote Explicit Agreement and Visible Union of God's People*, dozens of sermons, and two more biographies. But the point here is not to be exhaustive. The point is to introduce you to the work of Jonathan Edwards and illustrate his personal impact on one "modern evangelical"—an impact that I believe has been for the good, and for which I am profoundly thankful to God.

My own judgment is that, from generation to generation, giants like Edwards are needed to inspire us to think about our faith, and to guard us from settling superficially on small ideas about a small God. We need Edwards to waken us from our pragmatic stupor of indifference to doctrine in worship and prayer and evangelism and missions and church planting and social action. We need Edwards to show us again the beauty and the power of truth. Edwards does this so well because he is relentlessly God-besotted and God-exalting. He helps us recover truth because he never loses sight of the unspeakable reality of God, where truth originates, and whom it exists to serve.

Edwards has taught me—as one modern evangelical—that our concern with truth is an inevitable expression of our concern with God. If God exists, then he is the measure of all things, and what he thinks about all things is the measure of what we should think. Not to care about truth is not to care about God. To love God passionately is to love truth passionately. Being God-centered in life means being truth-driven in ministry. What is not true is not of God. What is false is anti-God. Indifference to the truth is indifference to the mind of God. Pretense is rebellion against reality, and what makes reality reality is God. Our concern with truth is simply an echo of our concern with God. And all this is rooted in God's concern with God, or God's passion for the glory of God.

A Christian spirit . . . disposes a person to be public-spirited. A man of a right spirit is not of a narrow, private spirit; but is greatly concerned for the good of the public community to which he belongs, and particularly of the town where he dwells.

JONATHAN EDWARDS
Charity and Its Fruits

In some sense, the most benevolent, generous person in the world seeks his *own* happiness in doing good to others, because he places his happiness in their good.

The whole universe, in all its actings, proceedings, revolutions, and entire series of events, should proceed with a view to God as the supreme and last end. . . . Every wheel, in all its rotations, should move with a constant invariable regard to him as the ultimate end of all; as perfectly and uniformly as if the whole system were animated and directed by one common soul.

JONATHAN EDWARDS
The End for Which God Created the World

CHAPTER FOUR

Jonathan Edwards,
Enjoying God and the
Transformation of Culture

The Public Life of a Modern Evangelical

As Physics to Space Travel, So Theology to Culture

Jonathan Edwards expressed concern about public life, or what we might call culture—but not very much. Discussions of social issues and public policies and programs have about as much place in his writings as they do in the New Testament. Which does not mean that what he wrote was irrelevant to public life and culture, any more than the New Testament is irrelevant. It was relevant—and *is* relevant—the way physics is relevant to space travel. And the way microbiology is relevant to a ten-day round of tetracycline.

It mattered to Jonathan Edwards, just as it should matter to us, whether a culture is diseased and scarred by fraud and bribery and wife-burning and witchcraft and foot-binding and marital unfaithfulness and teenage promiscuity and pervasive pornography and vigilante justice and rape and murder and theft and sloth and misogyny and pedophilia and dozens of forms of insolence and arrogance. Jonathan Edwards could not imagine a Christian being indifferent to the morals and manners of his own city or country. He said,

A Christian spirit . . . disposes a person to be public-spirited. A man of a right spirit is not of a narrow, private spirit; but is greatly concerned for the good of the public community to which he belongs, and particularly of the town where he dwells. God commanded the Jews that were carried captive to seek the good of the city of Babylon, though it was not their own city, but the city which had captivated them (Jer. 29:7). . . . A Christian spirited man will be also concerned for the good of his country, and it disposes him to lay out himself for it. . . . It is spoken of as a thing very provoking to God that they were not grieved for the calamities of their country (Amos 6:6).[1]

The Smallness of Only Being Concerned with Culture

That quote from a sermon on 1 Corinthians 13 gives us a glimpse into the cultural scope of Edwards's concern for the world. But even that quote doesn't come close to the scope he really believed in. Edwards knew something that many social activists and culture-watchers in America—evangelicals and others—don't seem to know or care about, namely, that cultures and societies and peoples who have no Christian presence in them at all cannot even begin to experience Christ-exalting social or cultural transformation. In other words, Edwards was deeply committed to world evangelization and cared as much (or more) about the advance of the kingdom among unreached peoples of the world as he did about the morals of Northampton, Massachusetts. He wrote to the evangelist George Whitefield in 1740,

> May God send forth more Laborers into his Harvest of a like Spirit, until the kingdom of Satan shall shake, and his proud Empire fall throughout the Earth, and the Kingdom of Christ, that glorious Kingdom of Light, holiness, Peace and Love, shall be established from one end of the Earth unto the other![2]

---

[1] Jonathan Edwards, *Charity and Its Fruits, Ethical Writings*, ed. by Paul Ramsey, in: *The Works of Jonathan Edwards*, vol. 8 (New Haven: Yale University Press, 1989), pp. 260-261.

[2] Quoted in Ronald E. Davies, "Jonathan Edwards: Missionary Biographer, Theologian, Strategist, Administrator, Advocate—and Missionary," in: *International Bulletin of Missionary Research*, April, 1997, p. 64.

In other words, if you had asked Edwards what is the really pressing, crucial issue of culture transformation in the world, I think Edwards would have said, "The really pressing issue in culture *transformation* is culture *penetration*. If the glorious God-centered gospel of Christ does not penetrate a people and beget worshipping, nurturing, evangelizing churches, there is not the slightest hope of transformation."

I think Edwards would have considered it astonishing how many Americans say they care about social justice and cultural issues, but don't seem to have the slightest concern for the hundreds of unreached people groups who do not have a known church-planting effort in their midst. Two thousand years have passed since the Lord of the universe gave the Great Commission to his church; yet there is not a single church, or a band of disciples or a solitary missionary among hundreds or even thousands of unreached people groups, depending on how you define them[3]—not to mention several thousand other peoples with a barely discernible Christian presence and witness. Such peoples cannot even begin to trust Christ for the power and wisdom and love to transform cultural darkness into light.

How Would Edwards Use the Internet?

Jesus said to the apostle Paul on the Damascus road, "I am sending you, [to the Gentiles, the nations] to open their eyes so that they may turn from darkness to light and from the dominion of Satan to God" (Acts 26:17-18). Edwards knew that this was the only way transforming light would come to the peoples of the world—namely, by missionaries being *sent* with a message of truth about the triumph of Jesus over sin and Satan and death.

Edwards loved to get news of the works of God in advancing his kingdom among unreached people groups. If he were alive today he would probably be on the Internet from time to time, following what is happening in global efforts to complete the task of world evangelization. Such globally minded missions-driven peo-

---

[3] As I write this chapter, the *Joshua Project 2000* estimates that there are about 579 people groups with over 10,000 population but no church or mission agency even targeting them with a church planting effort. See the Web Page for the AD 2000 Movement (www.ad2000.org), specifically the "Joshua Project 2000," for the listing of the 1739 most unreached peoples.

ple are the Christians with the *really* "public life," as Edwards meant it.

Brainerd's Mission and the Impact on Culture

His publication of David Brainerd's journals was an effort to make this point, among others. In his appendix to *The Life of Brainerd*, he said, "There is much in the preceding account to excite and encourage God's people to earnest prayers and endeavors for the advancement and enlargement of the kingdom of Christ in the world."[4] When he contemplated the unreached "nations" of Indians in "the wilderness" of America, he thought not only of redeemed persons, but also of transformed cultures. He defended Brainerd's Calvinistic beliefs by pointing to the remarkable trans-formation that had come to the Native American communities Brainerd served. Of those who said that Calvinism undermined "the very foundation of all religion and morality" he said,

> Where can they find an instance of so great and signal an effect of their doctrines in bringing infidels, who were at such a distance from all that is civil, human, sober, rational, and Christian, and so full of inveterate prejudices against these things, to such a degree of humanity, civility, exercise of reason, self-denial, and Christian virtue? Arminians place religion in morality: Let them bring an instance of their doctrines producing such a transfor-mation of a people in point of morality.[5]

In other words, Edwards did not conceive of world missions and the reaching of unreached tribes as a merely individualistic thing. The God-centered gospel as he understood it had great power to transform a culture through the people it changed.

There Is More Than One Kind of Privatism

If there is a problem today with privatistic religion, the worst form of it is not with pietistic evangelicals who don't care about block clubs and social justice and structural sin. The worst form is with

---

[4] Jonathan Edwards, *The Life of David Brainerd*, ed. by Norman Pettit, *The Works of Jonathan Edwards*, vol. 7 (New Haven: Yale University Press, 1985), pp. 531-532.

[5] *The Life of David Brainerd*, p. 526.

evangelicals who think they are publicly- and socially-minded when they have no passion for millions of perishing people without the gospel that alone can give them eternal life, and without a saving knowledge of the Light of the world who can transform their culture.

So the first message of Jonathan Edwards to modern evangelicals about our public lives is: Don't limit your passion for justice and peace to such a limited concern as the church-saturated landscape of American culture. Lift up your eyes to the real crisis of our day: namely, several thousand[6] cultures still unpenetrated by the gospel, who can't even dream of the blessings we want to restore. That is his first message.

The Narrowness of Embracing All as the Echo of the Self's Worth

But even that is not the main thing Jonathan Edwards would want to say to us. Because the real narrowness of our souls is not signified by our failure to embrace the city and the nations, but by our failure to embrace God in all of our other embracing. Edwards's diagnosis of the narrow and confined and selfish interests of human nature is that we are all idolaters of the self and are only interested in ourselves, or—as an extension of ourselves—*our* own family or *our* own city or *our* own world or even our own God, to the degree that we see even God as a reflection of our own value. In other words, even embracing God can be narrow and limited and confined and merely selfish if we embrace him only because he makes much of *us*.

The Fall as the Shrinking of the Soul's Concern

In 1738 Edwards preached a series of messages on 1 Corinthians 13, later published under the title, *Charity and Its Fruits* His sermon on verse 5, "Charity . . . seeketh not her own," is entitled, "The Spirit of Charity, the Opposite of a Selfish Spirit." In it, he gives his diagnosis of the human heart. It all began with the fall of man into sin in the Garden of Eden:

> The ruin that the Fall brought upon the soul of man consists very
> much in that he lost the nobler and more extensive principles,

---

[6] The numbers you pick here depend on the degree of penetration you have in mind. Suffice it to say, compared to the densely evangelized American landscape, there are thousands of people groups with virtually no self-sustaining witness.

and fell wholly under the government of self-love. . . .
Immediately upon the Fall the mind of man shrunk from its primitive greatness and extensiveness into an exceeding diminution
and confinedness . . . whereas before his soul was under the government of that noble principle of divine love whereby it was, as
it were, enlarged to a kind of comprehension to all his fellow
creatures; and not only so, but was . . . extended to the Creator,
and dispersed itself abroad in that infinite ocean. . . . But as soon
as he had transgressed, those nobler principles were immediately
lost and all this excellent enlargedness of his soul was gone and
he thenceforward shrunk into a little point, circumscribed and
closely shut up within itself to the exclusion of others. God was
forsaken and fellow creatures forsaken, and man retired within
himself and became wholly governed by narrow, selfish principles. Self-love became absolute master of his soul, the more noble
and spiritual principles having taken warning and fled.[7]

What's important for our purposes here is that in the Fall, that is,
in original sin, the human heart shrank; it contracted to "an
exceeding diminution and confinedness"; it forsook God and
became the slave of private, narrow, limited self-love. This is the
main problem of the Christian and his public life—whether modern or ancient. We love ourselves in a narrow, confined way, and
are indifferent to others and society and the nations and God.

Can Christian Hedonism Survive
Edwards's Indictment of Self-love?

But now this raises a question—a problem for someone like
me—who likes to use the term "Christian Hedonism" to describe
Biblical obedience, and to describe the theology of Jonathan
Edwards. Christian Hedonism implies that all true worship and
virtue involves the pursuit of our ultimate satisfaction—which
sounds very much like a form of self-love.

Even the title of this chapter forces this issue with the words,
"*Enjoying* God and the Transformation of Culture." The term
"Enjoying God" seems to muddy things by implying that I should

---

[7] *Charity and Its Fruits*, pp. 252-253.

get some pleasure for myself, when Edwards says that the very essence of human depravity is our bondage to "self-love." If we tackle this problem head-on, we will get very close to the heart of Edwards's ethics and see what a truly public-spirited person is.

The Negative Use of "Self-love"—Narrow Selfishness

The first thing to say is that Edwards uses the term "self-love" in two very different ways, one negative and one neutral. The negative use is the most common. Here's what he says: "Self-love, as the phrase is used in common speech, most commonly signifies a man's regard to his confined *private self*, or love to himself with respect to his *private interest*."[8] That's what Edwards means by "self-love" in diagnosing our depravity.

It's virtually synonymous with selfishness. People who are governed by this self-love, he says, "place their happiness in good things which are confined or limited to themselves exclusive of others. And this is selfishness. This is the thing most directly intended by that self-love which the Scripture condemns."[9] This is what he says Paul has in mind when he says in 1 Corinthians 13:5, "Love seeks not its own." "When it is said that charity seeketh not her own, we are to understand it of her own private good, good limited to herself."[10] In other words, true spiritual love is not governed by a narrow, limited, confined pursuit of one's own pleasure.

The Neutral Use of Self-love—Desire for Our Happiness

But Edwards also used the term "self-love" in a neutral way that does not necessarily involve sin, though it might. He says,

> It is not a thing contrary to Christianity that a man should love himself; or what is the same thing, that he should love his own happiness. Christianity does not tend to destroy a man's love to his own happiness; it would therein tend to destroy the humanity. . . . That a man should love his own happiness, is necessary to his nature, as a faculty of the will is; and it is impossible that it

---

[8] Jonathan Edwards, *The Nature of True Virtue*, in: *Ethical Writings, The Works of Jonathan Edwards*, vol. 8, ed. by Paul Ramsey (New Haven: Yale University Press, 1989), p. 577.

[9] *Charity and Its Fruits*, p. 257.

[10] *Charity and Its Fruits*, p. 258.

should be destroyed in any other way than by destroying his being. The saints love their own happiness; yea, those that are perfect in holiness. The saints and angels in heaven love their own happiness. Otherwise their happiness, which God has given them would be no happiness to them; for that which anyone does not love he can enjoy no happiness in.[11]

In other words, self-love in this second, neutral sense is simply our built-in capacity to like and dislike, or approve and disapprove, or be pleased and displeased. It is neither good nor bad until some object is fastened upon—something that is liked and approved and pleasing. If the thing fastened on is evil, or the fastening on it is disproportionate to its true worth, then our being pleased by it is shown to be corrupt. But the sheer faculty of desiring and liking and approving and being pleased, or not, is neither virtuous nor evil.

Scripture Assumes This Kind of Self-love and Builds on It

He goes on to defend from Scripture this legitimate neutral use of self-love.

> That to love ourselves is not unlawful is evident from the fact, that the law of God makes it a rule and measure by which our love to others should be regulated. Thus Christ commands, "Thou shalt love thy neighbor as thyself" [Matt. 19:19]; which command certainly supposes that we may, and must love ourselves. . . . [NOTE: this has nothing to do with the recent modern notion of self-esteem. Edwards is miles from that idea.] And it appears also from this, that the Scripture, from one end of the Bible to the other is full of things which are there held forth to work upon a principle of self-love. Such are all the promises and threatenings of the word of God, and all its calls and invitations; its counsels to seek our own good, and its warnings to beware of misery.[12]

So Edwards sees that the Bible is replete with commands for us to "seek our own good" and with warnings to "beware of misery."

---

[11] *Charity and Its Fruits*, p. 254.

[12] *Charity and Its Fruits*, pp. 254-255.

This means that God's Word assumes the legitimacy of the principle of self-love in the simple meaning of desiring and being pleased by what we think is good for us. This, he says, is virtually synonymous with the faculty of the will. Self-love is to the soul what hunger is to the stomach. It is simply there with our creaturehood; it's the inescapable desire to be happy.

What Then Is the Real Evil of the Human Heart?

So now, when we compare these two kinds of self-love, we can see more clearly what Edwards really regards as the essential evil of the human heart and the great hindrance to a public life of virtue. What is evil about self-love is not its desire to be happy—that is essential to our nature as creatures, whether fallen or not. What is evil about self-love is its finding happiness in such small, narrow, limited, confined reality, namely, the self and all that makes much of the self. Our depravity is our being exactly the opposite of public-spirited.

So self-love is a natural trait that man has before and after the Fall, and it becomes evil only because of its narrowness and confinement. We are evil because we seek our satisfaction in our own private pleasures but do not seek it in the good of others. We cherish our health and our food and our homes and families and jobs and hobbies and leisure. And we do not seek to expand that joy by drawing others into it. Our self-love, our desire for happiness, is narrow and confined and limited.

When Our Happiness Is in the Happiness of Another

If self-love were not narrow but broad, it would not necessarily be bad. For example, Edwards said, "Some, although they love their own happiness, do not place that happiness in their own confined good, or in that good which is limited to themselves, but more in the common good, in that which is the good of others as well as their own, in good to be enjoyed *in* others and to be enjoyed *by* others."[13]

How Extensive Must True Virtue Be?

But that raises a serious question: if true virtue is the broadening of self-love so that what makes us happy is not just our private

---

[13] *Charity and Its Fruits*, p. 257.

pleasures, but the good of others, then how broad and inclusive does self-love have to be before it stops being narrow and becomes true virtue? How public and social, or even universal, must self-love be to count as virtue and not vice?

What makes this question so crucial is that Edwards knows that there are great acts of moral courage and sacrifice that are *not* truly virtuous. "If I give away all I have, and if I deliver my body to be burned, but have not love, I gain nothing" (1 Cor. 13:3). There are acts that seem to be noble, but are not virtuous. So what's *wrong* with these broad acts of self-love that even sacrifices life for others?

If We Don't Embrace God in Our Virtue, We Are Infinitely Parochial

Edwards gives a stunning answer, which is why he is the great man that he is and why he is the man we need to listen to today. He said, as we saw in Chapter One,

> If there could be an instinct or other cause [like self-love] determining a person to benevolence towards the whole world of mankind . . . exclusive of . . . love to God . . . [and] supreme regard to him . . . it cannot be of the nature of true virtue.[14]

He says that self-love is confined and narrow and selfish—and not virtuous—until it embraces or delights in the good of the whole *universe of being*, or more simply, until it embraces *God*. If self-love embraces family, but not God, it is not virtuous. If it embraces country, but not God, it is not virtuous. If it embraces all the nations of the world, and not God, it is not virtuous. Why not? Edwards simply says, until self-love rises to embrace God, it embraces "an infinitely small part of universal existence."[15] In other words, to delight in the good of all the universe, but not to delight in God, is like being glad that a candle is lit, but being indifferent to the rising sun. Apart from embracing God as our chief delight, we are (quite literally) infinitely parochial.

---

[14] *The Nature of True Virtue*, pp. 602-603.

[15] *The Nature of True Virtue*, p. 601.

No God, No Virtue

What Edwards is doing here—and this is the great achievement of his life, and the great message to modern evangelicals—is making God absolutely indispensable in the definition of true virtue. He is refusing to define virtue—no matter how public, no matter how broad—without reference to God. He meant to keep God at the center of all moral considerations, to stem the secularizing forces of his own day. And the need for such vigilance over God-centeredness is even more necessary today. Edwards could not conceive of calling any act truly virtuous that did not have in it a supreme regard to God. One of the great follies of modern evangelical public life is how much we are willing to say about public virtue without reference to God.

Preserving a Supreme Regard for God in All Things

So what Edwards was trying to do in his definition of depravity—by focusing on the negative, narrow, confined, constricted sense of self-love—was to show, in the end, that *every* act of love performed without a supreme regard for God as the object of delight has no true virtue in it. In other words, his treatment of self-love, like everything else he wrote, was aimed at defending the centrality and supremacy of God in all things. The only public life of an evangelical that counts as virtuous is one that savors and celebrates the supremacy of God as the ground and goal of its public acts.

He Has Not Gone as Far as He Can Go

Now one might think that Edwards has pushed the God-centeredness of virtue as far as it can go. What more can he say about the public virtue of Christians that would exalt God more or make him more central in it? Well, he has not gone as far as he can go. And there is one more crucial question he raises about self-love and public virtue.

Even Neutral "Self-love" Is Just Natural and Not Spiritual

He asks, What if self-love does rise high enough and expand broadly enough to embrace the world and even God? Is there a possible reason to think that this embracing of God might *not* be virtuous? His answer is, Yes. He points out that "self-love"—even the neutral kind that is not evil in itself, the kind that is simply a love of happiness—is still a merely human and natural trait. It is not spiritual. It is not wrought by the Spirit of God. It does not require a work of special grace.

This means that if embracing God can be accounted for merely from the root of such self-love, then it will be a merely natural thing wrought by what is resident in human nature. And though God be at the top of it, he will not be at the bottom of it. Man will be. If that were possible, we will have wrought our own virtue. And God would not be supreme in the cause of virtue, even when being the apparent goal.

Mere Self-love, Minus the Spirit, Embraces God for His Gifts

I say "apparent goal" because what Edwards shows is that when self-love alone is at work to produce virtue, without any special saving, transforming grace—without the awakening work of the Holy Spirit—then self-love inevitably embraces God not for the beauty of his glory in itself, but for the natural benefits God gives. Mere self-love savors the gifts of God without savoring fellowship with God himself. And this, Edwards says, is not a true embracing of God himself. It is an embracing of the self, and of God only inasmuch as he makes much of the self. It is not true virtue, though it can be very religious. Here's the way he puts it:

> This is . . . the difference between the joy of the hypocrite, and the joy of the true saint. The [hypocrite] rejoices in himself; self is the first foundation of his joy: the [true saint] rejoices in God. . . . True saints have their minds, in the first place, inexpressibly pleased and delighted with the sweet ideas of the glorious and amiable [i.e., pleasant, admirable] nature of the things of God. And this is the spring of all their delights, and the cream of all their pleasures. . . . But the dependence of the affections of hypocrites is in a contrary order: *they first rejoice . . . that they are made so much of by God; and then on that ground, he seems in a sort, lovely to them.*[16]

[16] Jonathan Edwards, *The Religious Affections*, ed. by John Smith, *The Works of Jonathan Edwards*, vol. 2 (New Haven: Yale University Press, 1959), pp. 249-250 (emphasis added).

In other words, self-love *alone* simply cannot produce true virtue—private or public—because it is merely natural and has no truly spiritual or supernatural taste or perception of divine beauty. Because of the Fall, self-love is blind and seared in its capacity to discern and delight in the glory of God. It is, as the apostle says, not merely *natural* but *"dead* in trespasses and sins."[17]

Self-love Cannot Make the Good Beautifully Compelling

Another way to say it is that self-love moves us to embrace what we perceive will make us happy, but self-love does not have the power to make what is good and true and beautiful look attractive. Self-love alone may move one person to make money, another to seek power, another to be a philanthropist, another to steal and kill, and another to pray and read the Bible and preach. But it is not self-love that decides what appears to the mind as most attractive and valuable.

So what does make the difference whether self-love embraces God or embraces money? Or more radically: what makes the difference whether self-love embraces God for his gifts or for himself?

The Miracle of New Birth Is the Root of Virtue Beneath Self-love

Edwards's answer is *regeneration*, new birth—a supernatural work of the Spirit of God in the soul, giving it a new capacity to see spiritual beauty and to savor the glory of God as something real and pleasurable in itself.

> The first effect of the power of God in the heart in *regeneration*, is to give the heart a Divine taste or sense; to cause it to have a relish of the loveliness and sweetness of the supreme excellency of the Divine nature.[18]

---

[17] Ephesians 2:1, 5. And not only is self-love dead to spiritual things, it is merely natural and cannot rise to have spiritual taste or desire which are essential in order to know and love God. Self-love, says Edwards, "cannot be a truly gracious and spiritual love . . . for self-love is a principle entirely natural, and as much in the hearts of devils as angels; and therefore surely nothing that is the mere result of it can be supernatural and divine" (Jonathan Edwards, *The Religious Affections*, p. 242).

[18] Jonathan Edwards, *Treatise on Grace*, ed. by Paul Helm (Cambridge: James Clarke and Co., 1971), pp. 48-49.

Self-love cannot give itself this taste or sense of divine beauty. That is why self-love cannot be the bottom or the final foundation of true virtue. "Something else," Edwards says, "entirely distinct from self-love [must] be the cause of this, viz. a change made in the views of his mind, and relish of his heart whereby he apprehends a beauty, glory, and supreme good, in God's nature, as it is in itself."[19] Very simply, a capacity to taste a thing must precede our desire for its sweetness. That is, *regeneration* (or new birth) must precede the pursuit of happiness *in God*.

God Touches the Blind Eyes of Self-love and Says, "See!"

Therefore regeneration is the foundation of true virtue. There is no public virtue without it. True virtue not only embraces God as its highest goal—and thus escapes the curse of "infinite parochialism"—it also confesses that God is the root and foundation of its origin. Here is the way the apostle Paul put it in 2 Corinthians 4:6, "It is God who said, 'Let light shine out of darkness,' who has shone in our hearts to give the light of the knowledge of the glory of God in the face of Christ." God touched the blind eyes of self-love and gave her an irresistible view of his own glory in the face of Christ. He did not kill self-love; he supernaturally and profoundly transformed it into a spiritual hunger for the glory of God.

So Edwards says, "The alteration which is made in a man when he is converted and sanctified is not by diminishing his love to happiness, but only by regulating it with respect to its exercises and influence, and the objects to which it leads."[20] Self-love now has a new spiritual, supernatural taste for what will truly satisfy. Self-love now says to God, "Thou dost show me the path of life; in thy presence there is fullness of joy, in thy right hand are pleasures for evermore" (Ps. 16:11).

Self-love as a Passion for the Supremacy of God in All Things

The message of Jonathan Edwards to modern evangelicals concerning our public life is not mainly a message about what party to belong to, or what social cause to trumpet, or even which

---

[19] Jonathan Edwards, *The Religious Affections*, p. 241.

[20] *Charity and Its Fruits*, p. 255.

unreached people to adopt and evangelize, *as important as these are*. His main message is that, if we would not be infinitely parochial, and thus fail in true virtue, then our private life, our public life, and our global life must be driven not by a narrow, constricted, merely natural self-love, but by passion for the supremacy of God in all things—a passion created through supernatural new birth by the Holy Spirit, giving us a new spiritual taste for the glory of God—a passion sustained by the ongoing, sanctifying influences of the Word of God—and a passion bent on spreading itself through all of culture and all the nations until Christ comes.

This passion is rooted finally in the passion of God for his own glory. Our passion for God's glory is the work of God's Spirit granting us participation in God's own delight in God. Thus Jesus prayed, "I have made Your name known to them, and will make it known, *so that the love with which You loved Me may be in them*, and I in them" (John 17:26). This foundation of our passion for God in God's passion for God is so crucial I have made available in the rest of this book the most important work of Edwards concerning this reality, *The End for Which God Created the World*. To that I now bid you a very slow and reflective Godspeed.

PART TWO

THE END FOR WHICH GOD CREATED THE WORLD

by Jonathan Edwards

A NOTE ON HOW TO READ

THE END FOR WHICH GOD CREATED THE WORLD

(by John Piper)

I have numbered each paragraph (¶) in *The End for Which God Created the World* so that reference can be made to particular places with ease. I hope that, when Edwards's work is read and discussed, it will be with the very words of Edwards in view and not merely with vague generalizations and impressions. That is the path of courtesy and of growth.

There is good reason to suggest that readers who are less philosophically and more Biblically oriented should read *The End for Which God Created the World* backwards—Part Two first. The reason is that the work begins most philosophically and ends most Biblically. Some comments on the three major divisions may help the reader decide how to proceed.

1. The Introduction (¶¶ 1-26) is a discussion of the meaning of terms, especially what Edwards means by "ultimate end" in creation. This is the most difficult of the divisions and will discourage all but the most determined reader. In my judgment, it can be skipped by those who are less philosophically oriented. One should simply keep in mind that the terms "last end" and "ultimate end" are synonymous, and that an "ultimate end" is an end that God values for its own sake and not as a means to some other end (see ¶ 3). Paul Ramsey, the editor of *The End for Which God Created the World* in the Yale critical edition, argues, in fact, that Edwards

"wrote his Introduction last of all parts of the *Two Dissertations*" (*The End* and *True Virtue*, published together as *Two Dissertations*), since he was, evidently, still making notes in his *Miscellanies* on the method to be used *after* he had essentially completed *The End*. In addition, he refers to his definitions expressly only once in the body of the work.[1] One may, then, use the Introduction as a resource to consult if one finds confusion in Edwards's definitions.

2. The second major division is Chapter One (¶¶ 27-124). It addresses the question "What does reason teach concerning this affair?" This is a philosophically oriented effort to show that Edwards's conclusion is rationally defensible. Edwards confesses that "it would be relying too much on reason to determine the affair of God's last end in the creation of the world, without being herein *principally* guided by divine revelation, since God has given a revelation containing instructions concerning this very matter" (¶ 29).

One may ask why Edwards devotes so much effort then to wrestle philosophically with the goal of creation when in the last analysis he settles the matter with Scripture.[2] His answer is that since "objections have chiefly been made against what I think the Scriptures have truly revealed from the pretended dictates of reason, I would, in the *first* place, soberly consider in a few things what seems rational to be supposed concerning this affair—and *then* proceed to consider what light divine revelation gives us in it" (¶ 30). Edwards is persuaded that all truth is one and that what reason truly teaches and what Scripture teaches will cohere.

If determination or time is lacking, and one must choose parts of Chapter One to read rather than the whole, I would suggest that one be sure to include Section Three (¶¶ 57-76) on God's making himself the ultimate end in creation, and especially Section Four where Edwards answers four objections to his own position (¶¶ 77-124). His answers to these objections are very helpful and get to the essence of the matter. I have found that these are the very

---

[1] *Two Dissertations, Ethical Writings*, ed. by Paul Ramsey, *The Works of Jonathan Edwards*, vol. 8 (New Haven: Yale University Press, 1989), p. 407, note 2.

[2] See Part One, Chapter Two (pp. 49-75) for the relationship between philosophy and Scripture in Edwards's thinking.

things that people raise questions about today when I teach on God's passion for his glory.

The position Edwards is defending in answering these objections is that, in creating the world, God is "seeking that his glory and excellent perfections should be known, esteemed, loved, and delighted in by his creatures" (¶ 99). The objections he answers are that: 1) this seems to indicate some dependence on the creation, or lack of self-sufficiency on God's part in regard to the creation (¶¶ 77-92); 2) it seems to make God look selfish (¶¶ 93-98); 3) it seems unworthy of God to pursue the applause of beings "infinitely beneath him" (¶¶ 99-111); and 4) it seems to contradict the freedom of God in his beneficence and lessen the duty of gratitude that creatures owe (¶¶ 112-124). Reading Edwards's answers to these objections is not only helpful in defense of his view but just as much in clarifying what he really means.

3. The third major division is Chapter Two (¶¶ 125-287), which answers the question, "What is to be learned from Holy Scriptures concerning God's last end in the creation of the world?" For those who are more Biblically oriented than philosophically this will be the most compelling division. Here Edwards brings together a vast array of Biblical texts to argue that the ultimate end of God in creation is the exhibition of his glory for the creature to know, love and enjoy. As impressed as I was with the philosophical arguments of Chapter One, it was this section that settled the matter for me. I found it totally persuasive.

The ideal, of course, is that the reader take up a pencil and read (little by little, if necessary) the entire text of *The End for Which God Created the World*, underlining, marking the margins, jotting questions and thinking earnestly about these great matters. But if this is not feasible, I want to stress that much benefit can come from reading only parts of the work. And I would recommend that Chapter One, Section Three (how God makes himself the last end of creation), and especially Section Four (the objections answered), and Chapter Two (the Biblical portion) not be overlooked.

CONCERNING THE TEXT
USED IN THIS EDITION OF

THE END FOR WHICH
GOD CREATED THE WORLD

(by John Piper)

The following text of *The End for Which God Created the World* has been taken from the two-volume *Works of Jonathan Edwards* edited by Edward Hickman and published in London in 1834. That edition, in turn, was based on the Worcester edition of 1808-1809, issued forty-three years after *The End for Which God Created the World* was first published in 1765 with a preface by the editor, Samuel Hopkins, a personal friend of Edwards.

The Hickman edition was continually reprinted for over forty years and is in print today as The Banner of Truth Trust edition (1974). The Trust has kindly given written permission to use their text as the basis for what is published here.

From correspondence dated January 4, 1764, we learn that Samuel Hopkins and Joseph Bellamy, contemporaries and friends of Edwards, divided the labor in transcribing and preparing the *Two Dissertations* (*The End* and *True Virtue* published together in 1765) for publication after Edwards died—"Hopkins assuming

responsibility for *End of Creation* and Bellamy for *True Virtue*."[1]
It was necessary to transcribe Edwards's papers into "a fair hand
for the press."[2] There is a special fitness that Hopkins and Bellamy
should prepare *The End for Which God Created the World* for the
press, because in 1755 they had both visited Edwards's home in
Stockbridge and heard him read the manuscript in person:
"February 12, 1755. Mr. Bellamy came to my house last Tuesday,
with whom I went to Stockbridge, and staid there two nights and
one day to hear Mr. Edwards read a treatise upon the Last End of
God in the Creation of the World. Returned home today. . . ."[3]

The critical Yale edition of *The End* was published in 1989 and
was based on the first edition of the work in 1765.[4] No handwrit-
ten manuscript or copy survives. What about the reliability of the
text of *The End* used in this book? Comparing the Banner of Truth
(Hickman) edition and the Yale University Press (Ramsey) edition
shows that there are numerous differences in the wording. These
are minor, as I judge, and do not change the meaning significantly.
The usual tendency of the later edition is to simplify Edwards's language by removing redundancies. For example, compare the first
sentence of the Introduction:

> Hickman (Banner of Truth, 1974): "To avoid all confusion in our
> inquiries concerning the end for which God created the world, a
> distinction should be observed between the *chief* end for which
> an agent performs any work and the *ultimate* end."

> Ramsey (Yale University Press, 1989): "To avoid all confusion in
> our inquiries and reasonings concerning the end for which God
> created the world, a distinction should be observed between the
> *chief* end for which an agent or efficient exerts any act and per-
> forms any work, and the *ultimate* end."

[1] "Editor's Introduction," *Ethical Writings*, ed. by Paul Ramsey, *The Works of Jonathan Edwards*, vol. 8 (New Haven: Yale University Press, 1989), p. 113.

[2] Iain Murray, *Jonathan Edwards, A New Biography* (Edinburgh: The Banner of Truth Trust, 1989), p. 448.

[3] From Samuel Hopkins's diary quoted in Iain Murray, *Jonathan Edwards*, p. 391.

[4] "Editor's Introduction," *Ethical Writings*, p. 5, note 3. The texts may be compared with the original 1765 edition "available in the Evans microtext editions of works published in America before 1800, #9962" (*Ethical Writings*, p. 113).

The underlined parts were evidently omitted by Hickman, the later editor. These kinds of changes seemed insignificant enough to justify using the 1834/1974 readily-available Hickman edition.

With regard to punctuation, I have felt at liberty to add or remove commas and semicolons, for example, to make the flow of the sentences as clear as possible. This is warranted by the fact that we have little confidence in either the 1765 edition or the 1834 edition that we are looking at Edwards's own punctuation.[5] The same applies to Edwards's use of italics, capitalization, dashes, parentheses, spelling, contractions and abbreviations. I follow Paul Ramsey, who edited the Yale critical edition in bringing such things into consistency by more readable standards.[6]

I have left the italicization and most of the small caps of the Hickman edition as is, adding only a very few italics of my own to highlight parallels. In addition I have occasionally divided long paragraphs into two or more. Wherever I have added any words or changed any grammatical constructions I have indicated this in brackets. All the brackets used are mine. All the parentheses are from the Hickman edition. The modern reader may be confident that the wording of the text used here represents Edwards's wording closely enough so that a careful reading will not go astray because of inaccuracies. Where there may be rare, fine points of meaning that might be affected by the wording, the careful reader can compare the Yale edition.

With regard to the subheadings, the ones that are centered and in brackets are my own to provide a kind of road map. The numerous bold italicized subheadings that are justified on the left margin are also my effort to give the reader guidance and encouragement to press on. All other headings are Edwards's own.

Of the footnotes, twenty-three of them come from Edwards himself and are marked as such. The rest are mine and are meant to give clarifications and correlations and implications. They represent my own views and have no authority beyond what good judgment and Biblical teaching may warrant.

---

[5] Ramsey explains why in *Ethical Writings*, p. 115.

[6] *Ethical Writings*, pp. 115-121. This includes the abbreviations and punctuation of the Biblical references.

No notion of God's last end in the creation of the world is agreeable to reason, which would truly imply any indigence, insufficiency and mutability in God, or any dependence of the Creator on the creature for any part of his perfection or happiness.

Though it be true that God's glory and happiness . . . are infinite and cannot be added to, and . . . [are] perfectly independent of the creature; yet it does not hence follow, nor is it true, that God has no real and proper delight, pleasure, or happiness in any of his acts or communications relative to the creature.

[God] had respect to himself, as his last and highest end, in this work; because he is worthy in himself to be so, being infinitely the greatest and best of beings. All things else, with regard to worthiness, importance, and excellence, are perfectly as nothing in comparison of him.

All that is ever spoken of in the Scripture as an ultimate end of God's works is included in that one phrase, the glory of God.

JONATHAN EDWARDS
The End for Which God Created the World

THE END FOR WHICH GOD CREATED THE WORLD

by Jonathan Edwards

INTRODUCTION

CONTAINING EXPLANATIONS OF TERMS AND GENERAL POSITIONS

The difference between "ultimate" ends and "chief" ends

[1] To avoid all confusion in our inquiries concerning the end for which God created the world, a distinction should be observed between the *chief* end for which an agent performs any work and the *ultimate* end. These two phrases are not always precisely of the same signification, and though the *chief* end be always an *ultimate* end, yet every ultimate end is not always a chief end. A *chief* end is opposite to an *inferior* end; an *ultimate* end is opposite to a *subordinate* end.

"Subordinate" ends are the means of "ultimate" ends

[2] A *subordinate* end is what an agent aims at, not at all upon its own account, but wholly on the account of a *further* end of which it is considered as a means. Thus when a man goes [on] a journey to obtain a medicine to restore his health, the obtaining of that medicine is his subordinate end, because it is not an end that he

values at all upon its own account, but wholly as a means of a further end, *viz.* his health. Separate the medicine from that further end, and it is not at all desired.

[3] An *ultimate* end is that which the agent seeks, in what he does, for its *own* sake; what he loves, values, and takes pleasure in on its own account, and not merely as a means of a further end. As when a man loves the taste of some particular sort of fruit, and is at pains and cost to obtain it for the sake of the pleasure of that taste which he values upon its own account, as he loves his own pleasure, and not merely for the sake of any other good which he supposes his enjoying that pleasure will be the means of.

[4] Some ends are subordinate, not only as they are subordinated to an ultimate end, but also to another end that is itself but subordinate. Yea, there may be a succession or chain of many subordinate ends, one dependent on another, one sought for another, before you come to anything that the agent aims at and seeks for its *own* sake. As when a man sells a garment to get money—to buy tools—to till his land—to obtain a crop—to supply him with food—to gratify the appetite. And he seeks to gratify his appetite, on its *own* account, as what is grateful[1] in itself. Here the end of his selling his garment to get money is only a subordinate end, and it is not only subordinate to the *ultimate* end—gratifying his appetite—but to a *nearer* end—buying husbandry tools, and his obtaining these is only a subordinate end, being only for the sake of tilling land. And the tillage of land is an end not sought on its own account, but for the sake of the crop to be produced, and the crop produced is an end sought only for the sake of making bread; and bread is sought for the sake of gratifying the appetite.

[5] Here gratifying the appetite is called the *ultimate* end, because it is the *last* in the chain where a man's aim rests, obtaining in that, the thing finally aimed at. So whenever a man comes to that in which his desire terminates and rests, it being something valued on its *own* account, then he comes to an *ultimate* end, let the chain be longer or shorter; yea, if there be but one link or one step that he takes before he comes to this end. As when a man that

---

[1] In Edwards's language, "grateful" does not have the modern meaning of "thankful," but the old meaning of "pleasing."

loves honey puts it into his mouth, for the sake of the pleasure of the taste, without aiming at any thing further. So an end, which an agent has in view, may be both his *immediate* and his *ultimate* end; his *next* and his *last* end.[2] That end which is sought for the sake of itself, and not for the sake of a further end, is an ultimate end; there the aim of the agent stops and rests.[3]

[6] A thing sought may have the nature of an ultimate, and also of a subordinate end; as it may be sought partly on its own account, and partly for the sake of a further end. Thus a man, in what he does, may seek the love and respect of a particular person, partly on its own account, because it is in itself agreeable to men to be the objects of others' esteem and love; and partly because he hopes, through the friendship of that person, to have his assistance in other affairs; and so to be put under advantage for obtaining further ends.

Among "ultimate" ends, the "chief" or "highest" end is the one most valued[4]

[7] A *chief* end, which is opposite to an *inferior* end, is something diverse from an ultimate end; it is most valued, and therefore most sought after by the agent in what he does. It is evident that to be an end *more* valued than another end is not exactly the same thing as to be an end valued *ultimately*, or for its own sake. This will appear if it be considered,

[8] That two different ends may be both ultimate, and yet not

---

[2] Edwards will use "ultimate end" and "last end" interchangeably in what follows.

[3] Notice that, when Edwards speaks of something being "valued on its own account" or something being "sought for the sake of itself," he is *not* saying that this "valuing" or "seeking" is different from delighting in or taking pleasure in. Sometimes in our own day people contrast pursuing God "for his *own* sake" with pursuing God "for the *joy* there is in God." Someone may say, "Don't pursue God because he makes you happy; pursue God as an end in himself." The person who thinks this way will not be able to grasp Edwards's meaning here. Edwards does not make such a distinction between delighting in our ultimate end, on the one hand, and loving that end *for its own sake*, on the other hand. We love honey "for its *own* sake," he would say, because the *delight* we have in it is not a means to anything else. The delight that makes something an ultimate end is delight in the thing itself, not a subsequent delight in some gift or blessing. So pursuing pleasure *in* a thing and pursuing the thing "for its own sake" are the same.

[4] If it strikes the reader as strange to speak of more than one "ultimate end," keep in mind two things. 1) Edwards is using the term here in relation to a *limited* sequence of events, the last of which is ultimate as the one *in the sequence*, valued for its own sake. 2) Edwards will explain below that we can speak of "ultimate ends" in a "lower sense" and a "highest sense." The "lower sense" is in a limited, finite series of events where the ultimate end may not be the universally ultimate one, but only ultimate in relation to the finite sequence. The "highest sense" is the universally last end for which everything exists. See ¶¶ 20, 24, 26.

be chief ends. They may be both valued for their *own* sake, and both sought in the same work or acts; and yet one valued more highly, and sought more than another. Thus a man may go [on] a journey to obtain two different benefits or enjoyments, both which may be agreeable to him in *themselves* considered; and yet one may be much more agreeable than the other; and so be what he sets his heart *chiefly* upon. Thus a man may go [on] a journey, partly to obtain the possession and enjoyment of a bride that is very dear to him, and partly to gratify his curiosity in looking in a telescope, or some new-invented and extraordinary optic glass, and the one not [be] properly subordinate to the other, and therefore *both* may be *ultimate* ends. But yet obtaining his beloved bride may be his *chief* end, and the benefit of the optic glass his *inferior* end.

[9] An ultimate end is not always the chief end, because some *subordinate* ends may be *more* valued and sought after than some *ultimate* ends. Thus, for instance, a man may aim at two things in his journey: one, to visit his friends, and another, to receive a large sum of money. The latter may be but a *subordinate* end; he may not value the silver and gold on their *own* account, but only for pleasure, gratification, and honor; the money is valued only as a means of the other. But yet, obtaining the money may be *more* valued, and so is a *higher* end of his journey than the pleasure of seeing his friends; though the latter is valued on its *own* account, and so is an *ultimate* end.

But here several things may be noted:[5]

[POSITION ONE]
[A subordinate end is never valued (as a chief end) above its own ultimate end]

[10] *First*, when it is said that some *subordinate* ends may be *more* valued than some *ultimate* ends, it is [never] supposed that[6] a subordinate end is more valued than *that* to which it is subordinate. For that reason it is called a *subordinate* end, because it is valued

---

[5] Here the second part of the Introduction begins, namely, the nine "General Positions" mentioned in the title.

[6] In the original it reads: "it is not supposed that ever."

and sought not for its own sake, but only in subordination to a *further* end. But yet a subordinate end may be valued more than some *other* ultimate end that it is not subordinate to. Thus, for instance, a man goes [on] a journey to receive a sum of money, only for the value of the pleasure and honor that the money may be a means of. In this case it is impossible that the *subordinate* end, *viz.* his having the money, should be *more* valued by him than the pleasure and honor for which he values it. It would be absurd to suppose that he values the means more than the end, when he has no value for the means, but for the sake of the end of which it is the means. But yet he may value the money, though but a subordinate end, *more* than some *other ultimate* end to which it is not subordinate, and with which it has no connection. For instance, *more* than the comfort of a friendly visit, which was one ultimate end of his journey.

[POSITION TWO]
*[A subordinate end may be equally valued with an ultimate end
if it is necessary and sufficient to the ultimate end]*

[11] *Secondly*, the ultimate end is always *superior* to its subordinate end, and more valued by the agent, unless it be when the ultimate end entirely depends on the subordinate. If he has no other means by which to obtain his last end, then the subordinate may be *as much* valued as the last end; because the last end, in such a case, altogether depends upon, and is wholly and certainly conveyed by it.

[12] As for instance, if a pregnant woman has a peculiar appetite [for] a certain rare fruit that is to be found only in the garden of a particular friend of hers at a distance—and she goes [on] a journey to her friend's house or garden to obtain that fruit—the *ultimate* end of her journey is to gratify that strong appetite; the obtaining that fruit is the *subordinate* end of it. If she looks upon it [in such a way] that the appetite can be gratified by *no other* means than the obtaining of that fruit, and that it will *certainly* be gratified if she obtain it, then she will value the fruit *as much* as she values the gratification of her appetite.

[13] But otherwise it will not be so. If she be *doubtful* whether

that fruit will satisfy her craving, then she will not value it *equally* with the gratification of her appetite itself. Or if there be some *other fruit* that she knows of that will gratify her desire, at least *in part*, which she can obtain without such trouble as shall counter-vail the gratification—or if her appetite cannot be gratified with-out this fruit, nor yet with it *alone*, without something else to be compounded with it—then her *value* for her last end will be *divided* between these several ingredients as so many subordinate ends, and *no one alone* will be equally valued with the last end. Hence it rarely happens that a subordinate end is *equally* valued with its last end, because the obtaining of a last end rarely depends on *one* single, uncompounded means, infallibly connected with it. Therefore, men's *last* ends are *commonly* their *highest*[7] ends.

[POSITION THREE]
[When there is only one ultimate end,
it is chief above all other ends]

[14] *Thirdly,* if any being has but *one* ultimate end in all that he does, and there be a great variety of operations, his *last* end may justly be looked upon as his *supreme* end.[8] For in such a case, *every other* end but that one is in order to that end, and therefore no other can be superior to it. Because, as was observed before, a subordi-nate end is never *more* valued than the end to which it is subordi-nate. Moreover, the subordinate effects or events brought to pass, as means of this end, all uniting to contribute their share towards obtaining the one last end, are very various; and therefore, by what has been now observed, the ultimate end of all must be valued more than any one of the particular means. This seems to be the case with the works of God, as may more fully appear in the sequel.[9]

---

[7] Edwards uses "highest" interchangeably with "chief," and "last" interchangeably with "ulti-mate." "Highest" is the opposite of inferior (or less desired); "last" is the opposite of subordi-nate or means to the end. See footnote 2.

[8] In this sentence "last end" and "supreme end" are used interchangeably with "ultimate end" and "chief end" respectively.

[9] The logic of this paragraph is this: Since all subordinate ends are inferior to *their own* ultimate ends, this means that if there is *only one* ultimate end, then all other ends are subordinate to it and are therefore inferior to it, so that the ultimate end is the chief and highest end. This, he tells us, is where he is going with regard to God's end in all his works: there is only one ultimate end.

[POSITION FOUR]
[What we seek for its own sake is our "last" or "ultimate" end]

[15] *Fourthly*, whatsoever any agent has in view in any thing he does, which is agreeable to him *in itself*, and not merely for the sake of something else, is regarded by that agent as his *last* end. The same may be said of avoiding that which is in itself painful or disagreeable, for the avoiding of what is disagreeable is agreeable. This will be evident to any, bearing in mind the meaning of the terms. By *last* end is[10] meant that which is regarded and sought by an agent, as agreeable or desirable for its *own* sake; a *subordinate*, that which is sought only for the sake of something *else*.

[POSITION FIVE]
*[There is only one ultimate end
when one thing only is sought on its own account]*

[16] *Fifthly*, from hence it will follow that if an agent has in view *more things than one* that will be brought to pass by what he does, which he loves and delights in on their *own* account, then he must have *more things than one* that he regards as his *last* ends in what he does. But if there be *but one thing* that an agent seeks, on its *own* account, then there can be *but one* last end which he has in all his actions and operations.[11]

[17] But only here a distinction must be observed of things which may be said to be *agreeable* to an agent, in *themselves* considered:[12]

---

[10] The original has "being" instead of "is."

[11] To keep these thoughts from being a mere tangle of words, a discerning reader will probably begin to ask if Edwards is preparing to show us that God has but one last or ultimate end in creation, and if so, is he saying that all the other things that God delights in or loves are in some way enjoyed and loved for the sake of that one last end? Asking and thinking about such questions will help us endure what might seem to be an overkill of complex thoughts.

[12] This footnote may need to be read before and after "Position Five" in order to make fullest sense. This is a very difficult section. The point of this and the next four paragraphs of Position Five is that there are "absolute" ultimate ends and there are "consequential" ultimate ends. Both are ultimate ends because they are pleasing to the one who pursues them "in themselves" and not as means to another; yet the occasion for the "consequential" ultimate ends is brought about as a consequence of pursuing some other end. This is a very rarefied distinction. The importance of it seems to be at least this: Edwards is going to speak later of God's ultimate end as being only one, not many; and this one end will be the "highest end" and "original," not consequential, namely, the glory of God. Yet there are times when he speaks in his writings of God's delighting in the justice or faithfulness of an action in itself. These acts are "consequential" upon creation. Thus the creation of the category of "consequential ultimate ends" will help make sense of what Edwards means by God's delighting in something "for its own sake," which is nevertheless not his ultimate end in the highest sense, but only an ultimate end "consequentially." See footnote 15.

(1) what is in itself grateful [i.e., pleasing] to an agent, and valued on its own account, *simply* and *absolutely* considered; antecedent to, and *independent* of all conditions, or any supposition of particular cases and circumstances. And (2) what may be said to be in itself agreeable to an agent, *hypothetically* and consequentially, or on supposition of such and such circumstances, or on the happening of such a particular case.

[18] Thus, for instance, a man may originally love society.[13] An inclination to society may be implanted in his very nature; and society may be agreeable to him *antecedent* to all presupposed cases and circumstances; and this may cause him to seek a family. And the comfort of society may be originally his *last* end, in seeking a family. But after he has a family, peace, good order, and mutual justice and friendship in his family may be agreeable to him, and what he delights in for their *own* sake; and therefore these things may be his *last* end in many things he does in the government and regulation of his family. But they were not his *original* end with respect to his family. The justice and the peace of a family was not properly his last end *before* he had a family, that induced him to seek a family, but [justice and peace became his last end] *consequentially*. And the case being put of his having a family, then these things wherein the good order and beauty of a family consist, become his last end in many things he does in such circumstances.

[19] In like manner we must suppose that God, *before* he created the world, had some good in view, as a consequence of the world's existence, that was *originally* agreeable to him in itself considered, that inclined him to bring the universe into existence, in such a manner as he created it. But *after* the world was created, and such and such intelligent creatures actually had existence, in such and such circumstances, then a wise, just regulation of them was agreeable to God, *in itself* considered. And God's love of justice and hatred of injustice would be sufficient in such a case to induce God to deal *justly* with his creatures and to prevent all injustice in him towards them. But yet there is no necessity of sup-

---

[13] In Edwards's language "society" does not mean primarily the community, but rather the experience of being with other people. Loving society means being sociable and gregarious and liking to get together with others.

posing that God's love of doing justly to intelligent beings, and hatred of the contrary, was what *originally* induced God to create the world and make intelligent beings, and so to order the occasion of doing either justly or unjustly. The justice of God's nature makes a just regulation agreeable and the contrary disagreeable, as there is occasion; the *subject* being supposed and the *occasion* given. But we must suppose something else that should incline him to *create* the subjects or *order* the occasion.

[20] So [in the same way] that perfection of God which we call his faithfulness or his inclination to fulfill his promises to his creatures could not properly be what *moved* him to create the world; nor could such a fulfillment of his promises to his creatures be his *last* end in giving the creatures being. But yet *after* the world is created, *after* intelligent creatures are made, and God has bound himself by promise to them, then that disposition, which is called his faithfulness, may move him in his providential disposals towards them; and this may be the *end* of many of God's works of providence, even the exercise of his faithfulness in fulfilling his promises, and may be in the *lower* sense[14] his *last* end; because faithfulness and truth must be supposed to be what is in *itself* amiable [i.e., pleasant, admirable] to God, and what he delights in for its *own* sake. Thus God may have ends of particular works of *providence*, which are ultimate ends in a lower sense, which were not ultimate ends of the *creation*.

[21] So that here we have two sorts of ultimate ends: one of which may be called *original* and *independent*, the other *consequential* and *dependent*; for it is evident, the latter sort are truly of the nature of ultimate ends; because though their being agreeable to the agent be consequential on the existence, yet the subject and occasion being supposed, they are agreeable and amiable [i.e., pleasant, admirable] in themselves. We may suppose that, to a righteous Being, doing justice between two parties with whom he is concerned is agreeable in *itself* and not merely for the sake of some *other* end. Yet we may suppose that a desire of doing justice between two parties may be *consequential* on the being of those

---

[14] See footnote 4 and ¶¶ 24, 26. The "lower sense" refers to "last (or ultimate) ends" in the sense of being *subordinate* ends that are *last* in a limited sequence, but may not be last in the "highest" sense after which there are no other ends.

parties and the occasion given. [Therefore I make a distinction between an end that in this manner is *consequential*, and a *subordinate* end.][15]

[22] It may be observed that when I speak of God's ultimate end in the creation of the world in the following discourse, I commonly mean in that *highest* sense, *viz.* the *original* ultimate end.

[POSITION SIX]
[The one "original" ultimate end of all creation
governs all God's works]

[23] *Sixthly*, it may be further observed that the *original* ultimate end or ends of the creation of the world is *alone* that which induces God to give the occasion for consequential ends, by the first creation of the world, and the original disposal of it. And the more original the end is, the more extensive and universal it is. That which God had *primarily* in view in creating, and the *original* ordination of the world, must be constantly kept in view, and have a governing influence in all God's works, or with respect to every thing he does towards his creatures. And therefore,

[POSITION SEVEN]
[In the "highest sense" of God's ultimate end in creation,
this end is also the end of all his works of providence]

[24] *Seventhly*, if we use the phrase *ultimate end* in this highest sense, then the same that is God's ultimate end in creating the world—if we suppose but one such end—must be what he makes his ultimate aim in all his works, in every thing he does either in creation or providence. But we must suppose that in the *use* to which God puts his creatures, he must evermore have a regard to the *end* for which he has made them. But if we take *ultimate end* in the *lower* sense, God may sometimes have regard to those

---

[15] The Yale edition includes this sentence that the Banner of Truth edition does not have (Jonathan Edwards, *Ethical Writings*, ed. by Paul Ramsey, in: *The Works of Jonathan Edwards*, vol. 8 [New Haven: Yale University Press, 1989], p. 413). The point of this difficult paragraph is that an end can be "consequential" and nevertheless "ultimate." The desirability of an act of justice is consequential on the existence of the persons and situation, but the act may be desirable in itself. See footnote 12.

things as ultimate ends, in particular works of providence, which could not in any proper sense be his *last* end in creating the world.

[POSITION EIGHT]
*[The ultimate end of providence in general
is the ultimate end of creation]*

[25] *Eighthly*, on the other hand, whatever appears to be God's ultimate end, in any sense, of his works of providence *in general*, that must be the ultimate end of the work of *creation* itself. For though God may act for an end that is ultimate in a lower sense in *some* of his works of providence which is not the ultimate end of the creation of the world, yet this doth not take place with regard to the works of providence *in general*; for God's works of providence in general are the *same* with the *general use* to which he puts the world he has made. And we may well argue from what we see of the general *use* which God makes of the world to the general *end* for which he designed the world. Though there may be some ends of particular works of providence that were not the *last* end of the creation, which are in themselves grateful [i.e., pleasing] to God in such particular emergent circumstances, and so are last ends in an inferior sense; yet this is only in certain cases or particular occasions. But if they are last ends of God's proceedings in the use of the world *in general*, this shows that his making them last ends doth not depend on particular cases and circumstances, but the nature of things in general, and his general design in the being and constitution of the universe.

[POSITION NINE]
*[There is only one ultimate end of creation
if only one end is agreeable in itself]*

[26] *Ninthly*, if there be but *one thing* that is originally and independent of[16] any future supposed cases, agreeable to God, to be

---

[16] The original has "on" instead of "of."

obtained by the creation of the world, then there can be *but one last end* of God's work in this highest sense.[17] But if there are *various* things, properly diverse one from another, that are absolutely and independently agreeable to the Divine Being, which are actually obtained by the creation of the world, then there were *several* ultimate ends of the creation in that highest sense.

---

[17] I take this difficult sentence to mean the following: If God is pleased to seek only one thing in creation that is agreeable to him in itself (that is, not as a means to some future, more agreeable thing), then there is only one last end in creation. Then the next sentence holds out the hypothetical possibility (that Edwards will later reject) that several things may be agreeable to God which are absolutely diverse and independent from each other—not a means to any other thing. These then could be ultimate ends of God in creation.

WHEREIN IS CONSIDERED WHAT REASON TEACHES CONCERNING THIS AFFAIR

SECTION ONE

*SOME THINGS OBSERVED IN GENERAL
WHICH REASON DICTATES*

[27] Having observed these things to prevent confusion, I now proceed to consider what *may*, and what may *not*, be supposed to be God's ultimate end in the creation of the world.

Reason by itself is a defective guide

[28] Indeed this affair seems properly to be an affair of divine revelation. In order to [determine]¹⁸ what was designed, in the creating of the astonishing fabric of the universe we behold, it becomes us to attend to and rely on what HE who was the architect has told us. He best knows his own heart and what his own ends and designs were, in the wonderful works which he has wrought. Nor is it to be supposed that mankind—who, while destitute of revelation, by the utmost improvements of their own reason and advances in science and philosophy could come to no clear and

---

¹⁸ Original "In order to be determined . . ."

established determination who the *author* of the world was—would ever have obtained any tolerable settled judgment of the end which the author of it proposed to himself in so vast, complicated, and wonderful a work of his hands.

Revelation has improved the use of reason, but not enough

[29] And though it be true that the revelation which God has given to men, as a light shining in a dark place, has been the occasion of great improvement of their faculties and has taught men how to use their reason; and though mankind now, through the long-continued assistance they have had by this divine light, have come to great attainments in the habitual exercise of reason; yet I confess it would be relying too much on reason to determine the affair of God's last end in the creation of the world, without being herein *principally* guided by divine revelation, since God has given a revelation containing instructions concerning this very matter.

But reason can help answer objections to revelation

[30] Nevertheless, as objections have chiefly been made against what I think the Scriptures have truly revealed from the pretended dictates of reason, I would, in the *first* place, soberly consider in a few things what seems rational to be supposed concerning this affair—and *then* proceed to consider what light divine revelation gives us in it.

Six things that seem rational to suppose

[31] As to the *first* of these, I think the following things appear to be the dictates of reason:

[DICTATE ONE]

God's acting for the sake of his ultimate end implies no insufficiency in himself

[32] That no notion of God's last end in the creation of the world is agreeable to reason, which would truly imply any indigence,[19] insufficiency, and mutability in God, or any dependence of the

---

[19] "Indigence" means poverty and deprivation.

Creator on the creature for any part of his perfection or happiness. Because it is evident, by both Scripture and reason, that God is infinitely, eternally, unchangeably, and independently glorious and happy; that he cannot be profited by, or receive anything from, the creature; or be the subject of any sufferings, or diminution of his glory and felicity, from any other being.

[33] The notion of God creating the world, in order to receive any thing properly from the creature, is not only contrary to the nature of God, but inconsistent with the notion of creation; which implies a being receiving its existence, and all that belongs to it, out of nothing. And this implies the most perfect, absolute, and universal derivation and dependence. Now, if the creature receives its ALL from God, entirely and perfectly, how is it possible that *it* should have any thing to add to God to make him in any respect more than he was before, and so the Creator become dependent on the creature?[20]

[DICTATE TWO]

God's existence precedes his action
and so can't be the end of God's action

[34] Whatsoever is good and valuable *in itself* is worthy that God should value it with an *ultimate* respect. It is therefore worthy to be made the *last end* of his operation, if it be properly *capable* of being attained. For it may be supposed that some things, valuable

---

[20] While this is compelling to me, as it was to Edwards, it is not at all assumed by some, who conceive of God creating other creators (angels and humans) who can originate reality that God neither wills nor foresees, and therefore must reckon with as coming from outside himself. Such theologians would then not agree with Edwards that God "cannot . . . receive anything from the creature" that he did not first supply. One recent form of this historically unorthodox theology is called the "Openness of God" or "Free-will Theism." For example, one popular exponent of this view says, "If the future is genuinely 'open'—if it is to some degree not yet created, *leaving room for self-creating beings to create it*—then the truth value of propositions regarding the future, insofar as the future is yet open, must themselves also be open, and God must know them as such, for God's knowledge is, by definition, exhaustively accurate" (emphasis added) (Greg Boyd, *Trinity and Process: A Critical Evaluation and Reconstruction of Hartshorne's Di-Polar Theism Towards a Trinitarian Metaphysics* [New York: Peter Lang Publishing, Inc., 1992], p. 307). Similarly, in Boyd's more popular *Letters from a Skeptic*, he says, "God can't foreknow the good or bad decisions of the people He creates until He creates these people and they, in turn, create their decisions" (Colorado Springs: Chariot Victor Publishing, 1994), p. 30. Boyd concedes that "until the time of the Socinians [Faustus Socinus died in 1604], the belief that God's omniscience included all future events was not generally questioned" (*Trinity and Process*, p. 296f.). That is true. Moreover, the Socinian view has never been viewed as orthodox since that time—which should give us pause, before we reject a view of God that has always and everywhere been considered orthodox by the church.

and excellent in themselves, are not properly capable of being *attained* in any divine operation; because their existence, in all possible respects, must be conceived of as *prior* to any divine operation. Thus God's existence and infinite perfection, though infinitely valuable in themselves, cannot be supposed to be the *end* of any divine operation; for we cannot conceive of them as in any respect *consequent* on any works of God. But whatever is *in itself valuable*, absolutely so, and is *capable* of being sought and *attained*, is worthy to be made a last end of the divine operation. Therefore,

[DICTATE THREE]

What is in itself most valuable and attainable by creation is God's ultimate end in creation

[35] Whatever that be which is *in itself* most valuable, and was so originally, prior to the creation of the world, and which is *attainable* by the creation, if there be any thing which was superior in value to all others, *that* must be worthy to be God's *last* end in the creation; and also worthy to be his *highest end*. In consequence of this it will follow,

[DICTATE FOUR]

God's moral rectitude consists in his valuing the most valuable, namely, himself

[36] That if God *himself* be, in *any respect*, properly *capable* of being his own end in the creation of the world, then it is reasonable to suppose that he had respect to *himself*, as his last and highest end, in this work; because he is *worthy* in himself to be so, being infinitely the greatest and best of beings. All things else, with regard to worthiness, importance, and excellence, are perfectly as nothing in comparison of him. And therefore, if God has respect to things according to their nature and proportions, he must necessarily have the greatest respect to himself. It would be against the perfection of his nature, his wisdom, holiness, and perfect rectitude, whereby he is disposed to do everything that is fit to be done, to suppose otherwise.

[37] At least, a great part of the moral rectitude of God,

whereby he is disposed to every thing that is fit, suitable, and amiable [i.e., pleasant, admirable] in itself, consists in his having the highest regard to that which is in itself highest and best. The moral rectitude of God must consist in a due respect to things that are objects of moral respect; that is, to intelligent beings capable of moral actions and relations. And therefore it must chiefly consist in giving due respect to that Being to whom most is due; for God is infinitely the most worthy of regard. The worthiness of others is as nothing to his; so that to him belongs all possible respect. To him belongs the *whole* of the respect that any intelligent being is capable of. To him belongs ALL the heart. Therefore, if moral rectitude of heart consists in paying the respect of the heart which is due, or which fitness and suitableness requires, fitness requires infinitely the greatest regard to be paid to God; and the denying of supreme regard here would be a conduct infinitely the most unfit. Hence it will follow, that the moral rectitude of the disposition, inclination, or affection of God CHIEFLY consists in a regard to HIMSELF, infinitely above his regard to all other beings; in other words, his holiness consists in this.[21]

It is fitting that God show by his works what he values most, himself

[38] And if it be thus fit that God should *have* a supreme regard to himself, then it is fit that this supreme regard should *appear* in those things by which he makes himself known, or by his *word* and *works*, i.e. in what he *says*, and in what he *does*. If it be an infi-

---

[21] The truth of the preceding two paragraphs has been enormously important in the shaping of my own understanding of reality. I would encourage the reader to wrestle earnestly with this truth: "That the moral rectitude of . . . God CHIEFLY consists in a regard to HIMSELF, infinitely above his regard to all other beings." This is a continental divide in theology. If you really believe this, all the rivers of your thinking run toward God. If you do not, all the rivers run toward man. The theological and practical implications are innumerable. Settling this issue is worth many nights of prayer and months of study. Edwards calls God's regard to himself his "holiness." It may be more proper to call it God's "righteousness." Thus his "holiness" would be the infinite worth that God has in his own estimation, and his righteousness would be his valuing and respecting that worth without wavering and upholding it in all that he does. In my book *The Justification of God*, I have tried to show that this understanding of God's righteousness is the key to unlocking the "justification of God" in Romans 9, and that it is a deeply Biblical definition, not merely a rationally compelling one. There I argue that in the Old Testament and in Paul, "the righteousness of God must be his unswerving commitment always to preserve the honor of his name and to display his glory." John Piper, *The Justification of God: An Exegetical and Theological Study of Romans 9:1-23* (Grand Rapids: Baker Book House, 1993), p. 219, see p. 97.

nitely amiable [i.e., pleasant, admirable] thing in God that he should have a supreme regard to himself, then it is an amiable [i.e., pleasant, admirable] thing that he should *act* as having a chief regard to himself, or act in such a manner as to *show* that he has such a regard: that what is highest in God's *heart* may be highest in his *actions* and *conduct*. And if it was God's intention, as there is great reason to think it was, that his *works* should exhibit an *image* of himself their author, that it might brightly appear by his works what manner of being he is, and afford a proper representation of his divine excellencies, and especially his *moral* excellence, consisting in the *disposition of his heart*; then it is reasonable to suppose that his works are so wrought as to *show* this supreme respect to himself, wherein his moral excellence primarily consists.

The degree of regard for a being is in proportion to its existence and excellence

[39] When we are considering what would be most fit for God *chiefly* to respect with regard to the universality of things, it may help us to judge with greater ease and satisfaction to consider what we can *suppose* would be determined by some third being of perfect wisdom and rectitude that should be perfectly indifferent and disinterested. Or if we make the supposition that infinitely wise justice and rectitude were a distinct, disinterested person whose office it was to determine how things shall be most properly ordered in the whole kingdom of existence, including king and subjects, God and his creatures; and upon a view of the whole, to decide what regard should prevail in all proceedings—how such a judge, in adjusting the proper measures and kinds of regard, would weigh things in an even balance; taking care that a greater part of the whole should be more respected than the lesser, in proportion (other things being equal) to the measure of existence. So that the *degree of regard* should always be in a *proportion compounded* of the *proportion* of *existence* and *proportion* of *excellence*, or according to the degree of *greatness* and *goodness*, considered *conjunctly*.

As the Creator is infinite, so he must have all possible regard

[40] Such an arbiter, in considering the system of *created* intelligent beings by itself, would determine that the *system in general*, consisting of many millions, was of greater importance, and worthy of a greater share of regard, than only one individual. For, however considerable some of the individuals might be, no one exceeds others so much as to countervail all the system. And if this judge consider not only the system of created beings, but the system of *being in general*, comprehending the *sum total* of universal existence, both Creator and creature; still every part must be considered according to its importance or the measure it has of *existence* and *excellence*.

[41] To determine then what proportion of regard is to be allotted to the Creator and all his creatures taken together, both must be as it were put in the balance; the *Supreme Being*, with all in him that is great and excellent, is to be compared with all that is to be found in the *whole creation*; and according as the former is found to outweigh, in such proportion is he to have a greater share of regard. And in this case, as the whole system of created beings, in comparison of the Creator, would be found as the light dust of the balance, or even as nothing and vanity; so the arbiter must determine accordingly with respect to the *degree* in which God should be regarded, by all intelligent existence, in all actions and proceedings, determinations and effects whatever, whether creating, preserving, using, disposing, changing, or destroying. And as the Creator is infinite, and has all possible existence, perfection, and excellence, so he must have all possible regard. As he is every way the first and supreme, and as his excellency is in all respects the supreme beauty and glory, the original good, and fountain of all good; so he must have in all respects the supreme regard. And as he is *God over all*, to whom all are properly subordinate and on whom all depend, worthy to reign as supreme Head, with absolute and universal dominion; so it is *fit* that he should be so regarded by all, and in all proceedings and effects through the whole system: The universality of things, in their whole compass and series, should look to him in such a manner as that respect to

him should reign over all respect to other things, and regard to creatures should, universally, be subordinate and subject.

Every wheel should move with invariable regard to God

[42] When I speak of *regard* to be thus adjusted in the universal system, I mean the regard of the *sum total*; all intelligent existence, created and uncreated. For it is fit, that the regard of the *Creator* should be proportioned to the worthiness of objects, as well as the regard of creatures. Thus, we must conclude that such an arbiter as I have supposed would determine that the whole universe, in all its actings, proceedings, revolutions, and entire series of events, should proceed with a view to *God* as the supreme and last end; that every wheel, in all its rotations, should move with a constant invariable regard to him as the ultimate end of all; as perfectly and uniformly as if the whole system were animated and directed by one common soul; or as if such an arbiter as I have before supposed, possessed of perfect wisdom and rectitude, became the common soul of the universe and actuated and governed it in all its motions.

Infinite wisdom and rectitude arbitrates what is fit and suitable in the universe

[43] Thus I have gone upon the supposition of a third disinterested person. The thing supposed is impossible; but the case is, nevertheless, just the same as to what is most fit and suitable in itself. For it is most certainly proper for God to act, according to the greatest *fitness*, and he knows what the greatest fitness is, as much as if perfect rectitude were a distinct person to direct him. God himself is possessed of that perfect discernment and rectitude which have been supposed. It belongs to him as supreme arbiter, and to his infinite wisdom and rectitude, to state all rules and measures of proceedings. And seeing these attributes of God are infinite and most absolutely perfect, they are not the less fit to order and dispose, because they are in him who is a being concerned, and not a third person that is disinterested. For being *interested* unfits a person to be an arbiter or judge no otherwise than as interest tends to mislead his judgment, or incline him to act contrary to it. But that God should be in danger of either is contrary to the sup-

position of his being absolutely perfect. And as there must be *some* supreme judge of fitness and propriety in the universality of things (otherwise there could be no order), it therefore belongs to God, whose are all things, who is perfectly fit for this office, and who alone is so, to state all things according to the most perfect fitness and rectitude, as much as if perfect rectitude were a distinct person. We may therefore be sure it is and will be done.

It should seem that God proposes himself as the chief end of creation

[44] I should think that these things might incline us to suppose that God has not forgot himself in the ends which he proposed in the creation of the world; but that he has so stated these ends (however self-sufficient, immutable, and independent), as therein plainly to show a supreme regard to himself. Whether this can be, or whether God has done thus, must be considered afterwards, as also what may be objected against this view of things.

[DICTATE FIVE]

What God values for its own sake in creation is his ultimate end in creation

[45] Whatsoever is good, amiable [i.e., pleasant, admirable], and valuable *in itself*, *absolutely* and *originally* (which facts and events show that God aimed at in the creation of the world), must be supposed to be regarded or aimed at by God *ultimately* or as an ultimate end of creation. For we must suppose from the perfection of God's nature that whatsoever is valuable and amiable [i.e., pleasant, admirable] in itself, simply and absolutely considered, God values simply for itself; because God's judgment and esteem are according to truth. But if God values a thing simply and absolutely on its own account, then it is the *ultimate* object of his value. For to suppose that he values it only for some *farther* end is in direct contradiction to the present supposition, which is that he values it absolutely and for itself. Hence it most clearly follows that, if that which God values *for itself*, appears, in fact and experience, to be what he seeks by any thing he does, he must regard it as an *ultimate* end. And therefore, if he seeks it in creating the world or any

part of the world, it is an ultimate end of the work of creation. Having got thus far, we may now proceed a step farther, and assert,

[DICTATE SIX]

What God attained in creating the world, he aimed at, and what he aimed at is his end

[46] Whatsoever thing is *actually* the *effect* of the creation of the world, which is simply and absolutely valuable in itself, that thing is an ultimate end of God's creating the world. We see that it is a good which God *aimed* at by the creation of the world; because he has *actually attained* it by that means. For we may justly infer what God *intends*, by what he actually *does*; because he does nothing inadvertently or without design. But whatever God *intends* to attain, from a value for it, in his actions and works, that he *seeks* in those acts and works. Because, for an agent to *intend* to attain something he values by the means he uses is the same thing as to *seek* it by those means. And this is the same as to make that thing his *end* in those means. Now, it being, by the supposition, what God *values ultimately*, it must therefore, by the preceding position, be *aimed at* by God, as an ultimate end of creating the world.

SECTION TWO

SOME FURTHER OBSERVATIONS CONCERNING THOSE THINGS WHICH REASON LEADS US TO SUPPOSE GOD AIMED AT IN THE CREATION OF THE WORLD

What is the actual effect or consequence of creation?

[47] From what was last observed, it *seems* to be the most proper way of proceeding—as we would see what light *reason* will give us, respecting the particular end or ends God had ultimately in view in the creation of the world—to consider what thing or things are *actually* the effect or *consequence* of the creation of the world that are simply and originally valuable in themselves. And this is what I would directly proceed to, without entering on any tedious metaphysical inquiries, wherein fitness or amiableness [i.e., pleas-

antness, admirableness] consists; referring what I say to the dictates of the reader's mind, on sedate and calm reflection.

[SUPPOSITION ONE]

If God is sufficient for great effects,
it is fitting that he effect them in creation

[48] It seems a thing in itself proper and desirable that the glorious attributes of God, which consist in a *sufficiency* to certain acts and effects, should be *exerted* in the production of such effects as might manifest his infinite power, wisdom, righteousness, goodness, &c.[22] If the world had not been created, these attributes never would have had any *exercise*.[23] The *power* of God, which is a sufficiency in him to produce great effects, must for ever have been dormant and useless as to any effect. The divine *wisdom* and prudence would have had no exercise in any wise contrivance, any prudent proceeding, or disposal of things; for there would have been no objects of contrivance or disposal. The same might be observed of God's *justice, goodness*, and *truth*.

[49] Indeed God might have *known* as perfectly that he pos-

---

[22] The words "sufficiency" and "exerted" are meant to contrast the ability of God to a thing and the actual effecting of the thing through his exerting himself. The point is that it would seem proper that God, out of highest respect to himself, should exert himself to make his glorious attributes manifest.

[23] This statement taken by itself would be misleading as to what Edwards really thinks. It sounds as though there is no exercise of these attributes in the triune being of God apart from creation. This illustrates the very difficult task Edwards had of always qualifying his statements to give them the careful nuances that such a difficult theme as this demands. To clarify what he thinks here, consider these words from Miscellany #553, "There are many of the divine attributes that, if God had not created the world, never would have had any exercise—the power of God, the wisdom of God, the prudence and contrivance of God, the goodness and mercy and grace of God, the justice of God. . . . 'Tis true that there was from eternity that act in God, within Himself and towards Himself, that was the exercise of the same perfections of His nature. But it was not the same kind of exercise. It virtually contained it, but was not explicitly the same exercise of His perfection. God, who delights in the exercise of His own perfection, delights in all the kinds of its exercise" (Harvey Townsend, ed., *The Philosophy of Jonathan Edwards* [Westport, CT: Greenwood Press, Publishers, 1972], p. 136). In other words, Edwards, when speaking more carefully, would not say that God's attributes lay dormant *in every way*. They were in exercise as the members of the Trinity know and love each other, yet they were not in exercise with "the same kind" of exercise as they would have in creation as a public shining forth of God's glory.

Edwards does not make it explicit, but Daniel Fuller draws out the implication from Edwards, that all the attributes of God find exercise in the eternal life of the Trinity except mercy, or grace. Yet it is not as though God would not have an essential divine attribute without creation, for grace is unique in that it is but the free overflow of all the other excellencies of God for weak and dependent creatures to enjoy. Grace is the overflow of fullness and sufficiency, not the effort to repair a divine defect. See Daniel Fuller, *Unity of the Bible* (Grand Rapids: Eerdmans Publishing Co., 1992), pp. 129-137.

sessed these attributes, if they never had been exerted or expressed in any effect. But then, if the attributes which consist in a *sufficiency* for correspondent effects, are in themselves excellent, the *exercises* of them must likewise be excellent. If it be an excellent thing that there should be a sufficiency for a certain kind of action or operation, the excellency of such a sufficiency must consist in its *relation* to this kind of operation or effect; but that could not be, unless the *operation itself* were excellent. A sufficiency for any work is no further valuable than the work itself is valuable.[24]

[50] As God therefore esteems these attributes *themselves* valuable and delights in them, so it is natural to suppose that he delights in their proper *exercise* and expression. For the same reason that he esteems his own sufficiency wisely to *contrive* and dispose effects, he also will esteem the wise *contrivance* and disposition itself. And for the same reason, as he delights in his own disposition to do justly and to dispose of things according to truth and just proportion, so he must delight in such a righteous disposal itself.

[SUPPOSITION TWO]

It is most fitting that beings exist to know what God can manifest of his excellency

[51] It seems to be a thing in itself fit and desirable that the glorious perfections of God should be *known*, and the operations and expressions of them seen, by *other beings* besides himself. If it be fit that God's power and wisdom, &c. should be exercised and *expressed* in some effects and not lie eternally dormant, then it seems proper that these exercises should *appear* and not be totally hidden and unknown. For if they are, it will be just the same as to the above purpose, as if they were not. God as perfectly knew himself and his perfections, [and] has as perfect an idea of the exer-

---

[24] Edwards's own footnote: "The *end* of wisdom" (says Mr. G. Tennent, in his sermon at the opening of the Presbyterian Church of Philadelphia) "is *design*; the *end* of power is *action*; the *end* of goodness is *doing* good. To suppose these perfections not to be *exerted* would be to represent them as insignificant. Of what use would God's *wisdom* be, if it had nothing to design or direct? To what purpose his *almightiness*, if it never brought any thing to pass? And of what avail his *goodness*, if it never did any good?" [In his own sentence, Edwards does not mean that God is no more valuable than creation is valuable. He means that when a divine attribute is regarded as a *sufficiency* for action, the value of the sufficiency *as such* is coordinate with the value of the potential operation. As the next paragraph makes plain, the value of the effect comes from the value of the attribute, not vice versa. This is the opposite of utilitarianism in God.]

cises and effects they were sufficient for, *antecedently* to any such actual operations of them, and since. If, therefore, it be nevertheless a thing in itself valuable and worthy to be desired, that these glorious perfections be actually *exhibited* in their correspondent effects, then it seems also that the *knowledge* of these perfections and discoveries is valuable in itself absolutely considered, and that it is *desirable* that this knowledge should exist.

[52] It is a thing infinitely good in itself that God's glory should be *known* by a glorious society of created beings. And that there should be in them an *increasing* knowledge of God to all eternity, is worthy to be regarded[25] by him, to whom it belongs to order what is fittest and best. If *existence* is more worthy than defect and non-entity, and if any *created* existence is in itself worthy to be, then *knowledge* is; and if any knowledge, then the most *excellent sort* of knowledge, *viz.* that of God and his glory. This knowledge is one of the highest, most real, and substantial parts of all created existence, most remote from non-entity and defect.

[SUPPOSITION THREE]

It is fitting that God's glory be delighted in as well as known

[53] As it is desirable in itself that God's glory should be known, so when known it seems equally reasonable it should be esteemed and delighted in, answerably to its dignity. There is no more reason to esteem it a suitable thing, that there should be an idea in the *understanding* corresponding unto the glorious object, than that there should be a corresponding *affection* in the will.[26] If the per-

---

[25] "Regarded," that is, esteemed and valued.

[26] In Edwards's thinking "God has endued the soul with two faculties: one is that by which it is capable of perception and speculation, or by which it discerns and views and judges of things; which is called the understanding. The other faculty is that by which the soul does not merely perceive and view things, but is some way inclined with respect to the things it views or considers; either is inclined to 'em, or is disinclined, and averse from 'em; or is the faculty by which the soul does not behold things, as an indifferent unaffected spectator, but either as liking or disliking, pleased or displeased, approving or rejecting. This faculty is called by various names; it is sometimes called the *inclination*; and, as it has respect to the actions that are determined and governed by it, is called the *will*: and the *mind*, with regard to the exercises of this faculty, is often called the *heart*" (Jonathan Edwards, *Religious Affections*, ed. by John E. Smith, *The Works of Jonathan Edwards*, vol. 2 [New Haven: Yale University Press, 1959], p. 96). Therefore, when Edwards talks about "delighting" or "esteeming" and so on, these are not the acts of a third faculty after "understanding" and "will." These "affections" are "no other, than the more vigorous and sensible exercises of the inclination and will of the soul" (p. 96). "The will, and the affections of the soul, are not two faculties; the affections are not essentially distinct from the will, nor do they differ from the mere actings of the will and inclination of the soul, but only in the liveliness and sensibleness of exercise" (p. 97).

fection itself be excellent, the knowledge of it is excellent, and so is the esteem and love of it excellent. And as it is fit that God should love and esteem his own *excellence*, it is also fit that he should value and esteem the *love* of his excellency. And if it becomes a being highly to *value* himself, it is fit that he should love to have himself *valued* and esteemed. If the idea of God's perfection in the understanding be valuable, then the love of the heart seems to be more especially valuable, as moral beauty especially consists in the disposition and affection of the heart.

[SUPPOSITION FOUR]

It is fitting that a full fountain should send forth abundant streams

[54] As there is an infinite fullness of all possible good in God—a fullness of every perfection, of all excellency and beauty, and of infinite happiness—and as this fullness is capable of communication, or emanation *ad extra;*[27] so it seems a thing amiable [i.e., pleasant, admirable] and valuable in *itself* that this infinite fountain of good should send forth abundant streams. And as this is in itself excellent, so a *disposition* to this in the Divine Being, must be looked upon as an *excellent* disposition. Such an emanation of good is, in some sense, a *multiplication* of it. So far as the stream may be looked upon as any thing besides the fountain, so far it may be looked on as an *increase* of good. And if the fullness of good that is in the fountain is in itself excellent, then the emanation, which is, as it were, an increase, repetition, or multiplication of it, is excellent.

[55] Thus it is fit, since there is an infinite fountain of light and knowledge, that this light should shine forth in beams of communicated knowledge and understanding; and, as there is an infinite fountain of holiness, moral excellence, and beauty, that so it should flow out in communicated holiness. And that, as there is an infinite fullness of joy and happiness, so these should have an emanation,

---

[27] This Latin phrase is standard in theological idiom for the works of God directed to reality outside himself. His *ad extra* work is "toward the outside," as opposed to what he does within himself and among the members of the Trinity. Thus his eternal begetting of the Son would be an *ad intra* work, but his creation of the world would be *ad extra*.

and become a fountain flowing out in abundant streams, as beams from the sun.[28] Thus it appears reasonable to suppose that it was God's last end that there might be a glorious and abundant emanation of his infinite fullness of good *ad extra*, or without[29] himself; and that the disposition to communicate himself, or diffuse his own FULLNESS,[30] was what moved him to create the world.

[56] But here I observe that there would be some impropriety in saying that a disposition in God to communicate himself *to the creature* moved him to create the world. For an inclination in God to communicate himself to an *object* seems to presuppose the *existence* of the object, at least in idea. But the diffusive disposition that excited God to give creatures existence was rather a communicative *disposition* in general, or a disposition in the fullness of the divinity to flow out and diffuse itself. Thus the disposition there is in the root and stock of a tree to diffuse sap and life is doubtless the reason of their communication to its buds, leaves, and fruits, *after* these exist. But a disposition to communicate of its life and sap to its *fruits*, is not so properly the cause of its *producing* those fruits, as its disposition to diffuse its sap and life in general. Therefore, to speak strictly according to truth, we may suppose *that a disposition in God, as an original property of his nature, to an emanation of his own infinite fullness, was what excited him to create the world; and so, that the emanation itself was aimed at by him as a last end of the creation.*

---

[28] Edwards nears the end of his answer already. Why did God create the world? He will have much more to say. But he does not get much beyond this image of fullness of joy that is disposed by its nature to overflow, not compelled from outside or drawn out by something other than God, but simply by virtue of the nature of fullness or goodness. In his Miscellany #87 he puts it like this: "'Tis not proper to ask what moved God to exert his goodness; for this is the notion of goodness, an inclination to show goodness. Therefore such a question would be no more proper than this, viz. what inclines God to exert his inclination to exert goodness—which is nonsense, for it is an asking and an answering a question in the same words" (Jonathan Edwards, *The "Miscellanies,"* ed. by Thomas Schafer, *The Works of Jonathan Edwards*, vol. 13 [New Haven, Yale University Press, 1994], p. 252).

[29] "Without" means "outside" in this context.

[30] Edwards's own footnote: I shall often use the phrase *God's fullness*, as signifying and comprehending all the good which is in God, natural and moral, either excellence or happiness: partly because I know of no better phrase to be used in this general meaning; and partly, because I am led hereto by some of the inspired writers, particularly the apostle Paul, who often useth the phrase in this sense. [The texts that Edwards has in mind would include Colossians 1:19, "For it was the Father's good pleasure for all the *fullness* to dwell in Him." Colossians 2:9, "For in Him all the *fullness* of Deity dwells in bodily form." Ephesians 1:22-23, "And He put all things in subjection under His feet, and gave Him as head over all things to the church, which is His body, the *fullness* of Him who fills all in all." Ephesians 4:13, ". . . until we all attain to the unity of the faith, and of the knowledge of the Son of God, to a mature man, to the measure of the stature which belongs to the *fullness* of Christ."]

SECTION THREE

WHEREIN IT IS CONSIDERED HOW, ON THE SUPPOSITION
OF GOD'S MAKING THE AFOREMENTIONED THINGS
HIS LAST END, HE MANIFESTS A SUPREME AND ULTIMATE
REGARD TO HIMSELF IN ALL HIS WORKS

[57] In the last section I observed some things which are actually the consequence of the creation of the world, which seem absolutely valuable in themselves and so worthy to be made God's last end in his work. I now proceed to inquire how God's making such things as these his last end is consistent with his making *himself* his last end, or his manifesting an ultimate respect to himself in his acts and works. Because it is agreeable to the dictates of reason that in all his proceedings he should set himself highest;[31] therefore, I would endeavor to show how his infinite love to and delight in himself will naturally cause him to value and delight in these things, or rather how a value to these things is implied in his value of that infinite fullness of good that is in himself.

Delighting in the exercise of his sufficiency, God delights in himself and makes himself his end

[58] Now, with regard to the first of the particulars mentioned above—God's regard to the *exercise* of those attributes of his nature, in their proper operations and effects, which consist in a *sufficiency* for these operations—it is not hard to conceive that God's regard to *himself*, and value for his own perfections, should cause him to value these exercises and expressions of his perfections; inasmuch as their excellency consists in their relation to use, exercise, and operation. God's love to himself, and his own attributes, will therefore make him delight in that which is the use, end, and operation of these attributes.

[59] If one highly esteem and delight in the virtues of a friend,

---

[31] See above, ¶¶ 36-44. Here in the following phrases Edwards introduces the language of God's "infinite love to and delight in himself." This should be read and understood in the context of God's infinite moral rectitude or righteousness or holiness that inclines him to delight in what is most beautiful and worthy, namely, himself. To many this sounds "selfish" or "egocentric" or "narcissistic" in a pejorative sense, because such a self-assessment and self-worship in us creatures would, in fact, be evil. But that is only because we are not worthy of such a self-assessment and self-worship. God is. In fact, he would be unrighteous if he failed to delight fully in what is most beautiful and worthy, namely, himself.

as wisdom, justice, &c. that have relation to action, this will make him delight in the *exercise* and genuine *effects* of these virtues. So if God both esteem and delight in his own perfections and virtues, he cannot but value and delight in the expressions and genuine effects of them. So that in delighting in the *expressions* of his perfections, he manifests a delight in himself; and in making these expressions of his own perfections his end, *he makes himself his end.*

Delighting in his glory being known and enjoyed, God delights in himself and makes himself his end

[60] And with respect to the second and third particulars, the matter is no less plain. For he that loves any being, and has a disposition highly to prize and greatly to delight in his virtues and perfections, must from the same disposition be well pleased to have his excellencies known, acknowledged, esteemed, and prized by others. He that loves any thing, naturally loves the *approbation* of that thing, and is opposite to the disapprobation of it. Thus it is when one loves the virtues of a friend. And thus it will necessarily be, if a being loves himself and highly prizes his own excellencies. And thus it is *fit* it should be, if it be fit he should thus love himself, and prize his own valuable qualities; that is, it is fit that he should take delight in his own excellencies being seen, acknowledged, esteemed, and delighted in. This is implied in a love to himself and his own perfections; and in making *this* his end, he makes himself his end.

In his disposition to overflow from fullness God makes himself his end

[61] And with respect to the fourth and last particular, viz. God's being disposed to an abundant communication, and glorious emanation, of that infinite fullness of good which he possesses, as of his own knowledge, excellency, and happiness, in the manner [which] he does; if we thoroughly consider the matter, it will appear that herein also God makes himself his end, in such a sense as plainly to manifest and testify a supreme and ultimate regard to himself.

The general disposition to overflow with fullness precedes and grounds the existence of creatures

[62] Merely in this *disposition* to cause an emanation of his glory and fullness—which is prior to the existence of any other being and is to be considered as the inciting cause of giving existence to other beings—God cannot so properly be said to make the *creature* his end, as *himself*. For the creature is not as yet considered as existing. This disposition or desire in God must be *prior* to the existence of the creature, even in foresight. For it is a disposition that is the original ground even of the future, intended, and foreseen existence of the creature.

[63] God's benevolence, as it respects the creature, may be taken either in a larger or stricter sense. In a larger sense, it may signify nothing diverse from that good disposition in his nature to communicate of his own fullness in general; [such] as his knowledge, his holiness, and happiness; and to give creatures existence in order to it. This may be called benevolence, or love, because it is the same good disposition that is exercised in love. It is the very fountain from whence love originally proceeds, when taken in the most proper sense; and it has the same general tendency and effect in the creature's well-being. But yet this cannot have any particular present or future created existence for its object, because it is prior to any such object and the very source of the futurition [i.e., the future coming into being] of its existence. Nor is it really diverse from God's love to himself; as will more clearly appear afterwards.

[64] But God's love may be taken more strictly for this general disposition to communicate good, as directed to *particular objects*. Love, in the most strict and proper sense, *presupposes* the existence of the object beloved, at least in idea and expectation, and represented to the mind as future. God did not love angels in the strictest sense, but in consequence of his intending to create them, and so having an idea of future existing angels. Therefore his love to them was not properly what *excited* him to *intend* to create them.[32] Love

---

[32] This is a difficult paragraph to grasp. The key is in seeing the difference between what moved God to "intend" to create, and what moved God to create. Once God has a creature in his foreknowledge and *intends* to create him, then benevolence, or love, *toward the creature* is properly the motive of his action. But before (in order of thought, if not time) the creature is foreseen, there is something that "excites" the "intention" to create. That is not properly love to the creature (who is not yet in view as an intention), but purely the disposition to emanate or communicate or overflow. This "disposition" is what Edwards wants to show now as an expression of love to God himself.

or benevolence, strictly taken, presupposes an *existing* object, as much as pity [presupposes] a miserable suffering object.

God's delight in overflowing is a delight in himself as one who overflows

[65] This propensity in God to diffuse himself may be considered as a propensity to himself diffused, or to his own glory existing in its emanation. A respect to himself, or an infinite propensity to and delight in his own glory, is that which causes him to incline to its being abundantly diffused, and to delight in the emanation of it.[33] Thus, that nature in a tree, by which it puts forth buds, shoots out branches, and brings forth leaves and fruit, is a disposition that terminates in its own complete self. And so the disposition in the sun to shine, or abundantly to diffuse its fullness, warmth, and brightness is only a tendency to its own most glorious and complete state. So God looks on the communication of himself and the emanation of his infinite glory to belong to the fullness and completeness of himself, as though he were not in his most glorious state without it.[34]

[66] Thus the church of Christ (toward whom and in whom are the emanations of his glory, and the communication of his fullness) is called the *fullness of Christ*, as though he were not in his complete state without her, like Adam without Eve. And the church is called the glory of Christ, as the woman is the glory of

---

[33] This is an extremely important sentence. It shows how close to the bottom line we are in explaining the origin of creation. Notice the steps toward the bottom line, that is, trace the causes back as far as you can: 1) *creation* by God comes from 2) the abundant *diffusion* of God's glory that comes from 3) God's *inclination* to an abundant diffusion of glory that comes from 4) God's infinite *delight* in his glory. The deepest source of it all is the mysterious power of delight in God's being God. This delight is in other places called love, and sheds much light on the Biblical assertion that "God is love" (1 John 4:8, 16)

[34] Edwards wrestles mightily with how God can be motivated to create the world by the desire to display his glory for the enjoyment of his creatures, and yet not seem to be deficient as God apart from the existence of creation (see Edwards's material at footnote 48). In other words, God's dependence on his creation for his happiness seems to be implied in God's creating from a desire to enjoy the display of his glory for the good of his people. Edwards is aware that some of his expressions come very close to saying that God is dependent on his creation. This is partly why he uses the phrase "as though" so often. For example, here he says, "God looks on the communication of himself and the emanation of his infinite glory to belong to the fullness and completeness of himself, as though he were not in his most glorious state without it." This phrase "as though" is Edwards's signal to us that there are complexities of reality and thought here, and we need to be sure to take into account what he has said elsewhere. In fact, the first objection Edwards will raise to his own viewpoint and then answer is that it makes God look dependent on creation. See his three Answers to Objection One in Section Four, ¶¶ 77-92.

None of these problems is new to Edwards. For example, the answer he gave in Miscellany #1208 goes like this: "God may have a true, proper, and real delight (and so a part of his happiness) in seeing the state of the creature, in seeing its happy state; or he may delight in the exercise of his own goodness (and so gratifying the inclination of his own heart); and yet all his happiness be eternal and immutable. He eternally has this disposition and eternally sees and enjoys this future grati-

the man, 1 Corinthians 11:7. Isaiah 46:13. "*I will place salvation in Zion, for Israel* MY GLORY."[35]

[67] Indeed, after the creatures are *intended*[36] to be created, God may be conceived of as being moved by benevolence to them, in the strictest sense in his dealings with them. His exercising his goodness, and gratifying his benevolence to them in particular, may be the spring of all God's proceedings through the universe; as being now the determined way of gratifying his general inclination to diffuse himself. Here God acting for *himself*, or making himself his last end, and his acting for *their* sake, are not to be set in opposition; they are rather to be considered as coinciding one with the other, and implied one in the other.[37] But yet God is to be considered as first and original in his regard; and the creature is the object of God's regard, consequently, and by implication, as being, as it were, comprehended in God; as it shall be more particularly observed presently.

Considering the specifics of what actually overflows in creation

[68] But how God's value for and delight in the emanations of his fullness in the work of creation argues his delight in the infinite fullness of good in himself, and the supreme regard he has for himself (and that in making these emanations, he ultimately makes himself his end in creation) will more clearly appear by considering

---

fication of it as though it were present. Indeed all things are present to him; with him is no succession, no past and future, and he is independent in this delight. He brings the thing to pass by which he is gratified by his own independent power. . . . Although God has truly delight in the creature's happiness and holiness, yet still, his happiness is in himself; for those are but communications of himself—they are wholly being from the fountain. God's delight in these things is only a delight in his own brightness, communicated and reflected, and in his own action of communicating, which is still to be resolved into a delight in himself" (Harvey Townsend, ed., *The Philosophy of Jonathan Edwards* [Westport, CT: Greenwood Press, Publishers, 1972], pp. 146-147). A key sentence that has helped me comprehend what Edwards is saying is, "It is no argument of the emptiness or deficiency of a fountain that it is inclined to overflow." See *The End for Which God Created the World*, ¶ 87.

[35] Edwards's own footnote: Very remarkable is the place, John 12:23, 24. "*And Jesus answered them, saying, The hour is come, that the Son of man should be glorified. Verily, I say unto you, except a corn of wheat fall into the ground and die, it abideth alone; but if it die, it bringeth forth much fruit.*" Christ had respect herein to the blessed fruits of his death, in the conversion, salvation, and eternal happiness of those that should be redeemed by him. This consequence of his death, he calls his glory; and his obtaining this fruit, he calls his being glorified; as the flourishing, beautiful produce of a corn of wheat sown in the ground is its glory. Without this he is alone, as Adam was before Eve was created. But from him, by his death, proceeds a glorious offspring; in which are communicated his fullness and glory: as to fill his emptiness, and relieve his solitariness; by Christ's death, his fullness is abundantly diffused in many streams; and expressed in the beauty and glory of a great multitude of his spiritual offspring.

more particularly the nature and circumstances of these communications of God's fullness.

In sharing the knowledge of himself he makes himself his end in creation

[69] One part of that divine fullness which is communicated is the divine *knowledge*. That communicated knowledge, which must be supposed to pertain to God's last end in creating the world, is the creature's knowledge of HIM. For this is the end of all other knowledge, and even the faculty of understanding would be vain without it. And this knowledge is most properly a communication of God's infinite knowledge, which primarily consists in the knowledge of himself. God, in making *this* his end, makes *himself* his end. This knowledge in the creature is but a conformity to God. It is the image of God's own knowledge of himself. It is a participation of the same, though infinitely less in degree: as particular beams of the sun communicated are the light and glory of the sun itself in part.[38]

[70] Besides, God's glory is the object of this knowledge or the thing known, so that God is glorified in it, as hereby his excellency is seen. As therefore God values himself, as he delights in his own knowledge, he must delight in every thing of that nature; as he delights in his own light, he must delight in every beam of that light; as he highly values his own excellency, he must be well pleased in having it *manifested* and so *glorified*.

---

[36] See note 32 for the significance of "intended."

[37] Here is another profound reality that transforms the way I think about everything. God's acting for his own sake and his acting for my sake are not at odds. They are, Edwards says, "not to be set in opposition" but "coincide with one another" and "are implied in one another." This is massively important. It comes to expression in the cross, where God vindicates his own righteousness in the very act of saving us for infinite joy at his right hand (Rom. 3:25-26; compare 1 Pet. 3:18; Ps. 16:11). It is the very heart of the gospel. I have tried to unfold this great vision of God-centered, man-satisfying gospel in *The Pleasures of God*: "The exaltation of [God's] glory is the driving force of the gospel. The gospel is a gospel of grace! And grace is the pleasure of God to magnify the worth of God by giving sinners the right and power to delight in God without obscuring the glory of God." John Piper, *The Pleasures of God* (Sisters, OR: Multnomah Press, 1991), p. 203, see p. 19.

[38] These words, and numerous others in the remainder of Section Three, could give the impression that Edwards failed to preserve the distinction between the essence of the creature and the essence of God. But be sure to take seriously the phrases "image of" and "conformity to." The creature participates in God's knowledge of God and God's love of God and so is in the image of God and conforms to God in greater and greater degree, but is not God, nor ever arrives at becoming God. See footnote 42 and related material at footnotes 41-46, 113, 115.

In sharing his holiness God makes himself his end in creation

[71] Another emanation of divine fullness is the communication of virtue and *holiness* to the creature; this is a communication of God's holiness, so that hereby the creature partakes of God's own moral excellency, which is properly the beauty of the divine nature. And as God delights in his own beauty, he must necessarily delight in the creature's holiness which is a conformity to and participation of it, as truly as a brightness of a jewel, held in the sun's beams, is a participation or derivation of the sun's brightness, though immensely less in degree. And then it must be considered wherein this holiness in the creature consists, viz. in love, which is the comprehension of all true virtue; and primarily in love to God, which is exercised in a high esteem of God, admiration of his perfections, complacency [i.e., satisfaction, delight] in them, and praise of them. All which things are nothing else but the heart exalting, magnifying, or glorifying God; which, as I showed before, God necessarily approves of and is pleased with, as he loves himself, and values the glory of his own nature.

In sharing his happiness he makes himself his end in creation

[72] Another part of God's fullness which he communicates, is his *happiness*. This happiness consists in enjoying and rejoicing in himself; so does also the creature's happiness.[39] It is a participation in what is in God, and God and his glory are the objective ground of it. The happiness of the creature consists in rejoicing in God, by which also God is magnified and exalted.[40] Joy, or the exulting of

[39] When we see that God's passion for his own glory leads him to share that passion with us, we also see why his passion for himself is not "selfish" in a pejorative sense. God is the one being in the universe for whom self-exaltation is the highest virtue and the most loving act, because in exalting himself he displays the one Reality in the universe that can satisfy our souls and he shares the very passion for that Reality that satisfies him. The object of our happiness is God, and our happiness is God's happiness. No greater happiness can be conceived.

[40] Here we see more clearly why (as we saw in footnote 34) God's creating for *his* sake and for *our* sake are not at odds but in fact "are implied in one another." God's pursuit of the happiness of the creature is a pursuit of our happiness *in God*—not in money or sex or family or career or health. And when we thus rejoice in God, Edwards says, "God is [by this] magnified and exalted." So God is glorified by our being satisfied in him. This means that God's radical God-centeredness and our passion for ultimate satisfaction cannot be in tension, but come to fulfillment in the continual act of worshipful rejoicing in God. The implications of this are all-pervasive. It implies that we may not be indifferent to our quest for joy in God, but must pursue it as our highest duty, which is what I have tried to unfold under the rubric "Christian Hedonism." See John Piper, *Desiring God: Meditations of a Christian Hedonist* (Sisters, OR: Multnomah Press, revised edition, 1996).

the heart in God's glory, is one thing that belongs to praise. So that God is all in all with respect to each part of that communication of the divine fullness which is made to the creature. What is communicated is divine or something of God,[41] and each communication is of that nature, that the creature to whom it is made is thereby conformed to God and united to him, and that in proportion as the communication is greater or less. And the communication itself is no other, in the very nature of it, than that wherein the very honor, exaltation, and praise of God consists.

In giving creatures an ever-increasing likeness to God, God makes himself first cause and last end

[73] And it is farther to be considered that what God aimed at in the creation of the world, as the end which he had ultimately in view, was that communication of himself which he intended through all eternity [from creation and forever into the future]. And if we attend to the nature and circumstances of this eternal emanation of divine good, it will more clearly show HOW, in making this his end, God testifies a supreme respect to himself and makes himself his end.

[74] There are many reasons to think that what God has in view, in an increasing communication of himself through eternity, is an *increasing* knowledge of God, love to him, and joy in him.[42] And it is to be considered that the more those divine communications *increase* in the creature, the more it becomes one with God;[43] for so much the more is it united to God in love, the heart

---

[41] "Something of God" must be construed carefully, lest we impute to Edwards a confusing of the creature and the Creator, which many of his words could lead us to do (as we saw in footnote 38). God's knowledge and love and joy are "something of God," and may be shared by the creature. This results, as the following words here signify, in the creature being "conformed to God and united to him." That ever-increasing *conformity* and *union* will be expounded in detail in what follows immediately and at the end of Chapter Two, Section Seven, ¶¶ 279-285. See related material in footnotes 38, 42-46, 104, 113, 115.

[42] This sentence is extremely important in view of how strongly Edwards will express the union of God and his people. When he speaks of God's communicating "himself" to the creature, and therefore speaks of a "strict" union between "himself" and his people, we must recall this sentence, which stresses that his knowledge and love and joy in himself is what he has chiefly in mind. In participating in these, man is drawn, as it were, into the very life of the Trinity ("Heaven Is a Progressive State," in *Ethical Writings*, ed. by Paul Ramsey, p. 730), but not in the sense of being divinized or confused in essence with God. See footnotes 38, 41, 43-46, 104, 113, 115.

[43] Becoming "one with God" is none other than the "conformity" and the "union" referred to in footnotes 38, 41, and 42, not a merging of human and divine essences into one.

is drawn nearer and nearer to God, and the union with him becomes more firm and close, and at the same time, the creature becomes more and more *conformed* to God. The image is more and more perfect, and so the good that is in the creature comes forever nearer and nearer to an identity[44] with that which is in God. In the view therefore of God, who has a comprehensive prospect of the increasing union and conformity through eternity, it must be an infinitely strict and perfect nearness, conformity, and oneness. For it will forever come nearer and nearer to that strictness and perfection of union which there is between the Father and the Son.[45] So that in the eyes of God, who perfectly sees the whole of it, in its infinite progress and increase, it must come to

---

[44] There are two cautions given here. One is that a creaturely "image" is always an image, no matter how closely it conforms to the original. The other is that "identity" is not conceived by Edwards any other way than by the sharing of God's knowledge, love, and joy that he has of himself.

[45] Here we are introduced powerfully to Edwards's view of the eternal state as one that will be an "increasing union and conformity through eternity." In other words, eternity will not be static. The perfected, holy creature will, in his perfection, make progress in conformity to God. Since God can see all of the infinite progress (which never comes to an end) as though the whole of it were present to him, he regards the union of his people to himself as an "infinitely strict and perfect nearness and conformity, and oneness." But beware of jumping to the unwarranted conclusion that this "nearness, conformity and oneness" involves a loss of distinction between Creator and creature. *The End for Which God Created the World* ends with Edwards's meditations on this final state of ever-increasing joy and union with God.

> Let the most perfect union with God be represented by something at an infinite height above us; and the eternally increasing union of the saints with God, by something that is ascending constantly towards that infinite height, moving upwards with a given velocity; and that is to continue thus to move to all eternity. God, who views the whole of this eternally increasing height, views it as an infinite height. And if he has respect to it, and makes it his end, as in the whole of it, he has respect to it as an infinite height, though the time will never come when it can be said it has already arrived at this infinite height. (¶ 280)

The importance of this vision in Edwards's argument has to do with the fact that God's glory and our joy are one great goal in creation. Edwards is at pains to show that God's last end in creation is both the display of his glorious fullness, on the one hand, and the blessing of his creatures with infinite joy, on the other hand. These are not separate ends, but one. "The happiness of the creature consists in rejoicing in God, by which also God is magnified and exalted" (see ¶ 72). This is why in Chapter Two there is an entire section (Section Five, ¶ 226 ff.) devoted to amassing Biblical texts that demonstrate that the "communication of good to the creature" was the ultimate end of God in creating the world.

Now how does this lead Edwards to an endless, increasing state of happiness in the age to come? There are Biblical reasons (see Paul Ramsey, Appendix II, "Heaven Is a Progressive State," in *Ethical Writings*, pp. 706-738, especially 707-712). But there is also a reason that flows from the nature of the case: since God is infinite, the creature cannot fathom the totality of his greatness or comprehend his infinite beauty or delight in all that he is. Rather it will take an eternity for us to know and to enjoy all that God is; that is, God will be progressively revealed to us. Thus, since the display of God's glory in our finite, creaturely experience of knowing and delighting in God is the aim of creation, the achievement of this aim will take all eternity—there will never be a time when there is no more glory for the redeemed to discover and enjoy.

Edwards speaks of this ever-increasing knowledge and joy as an increasing conformity and union with God. (See footnote 43 and the footnotes mentioned there.) In fact, he does so in an eminent fulfillment of Christ's request, in John 17:21, 23. *That they all may be* ONE, *as thou Father art in me, and I in thee, that they also may be* ONE *in us; I in them and thou in me, that they may be made perfect in* ONE.

[75] In this view, those elect creatures, which must be looked upon as the end of all the rest of the creation, considered with respect to the whole of their eternal duration and as such made God's end, must be viewed as being, as it were, one with God. They were respected as brought home to him, united with him, centering most perfectly, as if swallowed up in him: so that his respect to *them* finally coincides, and becomes one and the same, with respect to himself. The interest of the creature is, as it were, God's own interest, in proportion to the degree of their relation and union to God.

[76] Thus the interest of a man's *family* is looked upon as the same with his *own* interest; because of the relation they stand in to him, his propriety in them, and their strict union with him.[46] But God's elect creatures, with respect to their eternal duration, are infinitely dearer to God, than a man's family is to him. What has been said shows that as all things are *from* God, as their first cause and fountain; so all things tend *to* him, and in their progress come nearer and nearer to him through all eternity, which argues that he who is their first cause is their last end.

---

ways that at times sound as if the creature and the Creator were metaphysically coalescing into one. But he does not lose sight of the distinction. For example, in Miscellany # 5 he says that in heaven "as [the holiest of all] see further into the divine perfections than others, so they shall penetrate further into the vast and infinite distance that is between them and God, and their delight of annihilating themselves, that God may be all in all, shall be the greater" (*Miscellanies*, ed. by Thomas Schafer, p. 202.). There is a mystery here that Edwards is happy to acknowledge: what does it really mean for spirits or minds to become united in knowledge and love and joy? "UNION, SPIRITUAL. What insight I have of the nature of minds, I am convinced that there is no guessing what kind of union and mixtion [sic], by consciousness or otherwise, there may be between them. So that all difficulty is removed in believing what the Scripture declares about spiritual unions—of the persons of the Trinity, of the two natures of Christ, of Christ and the minds of saints" (Miscellany, # 184, *Miscellanies*, ed. by Thomas Schafer, p. 330). Nevertheless, the matter is clear enough in Edwards that Paul Ramsey can say, "So if there is hope of increase of love in the society of heaven, this in no way promises merger with the divine or threatens the saints' collapse into identity one with another" (*Ethical Writings*, p. 534). See related material at footnotes 38, 41, 104, 113, 115.

[46] For a similar reference to the "strict union" among members of a family, see footnote 115.

SECTION FOUR

SOME OBJECTIONS CONSIDERED, WHICH MAY BE MADE
AGAINST THE REASONABLENESS OF WHAT HAS BEEN SAID OF
GOD MAKING HIMSELF HIS LAST END

[OBJECTION ONE]

Does not Edwards's view make God dependent on creation for his own completeness?

[77] **OBJECTION 1.** Some may object against what has been said as being inconsistent with God's absolute independence and immutability: particularly, as though God were inclined to a communication of his fullness and emanations of his own glory, as being his own most glorious and complete state.[47] It may be thought that this does not well consist with God, being self-existent from all eternity; absolutely perfect in himself, in the possession of infinite and independent good. And that, in general, to suppose that God makes himself his end in the creation of the world seems to suppose that he aims at some interest or happiness of his own, not easily reconcilable with his being perfectly and infinitely happy in himself.

[78] If it could be supposed that God needed any thing, or that the goodness of his creatures could extend to him, or that they could be profitable to him, it might be fit that God should make himself and his own interest his highest and last end in creating the world. But seeing that God is above all need and all capacity of being made better or happier in any respect, to what purpose should God make himself his end, or seek to advance himself in any respect by any of his works? How absurd is it to suppose that God should do such great things with a view to obtain what he is already most perfectly possessed of, and was so from all eternity, and therefore cannot now possibly need, nor with any color of reason be supposed to seek!

---

[47] That is, it may not seem that a state of overflowing communication in creation should be viewed "as being [God's] own most glorious and complete state." This may seem to imply dependence on creation for being in a "complete state."

[FIRST ANSWER TO OBJECTION ONE]

[79] *Answer 1.* Many have wrong notions of God's happiness, as resulting from his absolute self-sufficience, independence, and immutability. Though it be true that God's glory and happiness are in and of himself, are infinite and cannot be added to, and unchangeable, for the whole and every part of which he is perfectly independent of the creature; yet it does not hence follow, nor is it true, that God has no real and proper delight, pleasure, or happiness in any of his acts or communications relative to the creature or effects he produces in them, or in any thing he sees in the creature's qualifications, dispositions, actions and state.

God delights in our happiness, seeing it as a work of his own goodness

[80] God may have a real and proper pleasure or happiness in seeing the *happy state* of the creature; yet this may not be different from his delight in himself, being a delight in his own infinite goodness, or the exercise of that glorious propensity of his nature to diffuse and communicate himself, and so gratifying this inclination of his own heart. This delight which God has in his creature's happiness cannot properly be said to be what God receives from the creature. For it is only the effect of his own work in and communications to the creature, in making it and admitting it to a participation of his fullness, as the sun receives nothing from the jewel that receives its light and shines only by a participation of its brightness.

God delights in our holiness seeing it as an infusion of his own beauty

[81] With respect also to the creature's *holiness*; God may have a proper delight and joy in imparting this to the creature, as gratifying hereby his inclination to communicate of his own excellent fullness. God may delight, with true and great pleasure, in beholding that beauty which is an image and communication of his own beauty, an expression and manifestation of his own loveliness. And this is so far from being an instance of his happiness not being in and from himself, that it is an evidence that he is happy in himself, or delights and has pleasure in his own beauty.

[82] If he did not take pleasure in the *expression* of his own beauty, it would rather be an evidence that he does not *delight* in his own beauty, that he hath not his happiness and enjoyment in his own beauty and perfection. So that if we suppose God has real pleasure and happiness in the holy love and praise of his saints, as the image and communication of his own holiness, it is not properly any pleasure distinct from the pleasure he has in himself, but it is truly an instance of it.

God's delighting in the effulgence of his attributes is a delighting in himself

[83] And with respect to God's being glorified in those perfections wherein his glory consists, expressed in their corresponding effects—as his wisdom in wise designs and well-contrived works, his power in great effects, his justice in acts of righteousness, his goodness in communicating happiness—this does not argue that his pleasure is not in himself and his own glory, but the contrary. It is the *necessary consequence* of his delighting in the glory of his nature that he delights in the emanation and effulgence of it.

The pleasure God has in the creature is not properly pleasure from the creature

[84] Nor do these things argue any *dependence* in God on the creature for happiness. Though he has real pleasure in the creature's holiness and happiness, yet this is not properly any pleasure which he receives from the creature. For these things are what he *gives* the creature. They are wholly and entirely from him. His rejoicing therein is rather a rejoicing in his own acts and his own glory expressed in those acts, than a joy derived from the creature. God's joy is dependent on nothing besides his own act, which he exerts with an absolute and independent power.

Why God would not be so happy if his happiness were not shared by man, yet God not be dependent on the happiness of man

[85] And yet, in some sense, it can be truly said that God has the more delight and pleasure for the holiness and happiness of his creatures. Because God would be less happy if he were less good,

or if he had not that perfection of nature which consists in a propensity of nature to diffuse his own fullness. And he would be less happy if it were possible for him to be hindered in the exercise of his goodness, and his other perfections, in their proper effects. But he has complete happiness, because he has these perfections, and cannot be hindered in exercising and displaying them in their proper effects. And this surely is not because he is dependent, but because he is independent on any other that should hinder him.[48]

How man is not profitable to God

[86] From this view, it appears that nothing which has been said is in the least inconsistent with those expressions in Scripture that signify, "man cannot be profitable to God," &c. For these expressions plainly mean no more than that God is absolutely independent of us, that we have nothing of our own, no stock from whence we can give to God, and that no part of his happiness originates from man.

That a fountain is inclined to overflow is no deficiency

[87] From what has been said, it appears that the pleasure God hath in those things which have been mentioned is rather a pleasure in diffusing and *communicating* to, than in *receiving* from, the creature. Surely, it is no argument of indigence [i.e., deprivation, poverty] in God that he is inclined to communicate of his infinite fullness. It is no argument of the emptiness or deficiency of a fountain that it is inclined to overflow.

All God's overflowing has been eternally present to his mind

[88] Nothing from the creature alters God's happiness, as though it were changeable either by increase or diminution. For though these *communications* of God—these exercises, operations, and expressions of his glorious perfections, which God rejoices in—are in time; yet his *joy* in them is without beginning or

---

[48] See footnote 34. It is a crucial distinction to say "God would be less happy if he were less good," rather than to say, "God would be less happy if his creation did not exist." It is not the existence of the creation *per se* that elicits happiness in God; rather it is what creation says about the way God is, that elicits happiness in God. As Edwards said in the preceding paragraph, "God's joy is dependent on nothing besides his own act, which he exerts with an absolute and independent power."

change. They were always equally present in the divine mind.[49] He beheld them with equal clearness, certainty, and fullness, in every respect, as he does now. They were always equally present; as with him there is no variableness or succession. He ever beheld and enjoyed them perfectly in his own independent and immutable power and will.

[SECOND ANSWER TO OBJECTION ONE]

God was perfectly satisfied in himself, but was gratified in creating

[89] *Answer 2.* If any are not satisfied with the preceding answer, but still insist on the objection, let them consider whether they can devise any other scheme of God's last end in creating the world, but what will be equally obnoxious to this objection in its full force, if there be any force in it. For if God had any last end in creating the world, then there was something in some respect future, that he aimed at, and designed to bring to pass by creating the world; something that was agreeable to his inclination or will; let that be his own glory, or the happiness of his creatures, or what it will. Now, if there be something that God seeks as agreeable or grateful [i.e., pleasing] to him, then in the accomplishment of it, he is gratified. If the last end which he seeks in the creation of the world be truly a thing grateful [i.e., pleasing] to him (as certainly it is, if it be truly his end, and truly the object of his will), then it is what he takes a real delight and pleasure in. But then, according to the argument of the objection, how can he have any thing future to desire or seek, who is already perfectly, eternally, and immutably satisfied in himself? What can remain for him to take any delight in or to be further gratified by, whose eternal and unchangeable delight is in himself, as his own complete object of enjoyment. Thus the objector will be pressed with his own objection, let him embrace what notion he will of God's end in the cre-

---

[49] He probably has in mind Biblical teaching like that in 1 Peter 1:19-20, "[You were redeemed] with precious blood, as of a lamb unblemished and spotless, the blood of Christ. For *He was foreknown before the foundation of the world*, but has appeared in these last times for the sake of you" (emphasis added). If Christ was foreknown as a spotless lamb before the foundation of the world, then the whole plan of creation and redemption was foreknown before the world. God had the whole scope of creation and redemption in view from eternity.

ation. And I think he has no way left to answer but that which has been taken above.

[90] It may therefore be proper here to observe, that let what will be God's last end, *that* he must have a real and proper pleasure in. Whatever be the proper object of his will, he is gratified in [it]. And the thing is either grateful [i.e., pleasing] to him in itself, or for something else for which he wills it; and so is his further end. But whatever is God's last end, that he wills *for its own sake*; as grateful [i.e., pleasing] to him in itself, or in which he has some degree of true and proper pleasure. Otherwise we must deny any such thing as will in God with respect to any thing brought to pass in time; and so must deny his work of creation, or any work of his providence, to be truly voluntary.

[91] But we have as much reason to suppose that God's works in creating and governing the world are properly the fruits of his will, as of his understanding. And if there be any such thing at all as what we mean by *acts of will* in God, then he is not indifferent whether his will be fulfilled or not. And if he is not indifferent, then he is truly gratified and pleased in the fulfillment of his will. And if he has a real *pleasure* in attaining his end, then the attainment of it belongs to his *happiness*, that in which God's delight or pleasure in any measure consists. To suppose that God has pleasure in things that are brought to pass in time, only figuratively and metaphorically, is to suppose that he exercises will about these things and makes them his end only metaphorically.

[THIRD ANSWER TO OBJECTION ONE]

God goes not out of himself in what he seeks

[92] **Answer 3.** The doctrine that makes God's *creatures* and not *himself* to be his last end is a doctrine the furthest from having a favorable aspect on[50] God's absolute self-sufficiency and independence. It far less agrees therewith than the doctrine against which this is objected. For we must conceive of the efficient[51] as *depend-*

---

[50] ". . . favorable aspect on God's absolute self-sufficience . . ." = ". . . favorable view of God's absolute self-sufficience . . ." The meaning is that such a doctrine would undermine belief in God's self-sufficiency.

[51] "The efficient" refers to God who acts efficiently, that is, effectively.

ing on his ultimate end. He depends on this end, in his desires, aims, actions, and pursuits; so that he fails in all his desires, actions, and pursuits, if he fails of his end. Now if God himself be his last end, then in his dependence on his end, he depends on nothing but himself. If all things be of him and to him, and he the first and the last, this shows him to be all in all. He is all to himself. He goes not out of himself in what he seeks, but his desires and pursuits as they originate from, so they terminate in, himself; and he is dependent on none but himself in the beginning or end of any of his exercises or operations. But if not himself, but the creature, were his last end, then as he depends on his last end, he would be in some sort dependent on the creature.

[OBJECTION TWO]

Does God do everything from a selfish spirit?

[93] **OBJECTION 2.** Some may object that to suppose God makes himself his highest and last end is dishonorable to him, as it in effect supposes that God does everything from a selfish spirit. Selfishness is looked upon as mean and sordid in the creature; unbecoming and even hateful in such a worm of the dust as man. We should look upon a man as of a base and contemptible character who was governed, in everything he did, by selfish principles, and made his private interest his governing aim in all his conduct in life. How far then should we be from attributing any such thing to the Supreme Being, the blessed and only Potentate! Does it not become us to ascribe to him the most noble and generous dispositions and qualities, the most remote from every thing private, narrow, and sordid?

[FIRST ANSWER TO OBJECTION TWO]

If God is supremely valuable, he should value himself supremely

[94] *Answer 1.* Such an objection must arise from a very ignorant or inconsiderate notion of the vice of selfishness and the virtue of generosity. If by selfishness be meant a disposition in any being to regard himself, this is no otherwise vicious or unbecoming than as

one is less than a multitude; so the public weal is of greater value than his particular interest. Among created beings, one single person is inconsiderable in comparison of the generality, and so his interest is of little importance compared with the interest of the whole system. Therefore in them, a disposition to prefer self, as if it were more than all, is exceeding vicious. But it is vicious on no other account than as it is a disposition that does not agree with the nature of things, and [with] that which is indeed the greatest good. And a disposition in anyone to forego his own interest for the sake of others, is no further excellent, no further worthy [of] the name of generosity, than it is treating things according to their true value; prosecuting[52] something most worthy to be prosecuted; an expression of a disposition to prefer something to self-interest that is indeed preferable in itself.

[95] But if God be indeed so great and so excellent that all other beings are as nothing to him, and all other excellency be as nothing and less than nothing and vanity in comparison with his, and if God be omniscient and infallible, and perfectly knows that he is infinitely the most valuable being, then it is fit that his heart should be agreeable to this—which is indeed the true nature and proportion of things, and agreeable to this infallible and all-comprehending understanding which he has of them, and that perfectly clear light in which he views them—and that he should value himself infinitely more than his creatures.

[SECOND ANSWER TO OBJECTION TWO]

God's esteeming himself supremely is not contrary to his esteeming human happiness, since he is that happiness

[96] *Answer 2.* In created beings, a regard to self-interest may properly be set in *opposition* to the public welfare, because the private interest of one person may be inconsistent with the public good; at least it may be so in the apprehension [i.e., perception] of that person. That which this person looks upon as his interest, may interfere with or oppose the general good. Hence his private interest may be regarded and pursued in opposition to the public. But

---

[52] "Prosecuting" in the old sense of "pursuing" or "accomplishing."

this cannot be with respect to the Supreme Being, the author and head of the whole system, on whom all absolutely depend, who is the fountain of being and good to the whole. It is more absurd to suppose that his interest should be opposite to the interest of the universal system, than that the welfare of the head, heart, and vitals of the natural body, should be opposite to the welfare of the body. And it is impossible that God, who is omniscient, should apprehend his interest as being inconsistent with the good and interest of the whole.

[THIRD ANSWER TO OBJECTION TWO]

Nothing is more loving than for God to exalt himself for the enjoyment of man

[97] *Answer 3.* God seeking himself in the creation of the world, in the manner which has been supposed, is so far from being inconsistent with the good of his creatures that it is a kind of regard to himself that inclines him to seek the good of his creature. It is a regard to himself that disposes him to diffuse and communicate himself. It is such a delight in his own internal fullness and glory that disposes him to an abundant effusion and emanation of that glory. The same disposition that inclines him to delight in his glory causes him to delight in the exhibitions, expressions, and communications of it. If there were any person of such a taste and disposition of mind that the brightness and light of the sun seemed unlovely to him, he would be willing that the sun's brightness and light should be retained within itself. But they that delight in it, to whom it appears lovely and glorious, will esteem it an amiable [i.e., pleasant, admirable] and glorious thing to have it diffused and communicated through the world.

[98] Here, by the way, it may be properly considered, whether some writers are not chargeable with inconsistence in this respect. They speak against the doctrine of GOD making himself his own highest and last end, as though this were an ignoble selfishness—when indeed he only is fit to be made the highest end, by himself and all other beings, inasmuch as he is infinitely greater and more worthy than all others—yet with regard to *creatures*, who are infinitely less worthy of supreme and ultimate regard, they sup-

pose that they necessarily, at all times, seek their own happiness and make it their ultimate end in all, even their most virtuous actions; and that this principle, regulated by wisdom and prudence, as leading to that which is their true and highest happiness, is the foundation of all virtue and every thing that is morally good and excellent in them.

[OBJECTION THREE]

Is it not contemptible for God to do his works for the praise and applause of men?

[99] **OBJECTION 3.** To what has been supposed, that God makes himself his end—in seeking that his glory and excellent perfections should be known, esteemed, loved, and delighted in by his creatures—it may be objected that this seems unworthy of God. It is considered as below a truly great man to be much influenced in his conduct by a desire of popular applause. The notice and admiration of a gazing multitude would be esteemed but a low end to be aimed at by a prince or philosopher in any great and noble enterprise. How much more is it unworthy [for] the great God to perform his magnificent works, e.g. the creation of the vast universe, out of regard to the notice and admiration of worms of the dust, that the displays of his magnificence may be gazed at and applauded by those who are infinitely more beneath him, than the meanest rabble are beneath the greatest prince or philosopher.

[100] This objection is specious. It hath a show of argument, but it will appear to be nothing but a show, if we consider,

[FIRST ANSWER TO OBJECTION THREE]

[101] *Answer 1.* Whether it be not worthy of God to regard and value what is excellent and valuable in itself, and so to take pleasure in its existence.

If God's glory is infinitely worthy, delighting in it and praising it is an excellent thing

[102] It seems not liable to any doubt, that there could be no future existence worthy to be desired or sought by God, and so worthy

to be made his end, if no future existence was valuable and worthy to be brought to effect. If, when the world was not, there was
any possible future thing fit and valuable in itself, I think the
knowledge of God's glory, and the esteem and love of it, must be
so. Understanding and will are the highest kind of created existence. And if they be valuable, it must be in their exercise. But the
highest and most excellent kind of their exercise is in some actual
knowledge, and exercise of will. And certainly, the most excellent
actual knowledge and will that can be in the creature is the knowledge and the love of God. And the most true excellent knowledge
of God is the knowledge of his glory or moral excellence, and the
most excellent exercise of the will consists in esteem and love, and
a delight in his glory. If any created existence is in itself worthy to
be, or any thing that ever was future is worthy of existence, such
a communication of divine fullness, such an emanation and expression of the divine glory, is worthy of existence. But if nothing that
ever was future was worthy to exist, then no future thing was worthy to be aimed at by God in creating the world. And if nothing
was worthy to be aimed at in creation, then nothing was worthy
to be God's end in creation.

If praising God is excellent, God would be misguided not to delight in it

[103] If God's own excellency and glory is worthy to be highly valued and delighted in by him, then the value and esteem hereof by
others is worthy to be regarded by him; for this is a necessary consequence. To make this plain let it be considered, how it is with
regard to the excellent qualities of another. If we highly value the
virtues and excellencies of a *friend*, in proportion, we shall approve
of others' esteem of them, and shall disapprove the contempt of
them. If these virtues are truly valuable, they are worthy that we
should thus approve others' esteem, and disapprove their contempt
of them. And the case is the same with respect to any being's *own*
qualities or attributes. If he highly esteems them and greatly
delights in them, he will naturally and necessarily love to see
esteem of them in others and dislike their disesteem. And if the
attributes are worthy to be highly esteemed by the being who hath
them, so is the esteem of them in others worthy to be proportion-

ably approved and regarded. I desire it may be considered whether it be unfit that God should be displeased with contempt of himself? If not, but on the contrary, it be fit and suitable that he should be displeased with this, there is the same reason that he should be pleased with the proper love, esteem, and honor of himself.

[104] The matter may be also cleared by considering what it would become us to approve of and value with respect to any public society we belong to, e. g. our nation or country. It becomes us to love our country, and therefore it becomes us to value the just honor of our country. But the same that it becomes us to value and desire for a friend, and the same that it becomes us to desire and seek for the community, the same does it become God to value and seek for himself; that is, on supposition, that it becomes God to love himself as it does men to love a friend or the public, which I think has been before proved.

God prizes holiness in the creature, and holiness is essentially prizing God

[105] Here are two things that ought particularly to be adverted to. (1) That in God, the love of himself and the love of the public are not to be distinguished, as in man: because God's being, as it were, comprehends all. His existence, being infinite, must be equivalent to universal existence. And for the same reason, [the fact] that public affection in the creature is fit and beautiful, [therefore] God's regard to himself must be so likewise. (2) In God, the love of what is fit and decent, cannot be a distinct thing from the love of himself, because the love of God is that wherein all holiness primarily and chiefly consists, and God's own holiness must primarily consist in the love of himself. And if God's holiness consists in love to himself, then it will imply an approbation of the esteem and love of him in others. For a being that loves himself, necessarily loves love to himself. If holiness in God consist chiefly in love to himself, holiness in the creature must chiefly consist in love to him. And if God loves holiness in himself, he must love it in the creature.

[106] Virtue, by such of the late philosophers as seem to be in chief repute, is placed in public affection, or general benevolence. And if the essence of virtue lies primarily in this, then the love of

virtue itself is virtuous no otherwise, than as it is implied in, or arises from, this public affection or extensive benevolence of mind. Because if a man truly loves the public, he necessarily loves love to the public.

Where God makes virtue his end, he makes himself his end, since virtue is goodwill toward Being, namely God

[107] Now therefore, for the same reason, if universal benevolence in the highest sense be the same thing with benevolence to the Divine Being, who is in effect universal Being, it will follow that love to virtue itself is no otherwise virtuous, than as it is implied in, or arises from, love to the Divine Being.[53] Consequently, God's own love to virtue is implied in love to himself, and is virtuous no otherwise than as it arises from love to himself. So that God's virtuous disposition, appearing in love to holiness in the creature, is to be resolved into the same thing with love to himself. And consequently, whereinsoever he makes *virtue* his end, he makes *himself* his end. In fine, God being as it were an all-comprehending Being, all his moral perfections—his holiness, justice, grace, and benevolence—are some way or other to be resolved into a supreme and infinite regard to himself; if so, it will be easy to suppose that it becomes him to make himself his supreme and last end in his works.

[108] I would here observe, by the way, that if any insist that it becomes God to love and take delight in the virtue of his creature for its *own* sake, in such a manner as not to love it from regard to *himself*; this will contradict a former objection against God taking pleasure in communications of himself; *viz.* that inasmuch as God is perfectly independent and self-sufficient, therefore all his happiness and pleasure consists in the enjoyment of himself. So that if the same persons make both objections, they must be inconsistent with themselves.

---

[53] The idea that virtue is "benevolence to being in general" is the thesis of Edwards's treatise, *The Nature of True Virtue*, which was first published bound together with this treatise on *The End for Which God Created the World*, under the title *Two Dissertations*. Edwards intended them to be read together, as is shown in several places by his cross referencing. Today *True Virtue* may be read in Jonathan Edwards, *Ethical Writings*, ed. by Paul Ramsey, in: *The Works of Jonathan Edwards*, vol. 8 (New Haven: Yale University Press, 1989), pp. 537-628; or in: Jonathan Edwards, *The Works of Jonathan Edwards*, vol. 1 (Edinburgh: Banner of Truth Trust, 1974), pp. 122-142. Or Jonathan Edwards, *The Nature of True Virtue*, ed. by William K. Frankena (Ann Arbor, MI, The University of Michigan Press, 1960).

[SECOND ANSWER TO OBJECTION THREE]

That the praise of God comes from lowly creatures only highlights the glory of grace

[109] *Answer 2.* I would observe, that it is not unworthy of God to take pleasure in that which is in itself fit and amiable [i.e., pleasant, admirable], even in those that are infinitely below him. If there be infinite grace and condescension in it, yet these are not unworthy of God, but infinitely to his honor and glory.

[110] They who insist that God's own glory was not an ultimate end of his creation of the world, but the happiness of his creatures, do it under a color of exalting God's benevolence to his creatures. But if his love to them be so great, and he so highly values them as to look upon them [as] worthy to be his *end* in all his great works, as they suppose, they are not consistent with themselves in supposing that God has so little value for their love and esteem. For as the nature of love, especially great love, causes him that loves to value the esteem of the person beloved; so, that God should take pleasure in the creature's just love and esteem will follow from God's love both to himself and to his creatures. If he esteem and love himself, he must approve of esteem and love to himself, and disapprove the contrary. And if he loves and values the creature, he must value and take delight in their *mutual* love and esteem.

[THIRD ANSWER TO OBJECTION THREE]

[111] *Answer 3.* As to what is alleged, that it is unworthy of great men to be governed in their conduct and achievements by a regard to the applause of the populace, I would observe, What makes their applause worthy of so little regard is their ignorance, giddiness, and injustice. The applause of the multitude very frequently is not founded on any just view of things, but on humour, mistake, folly, and unreasonable affections. Such applause deserves to be disregarded. But it is not beneath a man of the greatest dignity and wisdom, to value the wise and just esteem of others, however inferior to him. The contrary, instead of being an expression of greatness of mind, would show a haughty and mean spirit. It is such an

esteem in his creatures that God regards, for such an esteem only is fit and amiable [i.e., pleasant, admirable] in itself.

Creatures are less obliged to be thankful to God for what he does for his own sake

[112] **OBJECTION 4.** To suppose that God makes himself his ultimate end in the creation of the world derogates from the freeness of his goodness in his beneficence to his creatures, and from their obligations to gratitude for the good communicated. For if God, in communicating his fullness, makes himself his end, and not the creatures, then what good he does, he does for himself, and not for them; for his sake, and not theirs.

God's glory and the creature's good are not at odds

[113] *Answer.* God and the creature, in the emanation of the divine fullness, are not properly set in opposition, or made the opposite parts of a disjunction. Nor ought God's glory and the creature's good to be viewed as if they were properly and entirely distinct in the objection. This supposes that God having respect to his glory, and [to] the communication of good to his creatures, are things altogether different; that God communicating his fullness for *himself*, and his doing it for *them*, are things standing in a proper disjunction and opposition. Whereas, if we were capable of more perfect views of God and divine things, which are so much above us, it probably would appear very clear, that the matter is quite otherwise, and that these things, instead of appearing entirely distinct, are *implied* one in the other.

God, in seeking the diffusion of his glory, seeks the creature's glory and happiness

[114] God in seeking his glory seeks the good of his creatures, because the emanation of his glory (which he seeks and delights in, as he delights in himself and his own eternal glory) implies the communicated excellency and happiness of his creatures. And in

communicating his fullness for them, he does it for himself, because their good, which he seeks, is so much in union and communion with himself. God is their good. Their excellency and happiness is nothing but the emanation and expression of God's glory. God, in seeking their glory and happiness, seeks himself, and in seeking himself, *i.e.* himself diffused and expressed (which he delights in, as he delights in his own beauty and fullness), he seeks their glory and happiness.

The creature moves forever nearer to union with God, so that God's respect to the creature is an ever more perfect respect to himself

[115] This will the better appear if we consider the degree and manner in which he aimed at the creature's excellency and happiness in creating the world, *viz.* during the whole of its designed eternal duration, in greater and greater nearness and strictness of union with himself, in his own glory and happiness, in constant progression, through all eternity. As the creature's good was viewed when God made the world, with respect to its whole duration, and eternally progressive union to, and communion with him; so the creature must be viewed as in infinitely strict union with himself.[54] In this view it appears that God's respect to the *creature*, in the whole, *unites* with his respect to *himself*. Both regards are like two lines which at the beginning appear separate, but finally meet in one, both being directed to the same center. And as to the *good* of the creature itself, in its whole duration and infinite progression, it must be viewed as *infinite*, and as coming nearer and nearer to the same thing in its infinite fullness. The nearer anything comes to infinite, the nearer it comes to an identity with God.[55] And if any *good*, as viewed by God, is beheld as infinite, it cannot be viewed as a distinct thing from God's own infinite glory.

---

[54] See footnote 45. Also notice that the concept of a "strict union" is applied, in the next paragraph, to the union between Christ and the church.

[55] "Identity" is a strong word. But it can be used in different senses. There are good reasons to believe that Edwards did not intend for us to take it in the sense that God and man would merge *essentially*, or *in being*, without distinction, even though there are Biblical texts that Edwards is eager to come to terms with, such as, "that God may be all in all" (1 Cor. 15:58). See footnotes 38, 41, 45, 104, 113, 115.

St. Paul teaches that Christ's love to the Church is love to himself

[116] The apostle's discourse of the great love of Christ to men, (Eph. 5:25, &c.) leads us thus to think of the love of Christ to his church, as coinciding with his love to himself, by virtue of the strict union of the church with him. "Husbands, love your wives, as Christ also loved the church, and gave himself for it—that he might present it to himself a glorious church. So ought men to love their wives, as their own bodies. He that loveth his wife loveth himself—even as the Lord [loves] the church; for we are members of his body, of his flesh, and of his bones." Now I apprehend that there is nothing in God's disposition to communicate of his own fullness to the creatures that at all derogates from the excellence of it, or the creature's obligation.

God is no less good because the good he imparts is himself

[117] God's disposition to cause his own infinite fullness to flow forth is not the less properly called his *goodness* because the good he communicates is what he delights in, as he delights in his own glory. The creature has no less benefit by it; neither has such a disposition less of a direct tendency to the creature's benefit. Nor is this disposition in God to diffuse his own good the less excellent, because it is implied in his love to himself. For his love to himself does not imply it any otherwise, but as it implies a love to whatever is worthy and excellent. The emanation of God's glory is in itself worthy and excellent, and so God delights in it; and this delight is implied in his love to his own fullness, because that is the fountain, the sum and comprehension of every thing that is excellent.

God's acting from delight in his glory does not diminish the freedom of his action

[118] Nor does God's inclination to communicate good from regard to himself, or delight in his own glory, at all diminish the freeness of his beneficence. This will appear, if we consider particularly in what ways doing good to others from self-love, may be inconsistent with the freeness of beneficence. And I conceive there are only these two ways,

Free benevolence consists in acting benevolently from delight in it

[119] When any does good to another from confined self-love, which is *opposite* to a general benevolence. This kind of self-love is properly called *selfishness*. In some sense, the most benevolent, generous person in the world seeks his *own* happiness in doing good to others, because he places his happiness in their good. His mind is so enlarged as to take them, as it were, into himself. Thus when they are happy, he feels it; he partakes with them and is happy in their happiness. This is so far from being inconsistent with the freeness of beneficence that, on the contrary, free benevolence and kindness consists in it. The most free beneficence that can be in men is doing good, not from a confined selfishness, but from a disposition to general benevolence or love to being in general.

God's self-love cannot be selfishly confined because the whole of creation is an expression of himself

[120] But now, with respect to the Divine Being there is no such thing as confined selfishness in him, or a love to himself *opposite* to general benevolence. It is impossible, because he comprehends all entity and all excellence in his own essence.[56] The eternal and infinite Being is, in effect, *being in general,* and comprehends universal existence. God, in his benevolence to his creatures, cannot have his heart enlarged in such a manner as to take in beings who are originally out of himself, distinct and independent. This can-

---

[56] Before jumping to the conclusion that Edwards is a pantheist, one must ponder what he says a few lines later at the end of this chapter: "I confess there is a degree of indistinctness and obscurity in the close consideration of such subjects and a great imperfection [!] in the expressions we use concerning them, arising unavoidably from the infinite sublimity of the subject and the incomprehensibleness of those things that are divine" (¶ 124). What does "comprehend" mean in this sentence? And what about the next sentence: "The eternal and infinite Being is, in effect, *being in general* and comprehends universal existence"—do these words only allow a pantheistic interpretation? What does "in effect" signal? Does the use of the word "creatures" in the next sentence affect the way we think of all being *comprehended* in God? Moreover, we must keep many other things in mind that Edwards has said elsewhere, especially footnote 45, where we argued against the merging of creation and Creator in a final metaphysical sense. It seems to me that Edwards is trying to come to terms with at least two things here. One is the philosophical implication that "an infinite Being, who exists alone from eternity" (read further in ¶ 120) cannot confront being except what comes from his own being and is absolutely dependent on him. In this sense he comprehends all being. The other thing he is trying to come to terms with is the Biblical witness in texts like Acts 17:28, "For in him we live, and move, and have our being," Colossians 1:17, "By [in] him all things consist," 1 Corinthians 15:28, "That God may be all in all."

not be in an infinite Being, who exists alone from eternity. But he, from his goodness, as it were, enlarges himself in a more excellent and divine manner. This is by communicating and diffusing himself; and *so*, instead of *finding*, he *makes* objects of his benevolence—not by taking what he finds distinct from himself, and so partaking of their good, and being happy in them, but—by flowing forth, and expressing himself in them, and making them to partake of him, and then rejoicing in himself expressed in them, and communicated to them.

God's beneficence is free because it is not constrained by anything outside himself

[121] Another thing, in doing good to others from self-love, that derogates from the freeness of the goodness is acting from *dependence* on them for the good we need or desire. So that in our beneficence we are not self-moved, but, as it were, constrained by something without [i.e., outside] ourselves. But it has been particularly shown already that God making himself his end argues no dependence, but is consistent with absolute independence and self-sufficiency.

[122] And I would here observe that there is something in that disposition to communicate goodness that shows God to be independent and self-moved in it, in a manner that is peculiar and above the beneficence of creatures. Creatures, even the most excellent, are not independent and self-moved in their goodness, but in all its exercises they are excited by some object they find; something appearing good, or in some respect worthy of regard, presents itself, and moves their kindness. But God, being all and alone, is absolutely self-moved. The exercises of his communicative disposition are absolutely from within himself; all that is good and worthy in the object, and its very *being*, proceeding from the overflowing of his fullness.

Therefore, we are no less obliged to feel gratitude to God, though his beneficence is for his glory

[123] These things show that the supposition of God making himself his ultimate end does not at all diminish the creature's obligation to gratitude for communications of good received. For if it

lessen its obligation, it must be on one of the following accounts. Either that the creature has not so much benefit by it; or that the disposition it flows from is not proper goodness, not having so direct a tendency to the creature's benefit; or that the disposition is not so virtuous and excellent in its kind; or that the beneficence is not so free. But it has been observed that none of these things take place, with regard to that disposition, which has been supposed to have excited God to create the world.

Finally, revelation is the surest guide

[124] I confess there is a degree of indistinctness and obscurity in the close consideration of such subjects and a great imperfection in the expressions we use concerning them, arising unavoidably from the infinite sublimity of the subject and the incomprehensibleness of those things that are divine. Hence revelation is the surest guide in these matters, and what that teaches shall in the next place be considered. Nevertheless, the endeavors used to discover what the voice of reason is, so far as it can go, may serve to prepare the way by obviating cavils insisted on by many, and to satisfy us that what the word of God says of the matter is not unreasonable.[57]

---

[57] Here he states what the two main functions of rational apologetics are: 1) to remove objections ("obviating cavils") and 2) to satisfy us that what the Scriptures teach are not unreasonable. But he makes plain that the "surest guide" in these great matters is "revelation," that is, Scripture, because of "the incomprehensibleness of those things that are divine" and because of the defect of reason by itself. He ends where he began in the first paragraphs of the Introduction concerning the inadequacy of reason alone.

WHEREIN IT IS INQUIRED WHAT IS TO BE LEARNED FROM HOLY SCRIPTURES CONCERNING GOD'S LAST END IN THE CREATION OF THE WORLD

SECTION ONE

THE SCRIPTURES REPRESENT GOD AS MAKING HIMSELF HIS OWN LAST END IN THE CREATION OF THE WORLD

Texts concerning God's making himself the ultimate end of creation

[125] It is manifest that the Scriptures speak on all occasions as though God made *himself* his end in all his works, and as though the same being, who is the *first cause* of all things, were the supreme and *last end* of all things. Thus in Isaiah 44:6: "Thus saith the Lord, the king of Israel, and his Redeemer the LORD of hosts, I am the first, I also am the last, and besides me there is no God." Chapter 48:12: "I am the first and I am the last." Revelation 1:8: "I am Alpha and Omega, the beginning and the ending, saith the Lord, which is, and was, and which is to come, the Almighty." Verse 11: "I am Alpha and Omega, the

first and the last." Verse 17: "I am the first and the last." Chapter 21:6: "And he said unto me, it is done; I am Alpha and Omega, the beginning and the end." Chapter 22:13: "I am Alpha and Omega, the beginning and the end, the first and the last."

The meaning of the texts and its Biblical confirmation

[126] When God is so often spoken of as the *last* as well as the *first*, the *end* as well as the *beginning*, it is implied that as he is the first, efficient[58] cause and fountain from whence all things originate; so, he is the last, final cause for which they are made; the final term to which they all tend in their ultimate issue. This seems to be the most natural import of these expressions; and is confirmed by other parallel passages; as Romans 11:36: "For of him, and through him, and to him, are all things." Colossians 1:16: "For by him were all things created, that are in heaven, and that are in earth, visible and invisible, whether they be thrones, or dominions, or principalities, or powers; all things were created by him, and for him." Hebrews 2:10: "For it became him, by whom are all things, and for whom are all things." And in Proverbs 16:4, it is said expressly, "The LORD hath made all things for himself."

[127] And the *manner* is observable, in which God is said to be the last, *to* whom and *for* whom are all things. It is evidently spoken of as a meet [i.e., fitting] and suitable thing, a branch of his glory; a meet prerogative of the great, infinite, and eternal Being; a thing becoming the dignity of him who is infinitely above all other beings; from whom all things are, and by whom they consist; and in comparison with whom all other things are as nothing.

---

[58] With the terms "efficient cause" and "final cause" Edwards uses classical terminology that goes back to Aristotle's four causes. Material cause: that out of which something is made; efficient cause: that by which something is made; formal cause: that into which something is made; final cause: that for the sake of which something is made. See Mortimer Adler's discussion of "The Four Causes" in *Aristotle for Everybody: Difficult Thought Made Easy* (New York: Macmillan Publishing Co., Inc., 1978), pp. 39-48.

SECTION TWO

WHEREIN SOME POSITIONS ARE ADVANCED
CONCERNING A JUST METHOD OF ARGUING IN THIS AFFAIR,
FROM WHAT WE FIND IN THE HOLY SCRIPTURES

God does not create that he may have existence or attributes or perfections

[128] We have seen that the Scriptures speak of the creation of the world as being *for God* as its end. What remains therefore to be inquired into is *which way do the Scriptures represent God as making himself his end*? It is evident that God does not make his *existence* or being the end of the creation, which cannot be supposed without great absurdity. His existence cannot be conceived of but as *prior* to any of God's designs. Therefore he cannot create the world to the end that he may have existence, or may have certain attributes and perfections. Nor do the Scriptures give the least intimation of any such thing. Therefore, what divine effect or what in relation to God is that which the Scripture teacheth us to be the end he aimed at in his works of creation and in designing which he makes *himself* his end?

[129] In order to [have] a right understanding of the Scripture doctrine and drawing just inferences from what we find said in the word of God relative to this matter, and so to open the way to a true and definite answer to the above inquiry, I would lay down the following positions.

[POSITION ONE]

God's ultimate end in providence is his ultimate end in creation

[130] *Position 1.* That which appears to be God's ultimate end in his works of *providence* in general, we may justly suppose to be his last[59] end in the work of *creation*. This appears from what was observed before, under the fifth particular of the introduction, which I need not now repeat.

---

[59] Edwards uses "ultimate end" and "last end" interchangeably. See the Introduction and footnote 2.

God's ultimate end in some works is his ultimate end in all

[131] *Position 2.* When anything appears in the Scripture to be the last end of *some* of the works of God, that thing appears to be the result of God's works in *general*. And although it be not mentioned as the end of those works, but only of *some* of them; yet as nothing appears *peculiar* in the nature of the case that renders it a fit, beautiful, and valuable result of those particular works, more than of the rest, we may justly infer that thing to be the last end of those *other* works also. For we must suppose it to be on account of the value of the effect, that it is made the end of those works of which it is *expressly* spoken as the end; and this effect, by the supposition being equally and in like manner, the result of the work and of the same value, it is but reasonable to suppose that it is the end of the work, of which it is naturally the consequence, in *one* case as well as in *another*.

An ultimate end of providence mentioned frequently is the ultimate end of creation

[132] *Position 3.* The ultimate end of God in creating the world, being also the last end of all his works of *providence*, we may well presume that if there be any *particular* thing more frequently mentioned in Scripture, as God's ultimate aim in his works of providence, than any thing else, this is the ultimate end of God's works in *general*, and so the end of the work of *creation*.

The ultimate end of the moral world is the ultimate end of the whole world

[133] *Position 4.* That which appears from the word of God to be his ultimate end with respect to the *moral* world, *or* the *intelligent* part of the system, that is God's last end in the work of creation in *general*. Because it is evident from the constitution of the world itself, as well as from the word of God, that the moral part is the

end of all the rest of the creation. The inanimate, unintelligent part is made for the rational, as much as a house is prepared for the inhabitant. And it is evident also from reason and the word of God that it is for the sake of some *moral good* in them, that moral agents are made and the world made for them. But it is further evident that whatsoever is the last end of *that part* of creation, which is the end of all the rest, and for which all the rest of the world was made, must be the last end of the *whole*. If all the other parts of a watch are made for the hand of the watch, in order to move that aright, then it will follow that the last end of the *hand* is the last end of the *whole* machine.

[POSITION FIVE]

God's ultimate end in his providential use of the world signifies the ultimate end of the world

[134] *Position 5.* That which appears from the Scripture to be God's ultimate end in the *chief* works of his providence, we may well determine is God's last end in creating the *world*. For, as observed, we may justly infer the *end* of a thing from the *use* of it. We must justly infer the end of a clock, a chariot, a ship, or water-engine, from the main *use* to which it is applied. But God's *providence* is his *use* of the *world* he has made. And if there be any works of providence which are evidently God's *main works*, herein appears and consists the *main use* that God makes of the creation. From these two last positions we may infer the next, *viz.*

[POSITION SIX]

God's ultimate end in his main works of providence toward the moral world is his ultimate end for the whole world

[135] *Position 6.* Whatever appears by the Scriptures to be God's ultimate end in his main works of *Providence* towards the *moral world*, that we may justly infer to be the last end of the *creation* of the world. Because, as was just now observed, the *moral* world is the *chief* part of the creation and the end of the rest, and God's last end in creating *that part* of the world, must be his last end in the creation of the *whole*. And it appears by the last position that

the end of God's main works of Providence towards moral beings, or the *main use* to which he puts them, shows the last end for which he has *made* them, and consequently the main end for which he has made the *whole world*.

The ultimate end of the goodness of moral agents is the ultimate end of creation

[136] *Position 7.* That which divine revelation shows to be God's ultimate end with respect to *that part* of the moral world which are *good*, in their *being* and in their being *good*, this we must suppose to be the last end of God's *creating* the world. For it has been already shown that God's last end in the *moral* part of creation must be the end of the *whole*. But his end in that part of the moral world that are *good* must be the last end for which he has made the moral world in *general*. For therein consists the goodness of a thing, its fitness to answer its end; at least this must be goodness in the eyes of its author. For goodness in his eyes is its agreeableness to his mind. But an agreeableness to his mind, in what he makes for some end or use, must be an agreeableness or fitness to that end. For his end in this case is his mind. That which he chiefly aims at in that thing is chiefly his mind with respect to that thing. And therefore, they are good moral agents who are fitted for the end for which God has made moral agents. And consequently, that which is the chief end to which *good* created moral agents, in being good, are fitted, this is the *chief* end of the moral part of the creation, and consequently of the *creation in general*.

The ultimate end commanded of moral creatures is the ultimate end of creation

[137] *Position 8.* That which the word of God requires the intelligent and moral part of the world to *seek*, as their ultimate and highest end, that we have reason to suppose is the last end for which God has *made them*; and consequently, by position fourth, the last end for which he has made the *whole world*. A main difference between the intelligent and moral parts, and the rest of the world, lies in this, that

the former are capable of *knowing* their Creator and the end for which he made them, and capable of *actively* complying with his design in their creation, and promoting it, while other creatures cannot promote the design of their creation, except *passively* and *eventually*.[60] And seeing they are capable of knowing the end for which their author has made them, it is doubtless their duty to fall in with it. Their wills ought to comply with the will of the Creator in this respect, in *mainly seeking* the same as *their* last end, which *God* mainly seeks as their last end. This must be the law of nature and reason with respect to them. And we must suppose that God's revealed law and the law of nature agree, and that his will as a *lawgiver* must agree with his will as a *Creator*. Therefore we justly infer that the same thing which God's *revealed* law requires intelligent creatures to seek as their last and greatest end, that God their *Creator* had made their last end, and so [is] the end of the *creation of the world*.

[POSITION NINE]

The ultimate end of the goodness of the moral world is the ultimate end of creation

[138] *Position 9.* We may well suppose that what is in Holy Scripture stated as the main end of the *goodness* of the moral world—so that the respect and relation their goodness has to that end is what chiefly makes it valuable and desirable—is God's ultimate end in the *creation* of the moral world; and so, by the fourth position, of the *whole world*. For the end of the *goodness* of a thing is the end of the *thing*.

[POSITION TEN]

The ultimate end sought by exemplary saints is the ultimate end of creation

[139] *Position 10.* That which persons who are described in Scripture as *approved* saints, and set forth as *examples* of piety, sought as their last and highest end (in the instances of their good

---

[60] An archaic meaning for "eventual" is "contingent" or "conditional." I take "eventually" in this context to mean that animals and stones and seas and mountains and planets comply with God's design not voluntarily, but when circumstances are brought about by some designer for them to fulfill such and such a design.

and approved behavior), that, we must suppose, was what they *ought* to seek as their last end, and consequently by the preceding position, was the same with *God's* last end in the *creation of the world*.

[POSITION ELEVEN]

The ultimate end longed for in the hearts of saints in their best frames of mind is the ultimate end of creation

[140] **Position 11.** What appears by the word of God to be that end, in the desires of which the souls of the best, and in their best frames, most naturally and directly *exercise* their goodness, and in expressing their desire of this end, they do most properly and directly express their respect to God;[61] we may well suppose that end to be the *chief* and *ultimate* end of a spirit of piety and *goodness*, and God's chief end in making the *moral* world, and so the *whole world*. For doubtless, the most direct tendency of a spirit of true goodness, in the best part of the moral world, is to the *chief end of goodness*, and so the chief end of the *creation* of the moral world. And in what else can the spirit of the true respect and friendship to God be expressed by way of desire, than in desires of the *same end* which God himself chiefly and ultimately desires in *making them and all other things*.

[POSITION TWELVE]

The ultimate end sought by Christ is the ultimate end of creation

[141] **Position 12.** Since the Holy Scriptures teach us that Jesus Christ is the Head of the moral world, and especially of all the good part of it; the chief of God's servants, appointed to be the Head of his saints and angels, and set forth as the chief and most perfect pattern and example of goodness; we may well suppose,

---

[61] This sentence is structurally obscure but not unintelligible. It says: The word of God expresses the goal that the best souls have in their desires. Moreover the word also expresses the goal of the desires of those saints when they are exercising their goodness in those desires during their best frames of mind. This goal is most obviously the ultimate end of their desires when they are expressed with respect to God.

by the foregoing positions, that what *he* sought as his last end, was God's last end in the *creation of the world*.

SECTION THREE

PARTICULAR TEXTS OF SCRIPTURE, WHICH SHOW THAT GOD'S GLORY IS AN ULTIMATE END OF THE CREATION

[PART ONE OF SECTION THREE]
[God's acting for his own sake is the same as acting for his glory]

[142] What God says in his word, naturally leads us to suppose that the way in which he makes himself his end in his work or works, which he does *for his own sake*, is in making *his glory his end*.

[143] Thus Isaiah 48:11. "For my own sake, even for my own sake, will I do it. For how should my name be polluted; and I will not give my glory to another." Which is as much as to say, I will obtain my end; I will not forego my glory; another shall not take this prize from me. It is pretty evident here that God's *name* and his *glory*, which seem to intend the same thing (as shall be observed more particularly afterwards), are spoken of as his *last end* in the great work mentioned; not as an inferior, subordinate end, subservient to the interest of others. The words are emphatical. The emphasis and repetition constrain us to understand that what God does is ultimately for his *own sake*: "For *my own sake*, even for *my own sake* will I do it."

[144] So the words of the apostle in Romans 11:36 naturally lead us to suppose that the way in which all things are *to* God, is in being *for his glory*. "For of him, and through him, and *to* him are all things, to whom be glory for ever and ever. Amen." In the preceding context, the apostle observes the marvelous disposals of divine wisdom, for causing all things to be *to* him, in their final issue and result, as they are *from* him at first and governed by him. His discourse shows how God contrived this and brought it to pass, by setting up the kingdom of Christ in the world; leaving the Jews and calling the Gentiles; including what he would hereafter

do in bringing in the Jews with the fullness of the Gentiles; with the circumstances of these wonderful works, so as greatly to show his justice and his goodness, to magnify his grace, and manifest the sovereignty and freeness of it, and the absolute dependence of all on him. And then, in the four last verses, he breaks out into a most pathetic[62] exclamation, expressing his great admiration of the *depth* of divine wisdom, in the steps he takes for attaining his end, and causing all things to be *to* him. Finally, he expresses a joyful consent to God's excellent design in all to *glorify himself*, in saying, "to him be glory for ever;" as much as to say, as all things are so wonderfully *ordered for his glory*, so let him *have the glory* of all for evermore.

[PART TWO OF SECTION THREE]
[The good parts of the moral world
are made for the glory of God]

[145] The glory of God is spoken of in Holy Scripture as the last end for which those parts of the moral world that are *good* were made.

[146] Thus in Isaiah 43:6, 7: "I will say to the north, Give up, and to the south, Keep not back; bring my sons from afar, and my daughters from the ends of the earth, even every one that is called by my name; for I have created him *for my glory*, I have formed him, yea I have made him." Again, Isaiah 60:21. "Thy people also shall be all righteous. They shall inherit the land for ever, the branch of my planting, the work of my hand, *that I may be glorified*." Also chapter 61:3: "That they may be called trees of righteousness, the planting of the LORD, *that he might be glorified*."

[147] In these places we see that the *glory of God* is spoken of as the end of God's saints, the end for which he makes them, *i.e.*, either gives them being, or gives them a being as saints, or both. It is said that God has made and formed them to be his sons and daughters *for his own glory*, that they are trees of his planting, the work of his hands, as trees of righteousness, *that he might be glo-*

---

[62] "Pathetic" is used in the older sense of "having great *pathos*," that is, great, earnest, deep feeling.

rified. And if we consider the words, especially as taken with the context in each of the places, it will appear quite unnatural[63] to suppose that God's glory is here spoken of only as an end inferior and subordinate to the happiness of God's people. On the contrary, they will appear rather as promises of making God's people happy, that God therein might be glorified.[64]

[148] So is that in Isaiah 43, as we shall see plainly, if we take the whole that is said from the beginning of the chapter, verses 1-7. It is wholly a promise of a future, great and wonderful work of God's power and grace, delivering his people from all misery, and making them exceeding happy; and then the end of all, or the sum of God's design in all, is declared to be *God's own glory.* "I have redeemed thee, I have called thee by thy name, thou art mine. I will be with thee. When thou walkest through the fire, thou shalt not be burnt, neither shall the flame kindle upon thee. Thou wast precious and honorable in my sight. I will give men for thee, and people for thy life. Fear not, I am with thee. I will bring my sons from far, and my daughters from the ends of the earth; every one that is called by my name: *for I have created him for my glory.*"

[149] So Isaiah 60:21. The whole chapter is made up of nothing but promises of future, exceeding happiness to God's church; but, for brevity's sake, let us take only the two preceding verses—19, 20. "The sun shall be no more thy light by day, neither for brightness shall the moon give light unto thee: but the LORD shall be unto thee an everlasting light, and thy God thy glory. Thy sun shall no more go down, neither shall thy moon withdraw itself; for the LORD shall be thine everlasting light, and

---

[63] "Unnatural" is a correction of the Banner of Truth edition ("natural"), which was no doubt an editorial oversight in the early edition. The Yale critical edition has "unnatural" (Jonathan Edwards, *The End for Which God Created the World,* in: *Ethical Writings,* ed. by Paul Ramsey, p. 476).

[64] It is extremely important that we not construe Edwards here to mean that God or we should seek God's glory *instead of* our happiness in him. He has made it crystal clear that God's glory is magnified *in* the creature's happiness in him. For example, in answering Objection Four (¶ 113) he said, "Nor ought God's glory and the creature's good to be viewed as if they were properly and entirely distinct. . . . Their excellency and happiness is nothing but the emanation and expression of God's glory. God, in seeking their glory and happiness, seeks himself, and in seeking himself, *i.e.* himself diffused and expressed . . . he seeks their glory and happiness." Therefore, what Edwards is stressing here in Part Two of Section Three is that no one should say God's glory is a subordinate means to the end of the happiness of the creature. He is not saying that the happiness of the creature *in God* is subordinate to the *manifestation* of the glory of God. The happiness of the creature in God is one *way* that God's glory is manifest. See footnote 69.

the days of thy mourning shall be ended. Thy people also shall be all righteous; they shall inherit the land for ever, the branch of my planting, the work of my hands . . ." and then the end of all is added, "*that I might be glorified.*" All the preceding promises are plainly mentioned as so many parts, or constituents, of the great and exceeding happiness of God's people; and *God's glory* is mentioned as the sum of his design in this happiness.

[150] In like manner is the promise in chapter 61:3. "To appoint unto them that mourn in Zion, to give unto them beauty for ashes, the oil of joy for mourning, the garment of praise for the spirit of heaviness, that they might be called trees of righteousness, the planting of the Lord, *that he might be glorified.*" The work of God promised to be effected is plainly an accomplishment of the joy, gladness, and happiness of God's people, instead of their mourning and sorrow; and the *end* in which God's design in this work is obtained and summed up is *his glory.* This proves, by the seventh position, that *God's glory* is the *end of the creation.*

[151] The same thing may be argued from Jeremiah 13:11. "For as a girdle cleaveth to the loins of a man, so have I caused to cleave unto me the whole house of Israel, and the whole house of Judah, saith the Lord: that they might be unto me for a people, and for a name, and for a praise, and *for a glory*: but they would not hear." That is, God sought to make them to be his own holy people, or as the apostle expresses it, his peculiar people, zealous of good works; that so they might be a *glory* to him; as girdles were used in those days for ornament and beauty, and as badges of dignity and honor.[65]

[152] Now when God speaks of himself as seeking a peculiar and holy people for himself, to be for his glory and honor, as a man that seeks an ornament and badge of honor for his glory, it is not natural to understand it merely of a *subordinate* end, as though God had no respect to himself in it, but only the good of others. If so, the comparison would not be natural; for men are commonly wont to seek their *own glory* and honor in adorning themselves and dignifying themselves with badges of honor.

---

[65] Edwards's own footnote: See verse 9 and also Isaiah 3:24 and 22:21 and 23:10; 2 Samuel 18:11; Exodus 28:8.

[153] The same doctrine seems to be taught, Ephesians 1:5.[66] "Having predestinated us to the adoption of children by Jesus Christ, unto himself, according to the good pleasure of his will, *to the praise of the glory of his grace.*" And the same may be argued from Isaiah 44:23: "For the LORD hath redeemed Jacob, he hath *glorified himself* in Israel." And chapter 49:3: "Thou art my servant Jacob, in whom I *will be glorified.*" John 17:10: "And all mine are thine, and thine are mine, and I *am glorified* in them." 2 Thessalonians 1:10: "When he shall come to be *glorified* in his saints." Verses 11, 12: "Wherefore also we pray always for you, that our God would count you worthy of his calling, and fulfil all the good pleasure of his goodness, and the work of faith with power: that the name of our Lord Jesus may be *glorified* in you, and ye in him, according to the grace of God and our Lord Jesus Christ."

[PART THREE OF SECTION THREE]
*[The ultimate end of the goodness of moral agents
is the glory of God]*

[154] The Scripture speaks of God's glory as his ultimate end of the *goodness* of the moral part of the creation; and that end, in relation to which chiefly the value of their virtue consists.

[155] As in Philippians 1:10, 11: "That ye may approve things that are excellent, that ye may be sincere, and without offence, till the day of Christ: being filled with the fruits of righteousness, which are by Jesus Christ, *unto the glory and praise of God.*" Here the apostle shows how the fruits of righteousness in them are valuable, and how they answer their end, viz. in being "by Jesus Christ *to the praise and glory of God.*" John 15:8: "Herein is my Father *glorified,* that ye bear much fruit." Signifying that by this means it is that the great *end* of religion is to be answered. And in 1 Peter 4:11 the apostle directs the Christians to regulate all their religious performances with reference to that one end. "If any man speak, let him speak as the oracles of God: if any man minister, let him

---

[66] The phrase "to the praise of the glory of his grace" occurs also in verse 6, and is repeated similarly in verses 12 and 14.

do it as of the ability which God giveth, *that God in all things may be glorified*; to whom be praise and dominion for ever and ever. Amen."

[156] And, from time to time, embracing and practicing true religion, and repenting of sin, and turning to holiness, is expressed by *glorifying God*, as though that were the sum and end of the whole matter. Revelation 11:13: "And in the earthquake were slain of men seven thousand; and the remnant were affrighted, and *gave glory to the God of heaven*." So Revelation 14:6, 7: "And I saw another angel fly in the midst of heaven, having the everlasting gospel to preach to them that dwell on the earth; saying with a loud voice, Fear God, and *give glory to him*." As though this were the sum and *end* of that virtue and religion, which was the grand design of preaching the gospel, everywhere through the world. Revelation 16:9: "And repented not to *give him glory*." Which is as much as to say, they did not forsake their sins and turn to true religion, that God might receive that which is the great end he seeks, in the religion he requires of men. (See to the same purpose, Ps. 22:21-23; Is. 66:19; 24:15; 25:3; Jer. 13:15, 16; Dan. 5:23; Rom. 15:5, 6.)

[157] And as the *exercise* of true religion and virtue in Christians is summarily expressed by their *glorifying God*, so, when the good influence of this on others is spoken of, it is expressed in the same manner. Matthew 5:16: "Let your light so shine before men, that others seeing your good works, may *glorify your Father* which is in heaven." 1 Peter 2:12: "Having your conversation honest among the Gentiles, that whereas they speak evil against you as evil-doers, they may, by your good works which they behold, glorify God in the day of visitation."

[158] That the ultimate end of moral goodness or righteousness is answered in God's glory being attained is *supposed* in the *objection* which the apostle makes, or supposes some will make, Romans 3:7. "For if the truth of God hath more abounded through my lie unto *his glory*, why am I judged as a sinner?" *i.e.*, seeing the great end of righteousness is answered by my sin, in God being glorified, why is my sin condemned and punished? And why is not my vice equivalent to virtue?

[159] And the glory of God is spoken of as that wherein con-

sists the value and end of particular graces. As of *faith*. Romans 4:20: "He staggered not at the promise of God through unbelief: but was strong in faith, *giving glory to God*." Philippians 2:11: "That every tongue should confess that Jesus is the Lord, *to the glory of God the Father*." Of *repentance*. Joshua 7:19: "Give, I pray thee, *glory to the LORD God of Israel*, and make confession unto him." Of *charity*. 2 Corinthians 8:19: "With this grace, which is administered by us, *to the glory of the same Lord*, and declaration of your ready mind." *Thanksgiving* and *praise*. Luke 17:18: "There are not found that returned to *give glory to God*, save this stranger." Psalm 50:23: "Whoso offereth praise *glorifieth me*; and to him that ordereth his conversation aright, will I show the salvation of God." Concerning which last place may be observed that God seems to say this to such as supposed, in their religious performances, that the *end of all religion was to glorify God*. They supposed they did this in the best manner, in offering a multitude of sacrifices; but God corrects their mistake, and informs them, that this grand end of religion is not attained this way, but in offering the more spiritual sacrifices of praise and a holy conversation [style of life].

[160] In fine, the words of the apostle in 1 Corinthians 6:20 are worthy of particular notice. "Ye are not your own; for ye are bought with a price: therefore glorify God in your body and in your spirit, which are his." Here, not only is glorifying God spoken of, as what summarily comprehends the end of religion, and of Christ redeeming us; but the apostle urges, that inasmuch as we are not our own, we ought not to act as if we were our own, but as God's; and should not use the members of our bodies, or faculties of our souls, for ourselves, but for God, as making him our end. And he expresses the way in which we are to make God our end, viz. in making his *glory* our end. "Therefore *glorify God* in your body and in your spirit, which are his."

[161] Here it cannot be pretended that though Christians are indeed required to make God's glory their end; yet it is but as a *subordinate* end, as subservient to their own happiness; for then, in acting chiefly and ultimately for their own selves, they would use themselves more as their *own* than as God's; which is directly contrary to the design of the apostle's exhortation and the argument he is upon;

which is, that we should give ourselves as it were away *from ourselves to God,* and use ourselves as *his,* and not our *own,* acting for his *sake,* and not our *own sakes.*[67] Thus it is evident, by the ninth position, that the *glory of God is the last end for which he created the world.*

[PART FOUR OF SECTION THREE]
*[God makes it the duty of man
to seek God's glory as their ultimate end]*

[162] There are some things in the word of God which lead us to suppose that it *requires* of men that they should *desire* and *seek* God's glory as their highest and last end in what they do.

[163] As particularly, from 1 Corinthians 10:31: "Whether therefore ye eat or drink, or whatsoever ye do, do all *to the glory of God.*" And 1 Peter 4:11: "That God in all things *may be glorified.*" And this may be argued, that Christ requires his followers should desire and seek God's glory in the *first place* and *above all* things else,[68] from that prayer which he gave his disciples, as the pattern and rule for the direction of his followers in their prayers. Its first petition is, *Hallowed be thy name,* which in Scripture language is the same with *glorified* be thy name; as is manifest from Leviticus 10:3 ["The LORD spake, saying, I will be *sanctified* (=hallowed) in them that come nigh me, and before all the people I will be *glorified*"], Ezekiel 28:22 and many other places.

---

[67] See footnote 64. Sometimes people take texts like this to mean that we should not pursue our own happiness, since that would be treating ourselves "as our own" rather than as a blood-bought possession of God. But this is not what Edwards would say, provided the happiness we seek is in God rather than in some gift of God that would glorify the gift above the Giver. Edwards makes it clear above, in answering Objection Four, (¶¶ 113-124) that, on the one hand, there is a "confined" pursuit of happiness that seeks it in private, limited ways rather than in the good of others or the beauty of God; and, on the other hand, there is an expansive pursuit of happiness in benevolence that is the very essence of virtue: "[This is] the very nature of benevolence—which is to have pleasure or happiness in the happiness of another" (Miscellany # 1182 in Harvey Townsend, ed., *The Philosophy of Jonathan Edwards,* p. 140). See the quote from *Charity and Its Fruits* in footnote 86. Edwards would say that selfishness includes doing good to another person from confined self-love, which is *opposite* to a general benevolence. In some sense, he says, the most benevolent, generous person in the world seeks his *own* happiness in doing good to others, because he places his happiness in their good. (See above, Answer to Objection Four, ¶¶ 113-124). When we seek our own happiness in God or in benevolently directing others to the love of God, we are not contradicting the aim of 2 Corinthians 6:20.

[68] Again he does not mean that we are to seek God's glory rather than seeking God's glory—which is nonsense. Seeking means doing one thing and not another thing. One of the things we do in seeking God's glory is to rejoice in God, and delight in God, and treasure God. See footnotes 64 and 69. Joy in God *is* the seeking of God "above all else."

[164] Now our last and highest end is doubtless what should be first in our *desires*, and consequently first in our *prayers*, and therefore we may argue that since Christ directs that God's glory should be first in our prayers, that therefore this is our last end. This is further confirmed by the conclusion of the Lord's prayer, *For thine is the kingdom, the power, and the glory,* which, as it stands in connection with the rest of the prayer, implies that we desire and ask all the things mentioned in each petition, with a subordination and in subservience to the dominion and glory of God; in which all our desires ultimately terminate, as their last end. God's glory and dominion are the two first things mentioned in the prayer, and are the subject of the first half of the prayer; and they are the two last things mentioned in the same prayer in its conclusion. God's glory is the Alpha and Omega in the prayer. From these things we may argue, according to the eighth position, that *God's glory is the last end of the creation.*

[PART FIVE OF SECTION THREE]
*[Saints, at their best, desire and delight
in the glory of God above all else]*

[165] By the account given in Scripture, the glory of God appears to be that event, in the earnest desires of which and in their delight in which, the *best part* of the moral world, when in their *best frames*, most naturally express the direct tendency of the spirit of true goodness, the virtuous and pious affections of their heart.

[166] This is the way in which the holy *apostles*, from time to time, gave vent to the ardent exercises of their piety and breathed forth their regard to the Supreme Being. Romans 11:36: "To whom be glory for ever and ever. Amen." Chapter 16:27: "To God only wise, be glory, through Jesus Christ, for ever. Amen." Galatians 1:4, 5: "Who gave himself for our sins, that he might deliver us from this present evil world, according to the will of God and our Father, to whom be glory for ever and ever. Amen." 2 Timothy 4:18: "And the Lord shall deliver me from every evil work, and will preserve me to his heavenly kingdom: to whom be glory for ever and ever. Amen." Ephesians 3:21: "Unto him be glory in the church by Christ Jesus, throughout all ages, world

without end." Hebrews 13:21: "Through Jesus Christ, to whom be glory for ever and ever. Amen." Philippians 4:20: "Now unto God and our Father be glory for ever and ever. Amen." 2 Peter 3:18: "To him be glory both now and for ever. Amen." Jude 25: "To the only wise God our Saviour, be glory and majesty, dominion and power, both now and ever. Amen." Revelation 1:5, 6: "Unto him that loved us, &c. to him be glory and dominion for ever and ever. Amen."

[167] It was in this way that holy *David*, the sweet psalmist of Israel, vented the ardent tendencies and desires of his pious heart. 1 Chronicles 16:28, 29: "Give unto the LORD, ye kindreds of the people, give unto the LORD *glory* and strength: give unto the LORD the *glory* due unto his name." We have much the same expressions again, Psalm 29:1, 2 ["Give unto the LORD the glory due unto his name; worship the LORD in the beauty of holiness."] and 69:7, 8. See also Psalm 57: 5 ["Be exalted above the heavens, O God; Let Your glory be above all the earth"]; 72:18, 19; 115:1. So the whole church of God through all parts of the earth, Isaiah 42:10-12 [". . . Let them give glory unto the LORD, and declare his praise in the islands"].

[168] In like manner the *saints and angels in heaven express* the piety of their hearts, Revelation 4:9 [And . . . those beasts give glory and honor and thanks to him that sat on the throne, who liveth for ever and ever"]; 11-14 and 7:12. This is the event that the hearts of the seraphim especially exult in, as appears by Isaiah 6:2, 3. "Above it stood the seraphim—And one cried unto another, and said, Holy, holy, holy is the Lord of hosts, the whole earth is full of his *glory.*" So at the birth of Christ, Luke 2:14. "*Glory* to God in the highest," &c.

[169] It is manifest that these holy persons in earth and heaven, in thus expressing their desires of the glory of God, have respect to it, not merely as a subordinate end, but as that which is in *itself* valuable in the *highest degree.* It would be absurd to say, that in these ardent exclamations, they are only giving vent to their vehement *benevolence to their fellow-creatures,* and expressing their earnest desire that *God might be glorified,* that so his *subjects* may be made happy by *that means.* It is evident, it is not so much their love, either to themselves or their fellow-

creatures, which they express, as their exalted and supreme regard to the most high and infinitely glorious Being. When the church says, *"Not unto us, not unto us, O Jehovah, but to thy name give glory"* [Ps. 115:1], it would be absurd to say that she only desires that God may have glory, as a necessary or *convenient means* of her own advancement and felicity.[69] From these things it appears by the eleventh position that *God's glory is the end of the creation.*

[PART SIX OF SECTION THREE]
[Christ's ultimate end in his ministry was the glory of God]

[170] The Scripture leads us to suppose that *Christ* sought God's glory as his highest and last end.

[171] John 7:18: "He that speaketh of himself, seeketh his own glory; but he that seeketh *his* glory that sent him, the same is true, and no unrighteousness is in him." When Christ says he did not seek his own glory, we cannot reasonably understand him, that he had no regard to his own glory, even the glory of the human nature; for the glory of that nature was part of the reward promised him and of the joy set before him. But we must understand him, that this was not his *ultimate* aim; it was not the end that *chiefly* governed his conduct. Therefore, when in opposition to this, in the latter part of the sentence he says, "But he that seeketh his glory that sent him, the same is true," &c. It is natural from the antithesis to understand him, that this was his ultimate aim, his supreme governing end.

[172] John 12:27, 28: "Now is my soul troubled, and what shall I say? Father, save me from this hour: but for this cause came I unto this hour, Father, *glorify thy name.*" Christ was now going to Jerusalem and expected in a few days there to be crucified; and the prospect of his last sufferings, in this near

---

[69] God's glory is not a stepping-stone to something higher, such as our joy. But this is not to say that God's glorification is ever at odds with the final happiness of the saints in God. See footnotes 64 and 67. When we cry, "Not to us, not to us, O Jehovah, but to thy name give glory," we mean that we want God to get all the glory for the help he gives us to know and love and rejoice in him. This is implied in the rest of the verse: "To thy name give glory, *because of Your lovingkindness.*" We don't want the glory, we want the free and unmerited lovingkindness. In this rejoice, and in rejoicing, God alone is glorified. He gets the glory, we get the merciful joy. So it is in Psalm 5:15 and 1 Peter 4:11 and Romans 15:9, etc.

approach, was very terrible to him. Under this distress of mind, he supports himself with a prospect of what would be the consequence of his sufferings, *viz. God's glory.* Now, it is the *end* that supports the agent in any difficult work that he undertakes, and above all others, his *ultimate* and supreme end; for this is above all others valuable in his eyes; and so, sufficient to countervail the difficulty of the means. That end, which is in itself agreeable and sweet to him and which ultimately terminates his desires, is the center of rest and support; and so must be the fountain and sum of all the delight and comfort he has in his prospects, with respect to his work. Now Christ has his soul straitened and distressed with a view of that which was infinitely the most difficult part of his work, and which was just at hand. Now certainly, if his mind seeks support in the conflict from a view of his end, it must most naturally repair to the *highest* end, which is the proper fountain of all support in this case. We may well suppose that when his soul conflicts with the most extreme difficulties, it would resort to the idea of his supreme and ultimate end, the fountain of all the support and comfort he has in the work.

[173] The same thing, Christ seeking the glory of God as his ultimate end, is manifest by what he says, when he comes yet nearer to the hour of his last sufferings, in that remarkable prayer, the last he ever made with his disciples, on the evening before his crucifixion, wherein he expresses the sum of his aims and desires. His first words are, "Father, the hour is come, glorify thy Son, that thy Son also may glorify thee" [John 17:1]. As this is his first request, we may suppose it to be his supreme request and desire, and what he ultimately aimed at in all. If we consider what follows to the end, all the rest that is said in the prayer, seems to be but an amplification of this great request. On the whole, I think it is pretty manifest that Jesus Christ sought the *glory of God* as his highest and last end, and that therefore, by position twelve, this was *God's last end in the creation of the world.*

[PART SEVEN OF SECTION THREE]
[The ultimate end of the work of redemption is the glory of God]

[174] It is manifest from Scripture that God's glory is the last end of that great work of providence, the work of *redemption* by Jesus Christ.

[175] This is manifest from what is just now observed, of its being the end ultimately sought by Jesus Christ the Redeemer. And if we further consider the texts mentioned in the proof of that, and take notice of the context, it will be very evident, that it was what Christ sought as his last end, in that great work which he came into the world upon, *viz.* to procure redemption for his people. It is manifest that Christ professes in John 7:18 that he did not seek his own glory in what he did, but the glory of him that sent him ["He who speaks from himself seeks his own glory; but He who is seeking the glory of the One who sent Him, He is true, and there is no unrighteousness in Him"]. He means in the work of his ministry, the work he performed and which he came into the world to perform, which is the work of redemption. And with respect to that text, John 12:27, 28 ["'Now My soul has become troubled; and what shall I say, 'Father, save Me from this hour'? But for this purpose I came to this hour. 'Father, glorify Your name.' Then a voice came out of heaven: 'I have both glorified it, and will glorify it again.'"], it has been already observed that Christ comforted himself in the view of the extreme difficulty of his work, in the prospect of the highest, ultimate, and most excellent end of that work, which he set his heart most upon and delighted most in.

[176] And in the answer that the Father made him from heaven at that time, in the latter part of the same verse, John 12:28: "I have both glorified it, and will glorify it again," the meaning plainly is that God had glorified his name in what Christ had done, in the work he sent him upon; and would glorify it again, and to a greater degree, in what he should further do, and in the success thereof. Christ shows that he understood it thus, in what he says upon it, when the people took notice of it, wondering at the voice; some saying that it thundered, others, that an angel spake to him. Christ says, "This voice came not because of me, but for your

sakes." And then he says, (exulting in the prospect of this glorious end and success,) "Now is the judgment of this world; now is the prince of this world cast out; and I, if I be lift up from the earth, will draw all men unto me." In the success of the same work of redemption, he places his own glory, as was observed before. John 12:23, 24: "The hour is come that the Son of man should be glorified. Verily, verily, I say unto you, except a corn of wheat fall into the ground, it abideth alone; but if it die, it bringeth forth much fruit."

[177] So it is manifest that when he seeks his own and his Father's glory, in that prayer, John 17, he seeks it as the end of that great work he came into the world upon, and which he is about to finish in his death. What follows through the whole prayer plainly shows this, particularly the 4th and 5th verses. "I have glorified thee on earth: I have finished the work which thou gavest me to do. And now, O Father, glorify thou me with thine own self." Here it is pretty plain, that declaring to his Father he had glorified him on earth and finished the work given him to do, meant that he had finished the work which God gave him to do *for this end*, that he might be *glorified*. He had now finished that foundation that he came into the world to lay for his glory. He had laid a foundation for his Father's obtaining his will, and the utmost that he designed, by which it is manifest that God's glory was the utmost of his design or his *ultimate* end in this great work.

[178] And it is manifest by John 13:31, 32 that the glory of the Father and his own glory are what Christ exulted in, in the prospect of his approaching sufferings, when Judas was gone out to betray him, as the end his heart was mainly set upon and supremely delighted in. "Therefore, when he was gone out, Jesus said, Now is the Son of man glorified, and God is glorified in him. If God be glorified in him, God shall also glorify him in himself, and shall straightway glorify him."

[179] That the glory of God is the highest and last end of the work of redemption, is confirmed by the song of the angels at Christ's birth. Luke 2:14: "Glory to God in the highest, and on earth peace, and good will toward men." It must be supposed that they knew what was God's last end in sending Christ into the world; and that in their rejoicing on the occasion, their minds

would most rejoice in that which was most valuable and glorious in it, which must consist in its relation to that which was its chief and ultimate end. And we may further suppose that the thing which chiefly engaged their minds was most glorious and joyful in the affair; and would be first in that song which was to express the sentiments of their minds, and exultation of their hearts.

[180] The glory of the Father and the Son is spoken of as the end of the work of redemption, in Philippians 2:6-11 (very much in the same manner as in John 12:23, 28 and 13:31, 32 and 17:1, 4, 5): "Who being in the form of God,—made himself of no reputation, and took upon him the form of a servant, and was made in the likeness of men: and being found in fashion as a man, he humbled himself, and became obedient unto death, even the death of the cross: wherefore God also hath highly exalted him, and given him a name, &c. that at the name of Jesus every knee should bow, and every tongue confess, that Jesus is the Lord, *to the glory of God the Father.*"

[181] So God's glory, or the praise of his glory, is spoken of as the end of the work of redemption, in Ephesians 1:3, &c. "Blessed be the God and Father of our Lord Jesus Christ, who hath blessed us with all spiritual blessings in heavenly places in Christ: according as he hath chosen us in him. Having predestinated us to the adoption of children, *to the praise of the glory of his grace.*" And in the continuance of the same discourse, concerning the redemption of Christ, God's glory is once and again mentioned as the great end of all [in Ephesians 1:12, 14].

[182] Several things belonging to that great redemption are mentioned in the following verses: Such as God's great wisdom in it, [Ephesians 1] verse 8. The clearness of light granted through Christ, verse 9. God's gathering together in one, all things in heaven and earth in Christ, verse 10. God's giving the Christians that were first converted to the Christian faith from among the Jews, an interest in this great redemption, verse 11. Then the great end is added, verse 12: "That we should be *to the praise of his glory,* who first trusted in Christ." And then is mentioned the bestowing of the same great salvation on the Gentiles, in its beginning or first fruits in the world, and in completing it in another world, in the two next verses. And then the same great end is added

again. "In whom ye also trusted, after that ye heard the word of truth, the gospel of your salvation: In whom also, after that ye believed, ye were sealed with the holy spirit of promise, which is the earnest of our inheritance, until the redemption of the purchased possession, *unto the praise of his glory.*"

[183] The same thing is expressed much in the same manner, in 2 Corinthians 4:14, 15. "He which raised up the Lord Jesus, shall raise us up also by Jesus, and shall present us with you. For all things are for your sakes, that the abundance of grace might, through the thanksgiving of many, redound *to the glory of God.*"

[184] The same is spoken of as the end of the work of redemption in the Old Testament, Psalm 79:9. "Help us, O God of our salvation, *for the glory of thy name*; deliver us and purge away our sins, for thy name's sake." So in the prophecies of the redemption of Jesus Christ, Isaiah 44:23: "Sing, O ye heavens; for the LORD hath done it: shout, ye lower parts of the earth: break forth into singing, ye mountains: O forest, and every tree therein: for the LORD hath redeemed Jacob, and *glorified himself* in Israel!" Thus the works of creation are called upon to rejoice at the attaining of the same end, by the redemption of God's people, that the angels rejoiced at when Christ was born. See also Isaiah 48:10, 11 ["Behold, I have refined you, but not as silver; I have tested you in the furnace of affliction. For My own sake, for My own sake, I will act; For how can *My name* be profaned? And My glory I will not give to another."] and 49:3 ["Thou art my servant, O Israel, in whom I will be glorified"].

[185] Thus it is evident, that the glory of God is the ultimate end of the work of redemption, which is the chief work of providence towards the moral world, as is abundantly manifest from Scripture. For the whole universe is put in subjection to Jesus Christ; all heaven and earth, angels and men, are subject to him [Phil. 2:10; 3:21; Col. 1:18; Eph. 1:21; Heb. 2:8], as executing this office; and are put under him to that end, that all things may be ordered by him, in subservience to the great designs of his redemption. All power, as he says, is given to him, in heaven and in earth [Matt. 28:18], that he may give eternal life to as many as the Father has given him [John 17:2]; and he is exalted far above all principality and power, and might and dominion, and made head over

all things to the church [Eph. 1:22]. The angels are put in subjection to him that he may employ them all as ministering spirits [Heb. 1:14], for the good of them that shall be the heirs of salvation; and all things are so governed by their Redeemer that all things are theirs, whether things present or things to come [1 Cor. 3:21-22]; and all God's works of providence in the moral government of the world, which we have an account of in Scripture history or that are foretold in Scripture prophecy, are evidently subordinate to the great purposes and ends of this great work. And besides, the work of redemption is that by which good men are, as it were, brought into being, as good men, or as restored to holiness and happiness. The work of redemption is a new creation, according to Scripture, whereby men are brought into a new existence or are made new creatures [2 Cor. 5:17; Gal. 6:15].

[186] From these things it follows, according to the 5th, 6th, and 7th positions, that *the glory of God is the last end of the creation of the world.*

[PART EIGHT OF SECTION THREE]
[The glory of God is the ultimate end
of God's moral government in wrath and mercy]

[187] The Scripture leads us to suppose that God's glory is his last end in his *moral government* of the world in general. This has been already shown concerning several things that belong to God's moral government of the world, as particularly in the work of redemption, the chief of all his dispensations in his moral government of the world. And I have also observed it, with respect to the duty which God requires of the subjects of his moral government in requiring them to seek his glory as their last end. And this is actually the last end of the moral goodness required of them, the end which gives their moral goodness its chief value. And also, that it is what that person which God has set at the head of the moral world, as its chief governor, even Jesus Christ, seeks as *his* chief end. And it has been shown that it is the chief end for which that part of the moral world which are good are made, or have their existence as good.

[188] I now further observe that this is the end of the estab-

lishment of the public *worship* and *ordinances* of God among mankind. Haggai 1:8: "Go up to the mountain, and bring wood, and build the house; and I will take pleasure in it, and I will *be glorified*, saith the LORD." This is spoken of as the end of God's promises of rewards and of their fulfillment. 2 Corinthians 1:20: "For all the promises of God in him are yea, and in him Amen, *to the glory of God* by us."

[189] And this is spoken of as the end of the execution of God's threatenings in the punishment of sin, Numbers 14:20, 21, 22, 23. "And the LORD said, I have pardoned according to thy word. But, as truly as I live, all the earth shall be filled with *the glory of Jehovah*." The glory of Jehovah is evidently here spoken of as that to which he had regard, as his highest and ultimate end, which therefore he could not fail of; but must take place everywhere, and in every case, through all parts of his dominion, whatever became of men. And whatever abatements might be made as to judgments deserved, and whatever changes might be made in the course of God's proceedings from compassion to sinners, yet the attaining of God's glory was an end, which, being ultimate and supreme, must in no case whatsoever give place.

[190] This is spoken of as the end of God executing judgments on his enemies in this world. Exodus 14:17, 18: "And I will get me honor (*w'ikabedah—I will be glorified*) upon Pharaoh, and upon all his host," &c. Ezekiel 28:22: "Thus saith the LORD God, Behold, I am against thee, O Zidon, and I *will be glorified* in the midst of thee: And they shall know that I am the LORD, when I shall have executed judgments in her, and shall be *sanctified* in her." So Ezekiel 39:13: "Yea, all the people of the land shall bury them; and it shall be to them a renown, the day *that I shall be glorified*, saith the LORD God."

[191] And this is spoken of as the end, both of the executions of wrath and in the glorious exercises of mercy, in the misery and happiness of another world. Romans 9:22, 23: "What if God, willing to show his wrath, and make his power known, endured with much long-suffering, the vessels of wrath fitted to destruction; and that he might make known the *riches of his glory* on the vessels of mercy, which he had afore prepared unto glory." And this is spoken of as the end of the day of judgment, which is the time

appointed for the highest exercises of God's authority as moral Governor of the world; and is, as it were, the day of the consummation of God's moral government, with respect to all his subjects in heaven, earth, and hell. 2 Thessalonians 1:9, 10: "Who shall be punished with everlasting destruction from the presence of the Lord, and from *the glory of his power;* when he shall come *to be glorified* in his saints, and *to be admired* in all them that believe." Then his glory shall be obtained with respect both to saints and sinners. From these things it is manifest, by the fourth position, that God's glory is the ultimate end of the creation of the world.

[PART NINE OF SECTION THREE]
[The glory of God is the ultimate end of God's works in the natural world]

[192] It appears from what has been already observed, that the glory of God is spoken of in Scripture as the last end of many of his works, and it is plain that this is, in fact, the result of the works of God's common providence and of the creation of the world. Let us take God's glory in what sense soever, consistent with its being a good attained by any work of God, certainly it is the consequence of these works; besides, it is expressly so spoken of in Scripture.

[193] This is implied in the eighth Psalm, wherein are celebrated the works of creation: the heavens, the work of God's fingers; the moon and the stars, ordained by Him; and man, made a little lower than angels, &c. The first verse is "O LORD, our LORD, how excellent is thy name in all the earth! Who hast set thy *glory* above the heavens," or upon the heavens. By *name* and *glory*, very much the same thing is intended here, as in many other places, as shall be particularly shown afterwards. The Psalm concludes as it began. "O LORD, our LORD, how excellent is thy name in all the earth!" So, in the 148th Psalm, after a particular mention of most of the works of creation, enumerating them in order, the psalmist says, verse 13: "Let them praise the name of the LORD, for his name alone is excellent, *his glory* is above the earth and the heaven." And in the 104th Psalm, after a very particular, orderly, and magnificent representation of God's works of creation and common providence, it is said in the 31st verse, "The *glory of the*

LORD shall endure for ever: the LORD shall rejoice in his works."
Here God's glory is spoken of as the grand result and blessed consequence, on account of which he rejoices in these works. And this
is one thing doubtless implied in the song of the seraphim, Isaiah
6:3: "Holy, holy, holy is the LORD of hosts, the whole earth is full
of his glory."

[194] The glory of God, in being the result and consequence
of those works of providence that have been mentioned, is in fact
the consequence of the creation. The good attained in the use of a
thing, made for use, is the result of the making of that thing; as signifying the time of day, when actually attained by the use of a
watch, is the consequence of making the watch. So it is apparent,
that the glory of God is actually the result and consequence of the
creation of the world. And from what has been already observed,
it appears that it is what God seeks as good, valuable, and excellent in itself. And I presume none will pretend that there is any
thing peculiar in the nature of the case, rendering it a thing valuable in some of the instances wherein it takes place, and not in others: or that the glory of God, though indeed an effect of all God's
works, is an exceeding desirable effect of some of them; but of others, a worthless and insignificant effect. God's glory therefore must
be a desirable, valuable consequence of the work of creation.
Therefore it is manifest, by the third position, that the glory of God
is an ultimate end in the creation of the world.

SECTION FOUR

*PLACES OF SCRIPTURE THAT LEAD US TO SUPPOSE THAT
GOD CREATED THE WORLD FOR HIS NAME, TO MAKE HIS
PERFECTIONS KNOWN; AND THAT HE MADE IT FOR HIS PRAISE*

[PART ONE OF SECTION FOUR]
*[God's name is the highest regard of his holy creatures
and of himself]*

[195] Here I shall first take notice of some passages of Scripture
that speak of God's *name* as being the object of his regard, and the

regard of his virtuous and holy intelligent creatures, much in the same manner as has been observed of *God's glory*.

[196] God's *name* is, in like manner, spoken of as the *end* of his acts of goodness towards the good part of the moral world, and of his works of mercy and salvation towards his people. As 1 Samuel 12:22: "The LORD will not forsake his people, *for his great name's sake*." Psalm 23:3: "He restoreth my soul, he leadeth me in the paths of righteousness, *for his name's sake*." Psalm 31:3: "For *thy name's sake*, lead me, and guide me." Psalm 109:21: "But do thou for me, *for thy name's sake*." The forgiveness of sin in particular, is often spoken of as being for God's *name's sake*. 1 John 2:12: "I write unto you, little children, because your sins are forgiven you *for his name's sake*." Psalm 25:11: "*For thy name's sake*, O LORD, pardon mine iniquity, for it is great." Psalm 79:9: "Help us, O God of our salvation, *for the glory of thy name*; and deliver us, and purge away our sins, *for thy name's sake*." Jeremiah 14:7: "O LORD, though our iniquities testify against us, do thou it *for thy name's sake*."

[197] These things seem to show that the *salvation of Christ* is for God's *name's sake*. Leading and guiding in the way of safety and happiness, restoring the soul, the forgiveness of sin; and that help, deliverance, and salvation, that is consequent therein, is *for God's name*. And here it is observable that those two great temporal salvations of God's people, the redemption from Egypt and that from Babylon, often represented as figures and similitudes of the redemption of Christ, are frequently spoken of as being wrought *for God's name's sake*.

[198] Thus that great work of God, in delivering his people from *Egypt*, and conducting them to Canaan. 2 Samuel 7:23: "And what one nation in the earth is like thy people, even like Israel, whom God went to redeem for a people to himself, and to *make him a name*." Psalm 106:8: "Nevertheless he saved them *for his name's sake*." Isaiah 63:12: "That led them by the right hand of Moses, with his glorious arm, dividing the waters before them, *to make himself an everlasting name*." In the 20th chapter of Ezekiel, God, rehearsing the various parts of this wonderful work, adds, from time to time, "*I wrought for my name's sake*, that it should not be polluted before the heathen," as in verses 9, 14, 22.

(See also Josh. 7:8, 9 ["And what will You do for Your great name?"]; Dan. 9:15 ["And now, O LORD our God, who have brought Your people out of the land of Egypt with a mighty hand and have made a name for Yourself"]).

[199] So is the redemption from the *Babylonish* captivity, Isaiah 48:9, 10: "*For my name's sake* will I defer mine anger. For mine own sake, even for mine own sake, will I do it; for how should *my name* be polluted?" In Ezekiel 36:21, 22, 23, the reason is given for God's mercy in restoring Israel. "But I had pity for my holy name. Thus saith the LORD, I do not this for your sakes,[70] O house of Israel, but *for my holy name's sake*; and I will *sanctify my great name*, which was profaned among the heathen." And chapter 39:25: "Therefore, thus saith the LORD God, now will I bring again the captivity of Jacob, and have mercy upon the whole house of Israel, *and will be jealous for my holy name*." Daniel prays, that God would forgive his people, and show them mercy *for his own sake*, Daniel 9:19.

[200] When God from time to time speaks of showing *mercy*, and exercising goodness, and promoting his people's happiness for his *name's sake,* we cannot understand it as of a merely subordinate end. How absurd would it be to say that he promotes their happiness for his name's sake, in subordination to their good, and that his name may be exalted only for their sakes, as a means of promoting their happiness![71] Especially when such expressions as these are used, "For mine own sake, even for mine own sake will I do it; for how should my name be polluted?" and "Not for your sakes do I this, but for my holy name's sake."

[201] Again, it is represented as though God's people had their existence, at least as God's people, for God's name's sake. God's redeeming or purchasing them, that they might be his people, *for his name*, implies this. As in that passage mentioned before, 2 Samuel 7:23: "Thy people Israel, whom God went to redeem for

---

[70] When God denies that he is acting "for the sake of his people," he means that he is not acting *because of any merit in them* or because any virtue or worth in them has constrained him. He does *not* mean that they are receiving no blessing and joy from his action. On the contrary, the very act in view is their salvation from Babylon. Thus he *is* acting for the sake of their rescue, but not for the sake of their desert.

[71] See footnotes 64, 69 and 70 to see how God's pursuit of his glory and of our joy are not at odds in Edwards's thinking.

a people to himself, and *to make him a name.*" So God making them a people for his name is implied in Jeremiah 13:11: "For as the girdle cleaveth to the loins of a man, so have I caused to cleave unto me the whole house of Israel, &c. that they may be unto me for a people, *and for a name.*" Acts 15:14: "Simeon hath declared how God at the first did visit the Gentiles, to take out of them a people *for his name.*"

[202] This is also spoken of as the end of the *virtue*, religion, and holy behavior of the saints. Romans 1:5: "By whom we have received grace and apostleship, for obedience to the faith among all nations *for his name.*" Matthew 19:29: "Every one that forsaketh houses, or brethren, &c. *for my name's sake*, shall receive an hundred fold, and shall inherit everlasting life." 3 John 7: "Because, that *for his name's sake*, they went forth, taking nothing of the Gentiles." Revelation 2:3: "And hast borne, and hast patience, and *for my name's sake* hast laboured and hast not fainted."

[203] And we find that holy persons express their *desire* of this, and their *joy* in it, in the same manner as in the glory of God. 2 Samuel 7:26: "Let thy *name* be magnified for ever." Psalm 76:1: "In Judah is God known, his *name* is great in Israel." Psalm 148:13: "Let them praise the *name* of the LORD; for his *name* alone is excellent, his *glory* is above the earth and heaven." Psalm 145:13: "Thy *name*, O LORD, endureth for ever, and thy memorial throughout all generations." Isaiah 12:4: "Declare his doings among the people, make mention that his *name* is exalted."

[204] The *judgments* God executes on the wicked are spoken of as being *for the sake of his name*, in like manner as for his glory. Exodus 9:16: "And in very deed, for this cause have I raised thee up, for to show in thee my power; and that my *name* may be declared throughout all the earth." Nehemiah 9:10: "And showedst signs and wonders upon Pharaoh, and on all his servants, and on all the people of his land; for thou knewedst that they dealt proudly against them: so didst thou *get thee a name*, as at this day."

[205] And this is spoken of as a *consequence* of the works of creation, in like manner as God's *glory*. Psalm 8:1: "O LORD, *how excellent is thy name* in all the earth! Who hast set thy glory above

the heavens." And then, at the conclusion of the observations on the works of creation, the Psalm ends thus, verse 9. "O LORD our LORD, *how excellent is thy name* in all the earth!" So Psalm 148:13, after a particular mention of the various works of creation. "Let them praise the name of the LORD, for *his name alone* is excellent in all the earth, his glory is above the earth and the heaven."

[PART TWO OF SECTION FOUR]
[God's perfections, greatness and excellency
are spoken of as his ultimate end in creation]

[206] So we find the manifestation of God's *perfections*, his *greatness*, and *excellency*, is spoken of very much in the same manner as God's glory.

[207] There are several Scriptures which would lead us to suppose this to be the great thing that God sought of the *moral world*, and the end aimed at in moral agents, wherein they are to be active in answering their end. This seems implied in that argument God's people sometimes made use of, in deprecating a state of death and destruction: that, in such a state, they cannot know, or make known, the glorious excellency of God. Psalm 88:11, 12: "Shall thy lovingkindness be declared in the grave, or thy faithfulness in destruction? Shall thy wonders be known in the dark, and thy righteousness in the land of forgetfulness?" So Psalm 30:9 ["What profit is there in my blood, when I go down to the pit? Shall the dust praise thee? shall it declare thy truth?"]; Isaiah 38:18, 19 ["For the grave cannot praise thee, death can not celebrate thee: they that go down into the pit cannot hope for thy truth. The living, the living, he shall praise thee, as I do this day: the father to the children shall make known thy truth"]. The argument seems to be this: Why should we perish? And how shall thine end, for which thou hast made us, be obtained in a state of destruction, in which thy glory cannot be known or declared?[72]

---

[72] The point of these psalms is not to dispute that there is such a thing as a resurrection when God will indeed be praised. Rather, the point is that God's will is for *this earth* to be filled with the praises of his perfections, and death silences any particular person's participation in that act on the earth. There are scattered evidences in the Psalms that this very purpose of God to be praised by his people forever would not allow death to have the last word. "God will redeem my soul from the power of the grave: for he shall receive me." (Ps. 49:15; see also Ps. 16:10-11; 17:15; 73:24-26; etc.)

[208] This is the end of the *good part* of the moral world, or the end of God's people in the same manner as the glory of God. Isaiah 43:21: "This people have I formed for myself, they shall show forth my *praise*." 1 Peter 2:9: "But ye are a chosen generation, a royal priesthood, an holy nation, a peculiar people, *that ye should show forth the praises of him* who hath called you out of darkness into marvelous light."

[209] And this seems to be represented as the thing wherein the *value*, the proper *fruit* and end of their virtue appears. Isaiah 60:6, speaking of the conversion of the Gentile nations to true religion: "They shall come and *show forth the praises* of the LORD." Isaiah 66:19: "I will send unto the nations and to the isles afar off, that have not *heard my fame*, neither have seen my glory; and they shall *declare* my *glory* among the Gentiles." To which we may add, the *proper tendency* and rest of true virtue, and holy dispositions. 1 Chronicles 17:8: "Make known his deeds among the people." Verses 23, 24: "Show forth from day to day thy salvation. Declare his glory among the heathen."[73]

[210] This seems to be spoken of as a great end of the acts of God's *moral government*; particularly the great *judgments* he executes for sin. Exodus 9:16: "And in very deed, for this cause have I raised thee up, to show in thee my power; and that my name might be declared throughout all the earth." Daniel 4:17: "This matter is by the decree of the watchers, &c. To the intent, that the living may know that the Most High ruleth in the kingdom of men, and giveth it to whomsoever he will; and setteth up over it the basest of men." But places to this purpose are too numerous to be particularly recited. See them in the margin.[74]

[211] This is also a great end of God's works of *favor* and *mercy* to his people. 2 Kings 19:19: "Now, therefore, O Lord our God, I beseech thee, save thou us out of his hand, that all the kingdoms of the earth *may know that thou art the LORD God*, even

---

[73] Edwards's own footnote: See also Psalm 9:1, 11, 14 and 19:1 and 26:7 and 71:18 and 75:9 and 76:1 and 79:13 and 96:2,3 and 101:1 and 107:22 and 145:6, 11, 12; Isaiah 42:12 and 64:1, 2; Jeremiah 51:10.

[74] Edwards's own footnote: Exodus 14:17, 18; 1 Samuel 17:46; Psalm 83:18; Isaiah 45:3; Ezekiel 6:7, 10, 13, 14 and 7:4, 9, 27 and 11:10, 11, 12 and 12:15, 16, 20 and 13:9, 14, 21, 23 and 14:8 and 15:7 and 21:5 and 22:16 and 25:7, 11, 17 and 26:6 and 28:22, 23, 24 and 29:9, 16 and 30:8, 19, 25, 26 and 32:15 and 33:29 and 35:4, 12, 15 and 38:23 and 39:6, 7, 21, 22.

thou only." 1 Kings 8:59, 60: "That he maintain the cause of his servant, and the cause of his people Israel, at all times, as the matter shall require, that all the people of the earth may know that the Lord is God, and that there is none else." See other passages to the same purpose referred to in the margin.[75]

[212] This is spoken of as the end of the eternal *damnation* of the wicked, and also the eternal *happiness* of the righteous. Romans 9:22, 23: "What if God, willing to show his wrath, and make his power known, endured with much long-suffering the vessels of wrath fitted to destruction: and that he might make known the riches of his glory on the vessels of mercy, which he hath afore prepared unto glory?"

[213] This is spoken of, from time to time, as a great end of the *miracles* which God wrought. (See Ex. 7:17 and 8:10 and 10:2; Deut. 29:5,6; Ezek. 24:17). And of the *ordinances* he has established, Exodus 29:44, 45, 46. "And I will sanctify also both Aaron and his sons, to minister to me in the priests' office. And I will dwell among the children of Israel, and will be their God. And they shall know that I am the LORD their God," &c. Chapter 31:13: "Verily, my sabbaths shall ye keep; for it is a sign between me and you, throughout your generations; that ye may know that I am the LORD that doth sanctify you." We have again almost the same words, Ezekiel 20:12 and verse 20.

[214] This was a great end of the redemption out of *Egypt.* Psalm 106:8: "Nevertheless he saved them for his name's sake, that *he might make his mighty power to be known.*" (See also Ex. 7:5 and Deut. 4:34, 35). And also of the redemption from the Babylonish captivity, Ezekiel 20:34-38. "And I will bring you out from the people, and will gather you out of the countries whither ye are scattered. And I will bring you into the wilderness of the people; and there I will plead with you, as I pleaded with your fathers in the wilderness of the land of Egypt. And I will bring you into the bond of the covenant. And I will purge out the rebels. *And ye shall know that I am the* Lord." Verse 42: "*And ye shall know that I am the Lord,* when I shall bring you into the land of Israel."

---

[75] Edwards's own footnote: Exodus 6:7 and 8:22 and 16:12; 1 Kings 8:43 and 20:28; Psalm 102:21; Ezekiel 23:49 and 24:21 and 25:5 and 35:9 and 39:21, 22.

Verse 44: "*And ye shall know that I am the Lord,* when I have wrought with you *for my name's sake.*" (See also chapter 28:25, 26 and 36:11 and 37: 6, 13.)

[215] This is also declared to be a great end of the work of *redemption by Jesus Christ*: both of its *purchase,* and its application. Romans 3:25, 26: "Whom God hath set forth to be a propitiation, through faith in his blood, *to declare his righteousness. To declare, I say, at this time, his righteousness:* that he might be just, and the justifier of him that believeth in Jesus." Ephesians 2:4-7: "But God, who is rich in mercy, &c. *That he might show the exceeding riches of his grace,* in his kindness towards us through Jesus Christ." Chapter 3:8, 9, 10: "To preach among the Gentiles the unsearchable riches of Christ, and to make all men see, what is the fellowship of that mystery which, from the beginning of the world, hath been hid in God, who created all things by Jesus Christ: *To the intent that now unto the principalities and powers* in heavenly places, might *be known by the church the manifold wisdom of God.*" Psalm 22:21, 22: "Save me from the lion's mouth. I *will declare thy name unto my brethren;* in the midst of the congregation will I praise thee." (Compared with Heb. 2:12 ["I will declare thy name unto my brethren, in the midst of the church will I sing praise unto thee"] and John 17:26 ["I have declared unto them thy name, and will declare it: that the love wherewith thou hast loved me may be in them, and I in them"]) Isaiah 64:4: "O that thou wouldest rend the heavens *to make thy name known to thine adversaries.*"

[216] And it is pronounced to be the end of the great, *actual salvation,* which should follow Christ's purchase of salvation, both among Jews and Gentiles. Isaiah 49:22, 23: "I will lift up my hand to the Gentiles, and they shall bring thy sons in their arms and kings shall be thy nursing-fathers *and thou shalt know that I am the Lord.*"[76]

[217] This appears to be the end of God's *common providence,* Job 37:6, 7. "For he saith to the snow, Be thou on the earth. Likewise to the small rain, and to the great rain of his strength. He

---

[76] Edwards's own footnote: See also Ezekiel 16:62 and 29:21 and 34:27 and 36:38 and 39:28, 29; Joel 3:17.

sealeth up the hand of every man, that all men may know his work." And of the *day of judgment*, that grand consummation of God's moral government of the world, and the day for bringing all things to their designed ultimate issue. It is called, "The day of the revelation of the righteous judgment of God," Romans 2:5.

[218] And the *declaration*, or openly manifesting of God's excellency, is spoken of as the actual, happy consequence and effect of the work of creation. Psalm 19:1, &c. "The heavens declare the glory of God, and the firmament showeth his handy-work. Day unto day uttereth speech, night unto night showeth knowledge. In them hath he placed a tabernacle for the sun, which is as a bridegroom coming out of his chamber, and rejoiceth as a strong man to run his race," &c.

[PART THREE OF SECTION FOUR]
[God's praise is the ultimate end of creation]

[219] In like manner, there are many Scriptures that speak of God's PRAISE, in many of the aforementioned respects, just in the same manner as of his *name* and *glory*.

[220] This is spoken of as the end of the very *being* of God's people, in the same manner as before, Jeremiah 13:11. "For as the girdle cleaveth to the loins of a man, so have I caused to cleave unto me the whole house of Israel, and the whole house of Judah, saith the LORD: that they might be unto me for a name, *and for a praise*, and a glory."

[221] It is spoken of as the end of the *moral world*. Matthew 21:16: "Out of the mouth of babes and sucklings *hast thou perfected praise*." That is, so hast thou in thy sovereignty and wisdom ordered it, that thou shouldest obtain the *great end* for which intelligent creatures are made, more especially from some of them that are in themselves weak, inferior, and more insufficient. (Compare Ps. 8:1, 2.)

[222] And the same thing that was observed before concerning the making known God's excellency, may also be observed concerning *God's praise*. That it is made use of as an argument in deprecating a state of destruction; that in such a state, this end cannot be answered in such a manner as seems to imply its being an ultimate end, for which God had made man, Psalm 88:10. "Shall the

dead arise and *praise thee*? Shall thy loving-kindness be declared in the grave? Shall thy wonders be known in the dark?" Psalm 30:9: "What profit is there in my blood? When I go down to the pit, *shall the dust praise thee*? Shall it declare thy truth? Psalm 115:17, 18: "The dead *praise not the LORD,* neither any that go down into silence: but we will *bless the LORD,* from this time forth and for evermore. *Praise ye the LORD.*" [77] Isaiah 38:18, 19: "For the grave *cannot praise thee,* death cannot celebrate thee; they that go down into the pit cannot hope for thy truth. The living, the living, *he shall praise thee.*" And God's praise is spoken of as the end of the *virtue* of God's people, in like manner as his glory. Philippians 1:11: "Being filled with the fruits of righteousness, which are by Jesus Christ *to the praise and glory of God.*"

[223] God's praise is the end of the *work of redemption.* In Ephesians 1, where that work in its various parts is particularly insisted on and set forth in its exceeding glory, this is mentioned from time to time as the great end of all, that it should be *"to the praise of his glory,"* as in verse 6, 12, 14. By which we may doubtless understand much the same thing with what in Philippians 1:11 is expressed, *"his praise and glory."* Agreeably to this, Jacob's fourth son, from whom the great Redeemer was to proceed by the special direction of God's providence, was called PRAISE.[78] This happy consequence, and glorious end of that great redemption, Messiah, one of his posterity, was to work out.

[224] In the Old Testament this praise is spoken of as the end of the forgiveness of God's people and their salvation, in the same manner as God's name and glory, Isaiah 48:9, 10, 11. "For my name's sake will I defer mine anger, and for my *praise* will I refrain for thee, that I cut thee not off. Behold I have refined thee for mine own sake, even for mine own sake will I do it; for how should my name be polluted? and my glory will I not give to another." Jeremiah 33:8, 9: "And I will cleanse them from all their iniquity—and I will pardon all their iniquities. And it shall be to me a name of joy, a *praise* and an honor."

---

[77] See footnote 72 for an explanation of how the Psalms see death and resurrection and praise.

[78] "Judah" means "praised," as it is taken from the Hebrew word *yadah.* See Genesis 29:35—"And she conceived again, and bare a son: and she said, Now will I praise the LORD: therefore she called his name Judah."

[225] And that the *holy* part of the moral world express desires of this, and delight in it, as the end which holy principles in them tend to reach after and rest in, in their highest exercises—just in the same manner as the glory of God, is abundantly manifest. It would be endless to enumerate particular places wherein this appears; wherein the saints declare this, by expressing their earnest desires of God's praise; calling on all nations and all beings in heaven and earth to praise him; in a rapturous manner calling on one another, crying, "Hallelujah; praise ye the Lord, praise him for ever." Expressing their resolutions to praise him as long as they live through all generations, and for ever; declaring how good, how pleasant and comely the *praise* of God is, &c. And it is manifest that God's *praise* is the desirable and glorious consequence and effect of all the works of creation by such places as these. Psalm 145:5-10 and 148 throughout, and 103:19-22.

SECTION FIVE

*PLACES OF SCRIPTURE FROM WHENCE IT MAY BE ARGUED
THAT COMMUNICATION OF GOOD TO THE CREATURE
WAS ONE THING WHICH GOD HAD IN VIEW
AS AN ULTIMATE END OF THE CREATION OF THE WORLD*

[PART ONE OF SECTION FIVE]
*[Doing good to his creatures is pleasing to God in itself,
while doing harm is pleasing only in relation to something else]*

[226] According to the Scripture, *communicating good* to the creatures is what is *in itself* pleasing to God. And this is not merely subordinately agreeable, and esteemed valuable on account of its *relation* to a further end, as it is in executing justice in punishing the sins of men;[79] but what God is inclined to on its own account,

---

[79] Thus there is, in Edwards's view, an asymmetry between damnation and salvation. They are both the works of God, and indeed, in some sense God approves and even delights in both salvation (Jer. 32:40-41; Zeph. 3:17; Eph. 2:7) and damnation (Deut. 28:63; Ps. 135:6-11). Nevertheless God does *not* delight in them both *in the same way*. He says that executing judgment is agreeable to God "on account of its relation to a further end," but communicating good to a creature is agreeable to God "in itself." For my Biblical reflections on how the death of the wicked can be agreeable in any sense to God, when he says in Ezekiel 18:32 that he does not have pleasure in him that dies, see John Piper, *The Pleasures of God: Meditations on God's Delight in Being God* (Sisters, OR: Multnomah Press, 1991), pp. 61-69.

and what he delights in simply and ultimately. For though God is sometimes in Scripture spoken of as taking pleasure in punishing men's sins—Deuteronomy 28:63: "The Lord will rejoice over you, to destroy you;" Ezekiel 5:13: "Then shall mine anger be accomplished, and I will cause my fury to rest upon them, and I will be comforted"—yet God is often spoken of as exercising goodness and showing mercy with delight, in a manner quite different and opposite to that of his executing wrath. For the latter is spoken of as what God proceeds to with backwardness and reluctance; the misery of the creature being not agreeable to him *on its own account.*

[227] [But now, on the contrary, he speaks of mercy not in this reluctant way but as the thing he delights to do in itself.] Nehemiah 9:17: "Thou art a God ready to pardon, gracious and merciful, slow to anger, and of great kindness." Psalm 103:8: "The LORD is merciful and gracious, slow to anger, and plenteous in mercy." Psalm 145:8: "The LORD is gracious and full of compassion, slow to anger, and of great mercy." We have again almost the same words, Jonah 4:2; Micah 7:18: "Who is a God like unto thee, that pardoneth iniquity, &c. He retaineth not his anger for ever, because he delighteth in mercy." Ezekiel 18:32: "I have no pleasure in the death of him that dieth, saith the LORD God; wherefore turn yourselves, and live ye." Lamentation 3:33: "He doth not afflict willingly, nor grieve the children of men." Ezekiel 33:11: "As I live, saith the LORD God, I have no pleasure in the death of the wicked, but that the wicked turn from his way and live: turn ye, turn ye from your evil ways; for why will ye die, O house of Israel!" 2 Peter 3:9: "Not willing that any should perish, but that all should come to repentance."[80]

---

[80] In Miscellany #461, Edwards uses these same texts to argue that "if God delights in the creatures' participation of his happiness for its own sake, then it is evident that the communication of good is not merely a subordinate end, but must be allowed the place of an ultimate end. . . . But 'tis evident that God delights in goodness for its own sake, by such places as [Lam. 3:33; Ezek. 18:23, 32; 33:11; Mic. 7:18]. . . . Such passages of Scripture show that God delighteth in the creatures' happiness in a sense that he doth not in their misery. 'Tis true that God delights in justice for its own sake, as well as in goodness; but it will by no means follow from thence, that he delights in the creatures' misery for its own sake as well as [in their] happiness" (Jonathan Edwards, *The Miscellanies*, ed. by Thomas Schafer, p. 502). Note that the good that God dispenses to his creatures as an end in itself is a "participation" in his own happiness. In other words, the good that creatures receive is the goodness of God in exhibition. Thus, making the good of the creature an ultimate end of creation is not contrary to saying that the glory of God is the ultimate end of creation, since doing good to creatures *in this way* is part of the glorification of God.

[PART TWO OF SECTION FIVE]
*[God delights in the saving work of Christ
as an ultimate end of creation]*

[228] The work of *redemption* wrought out by Jesus Christ is spoken of in such a manner as, being from the grace and love of God to men, does not well consist with his seeking a communication of good to them, *only subordinately*. Such expressions as that in John 3:16 carry another idea. "God so loved the world, that he gave his only-begotten Son, that whosoever believeth in him, should not perish, but have everlasting life." And 1 John 4:9, 10: "In this was manifested the love of God toward us, because that God sent his only-begotten Son into the world, that we might live through him. Herein is love; not that we loved God, but that he loved us, and sent his Son to be the propitiation for our sins." So Ephesians 2:4: "But God who is rich in mercy, for his great love wherewith he loved us," &c. But if indeed this was only from a regard to a *further* end, entirely diverse from our good,[81] then all the love is truly terminated in that, its ultimate object, and *therein* is his love manifested, strictly and properly speaking, and not in that he *loved* us or exercised such high regard towards us. For if our good be not at all regarded ultimately, but only subordinately, then our good or interest is, in itself considered, *nothing* in God's regard.[82]

[229] The Scripture everywhere represents it, as though the great things Christ did and suffered were in the most *direct* and proper sense from exceeding *love to us*. Thus the apostle Paul represents the matter, Galatians 2:20: "Who loved me, and gave himself for me." Ephesians 5:25: "Husbands, love your wives, even as Christ loved the church, and gave himself for it." And Christ himself, John 17:19: "For their sakes I sanctify myself." And the Scripture represents Christ as resting in the salvation and glory of his people, when obtained as in what he *ultimately* sought, as having therein reached the goal, obtained the prize he aimed at, enjoy-

---

[81] The good of the creature, however, is *not* "entirely diverse from" the glory of God. See footnotes 64 and 69. Therefore God's loving us and his loving himself and his own glory are not contrary or alternatives.

[82] In the Yale edition of Edwards's *Works* (vol. 8, *Ethical Writings*, p. 505) this sentence continues, ". . . or love: God's respect is all terminated upon, and swallowed up in something diverse, which is the end, and not in the means."

ing the travail of his soul in which he is satisfied, as the recompense of his labors and extreme agonies, Isaiah 53:10, 11. "When thou shalt make his soul an offering for sin, he shall see his seed, he shall prolong his days, and the pleasure of the LORD shall prosper in his hand. He shall see of the travail of his soul, and shall be satisfied; by his knowledge shall my righteous servant justify many, for he shall bear their iniquities." He sees the travail of his soul, in seeing his seed, the children brought forth as the result of his travail. This implies that Christ has his delight, most truly and properly, in obtaining the salvation of his church, not merely as a means, but as what he rejoices and is satisfied in, *most directly* and properly.

[230] This is proved by those Scriptures which represent him as rejoicing in his obtaining this fruit of his labour and purchase, as the bridegroom, when he obtains his bride, Isaiah 62:5. "As the bridegroom rejoices over the bride, so shall thy God rejoice over thee." And how emphatical and strong to the purpose are the expressions in Zephaniah 3:17. "The LORD thy God in the midst of thee is mighty; he will save, he will rejoice over thee with joy; he will rest in his love, he will rejoice over thee with singing." The same thing may be argued from Proverbs 8:30, 31. "Then was I by him, as one brought up with him: and I was daily his delight, rejoicing always before him: rejoicing in the habitable part of his earth, and my delights were with the sons of men." And from those places, that speak of the saints as God's portion, his jewels and peculiar treasure, these things are abundantly confirmed, John 12:23-32:

> [And Jesus answered them, saying, The hour is come, that the Son of man should be glorified. Verily, verily, I say unto you, Except a corn of wheat fall into the ground and die, it abideth alone: but if it die, it bringeth forth much fruit. He that loveth his life shall lose it; and he that hateth his life in this world shall keep it unto life eternal. If any man serve me, let him follow me; and where I am, there shall also my servant be: if any man serve me, him will my Father honour. Now is my soul troubled; and what shall I say? Father, save me from this hour: but for this cause came I unto this hour. Father, glorify thy name. Then came there a voice from heaven, saying, I have both glorified it, and

will glorify it again. The people therefore, that stood by, and heard it, said that it thundered: others said, An angel spake to him. Jesus answered and said, This voice came not because of me, but for your sakes. Now is the judgment of this world: now shall the prince of this world be cast out. And I, if I be lifted up from the earth, will draw all men unto me. (KJV)]

But the particular consideration of what may be observed to the present purpose, in that passage of Scripture, may be referred to the next section.

[PART THREE OF SECTION FIVE]

[The motive of showing goodness and mercy to his people is spoken of in the same way as doing it for his name's sake]

[231] The communications of divine goodness, particularly forgiveness of sin, and salvation, are spoken of, from time to time, as being for God's *goodness'* sake and for his *mercies'* sake, just in the same manner as they are spoken of as being for God's *name's* sake, in the places observed before. Psalm 25:7: "Remember not the sins of my youth, nor my transgressions: according to thy mercy remember thou me, *for thy goodness' sake*, O LORD." In the 11th verse, the psalmist says, "For thy name's sake, O LORD, pardon mine iniquity." Nehemiah 9:31: "Nevertheless, *for thy great mercies' sake*, thou hast not utterly consumed them, nor forsaken them; for thou art a gracious and a merciful God." Psalm 6:4: "Return, O LORD, deliver my soul: O save me *for thy mercies' sake*." Psalm 31:16: "Make thy face to shine upon thy servant: save me *for thy mercies' sake*." Psalm 44:26: "Arise for our help; redeem us *for thy mercies' sake*." And here it may be observed, after what a remarkable manner God speaks of his love to the children of Israel in the wilderness, as though his love were for love's sake, and his goodness were its own end and motive. Deuteronomy 8:7, 8: "The LORD did not set his love upon you, nor choose you, because ye were more in number than any people, for ye were the fewest of all people: *but because the LORD loved you*."

[PART FOUR OF SECTION FIVE]
*[The entire government of the universe by Christ
is for the good of God's people]*

[232] That the government of the world in all its parts is *for the
good* of such as are to be the eternal subjects of God's goodness is
implied in what the Scripture teaches us of Christ being set at God's
right hand, made king of angels and men; set at the head of the
universe, having all power given him in heaven and earth, *to that
end* that he may promote their *happiness*; being made head over
all things to the church, and having the government of the whole
creation for their good.[83] Christ mentions it, Mark 2:28, as the *reason* why the Son of man is made Lord of the Sabbath, because "the
Sabbath was made for man." And if so, we may in like manner
argue that *all things* were made for man, because the Son of man
is made *Lord of all things.*

[PART FIVE OF SECTION FIVE]
*[All the wheels of providence turn
for the sake of saving the people of God]*

[233] That God uses the whole creation, in his government of it, for
the good of his people, is most elegantly represented in Deuteronomy
33:26. "There is none like unto the God of Jeshurun,[84] who rideth
upon the heaven." The whole universe is a machine or chariot which
God hath made for his own use, as is represented in Ezekiel's vision.
God's seat is heaven, where he sits and governs, Ezekiel 1:22, 26-28.
The inferior part of the creation, this visible universe, subject to such
continual changes and revolutions, are the wheels of the chariot.
God's providence, in the constant revolutions, alterations, and successive events, is represented by the motion of the wheels of the chariot, by the Spirit of him who sits on his throne on the heavens or
above the firmament. Moses tells us for whose sake it is that God
moves the wheels of this chariot or rides in it, sitting in his heavenly

---

[83] Edwards's own footnote: Ephesians 1:20-23; John 17:2; Matthew 11:27 and 28:18, 19; John
3:35.

[84] "The upright one" (the Greek Old Testament has "the beloved one"). A poetic name for the
people of Israel found in Deut. 32:15; 33:5, 26; Is. 44:2.

seat, and to what end he is making his progress or goes his appointed journey in it, *viz. the salvation of his people.*

[PART SIX OF SECTION FIVE]

[God's judgment on the wicked
serves the final happiness of God's people]

[234] God's *judgments* on the wicked in this world and also their eternal damnation in the world to come are spoken of as being for the *happiness of God's people.* So are his judgments on them in this world. Isaiah 43:3, 4. "For I am the Lord thy God, the Holy One of Israel, thy Saviour. I gave Egypt for thy ransom, Ethiopia and Seba for thee. Since thou hast been precious in my sight, thou hast been honorable, and I have loved thee; therefore will I give men for thee, and people for thy life." So the works of God's vindictive justice and wrath are spoken of as works of mercy to his people, Psalm 136:10, 15, 17-20 ["To him that smote Egypt in their firstborn: for his mercy endureth for ever. . . . But overthrew Pharaoh and his host in the Red sea: for his mercy endureth for ever. . . . To him which smote great kings: for his mercy endureth for ever: And slew famous kings: for his mercy endureth for ever: Sihon king of the Amorites: for his mercy endureth for ever: And Og the king of Bashan: for his mercy endureth for ever"].

[235] And so is their eternal damnation in another world. Romans 9:22, 23: "What if God, willing to show his wrath and make his power known, endured with much long-suffering the vessels of wrath fitted to destruction: and that he might make known the riches of his glory on the vessels of mercy, which he had afore prepared unto glory." Here it is evident the last verse comes in, in connection with the foregoing, as giving *another* reason of the destruction of the wicked, *viz. showing the riches of his glory on the vessels of mercy: higher degrees* of their glory and happiness, in a relish of their own enjoyments, and a greater sense of their value and of God's free grace in bestowing them.[85]

---

[85] Edwards wrote in Miscellany # 279 (ed. by Thomas Schafer, p. 379), "I am convinced that hell torments will be eternal from one great good the wisdom of God proposes by them, which is by the sight of them to exalt the happiness, the love, and joyful thanksgivings of the angels and men that are saved; which it tends exceedingly to do. I am ready to think that beholding the sight of the great miseries of those of their species that are damned will double the ardor of their love, and the fullness of the joy of the elect angels and men. It will do it many ways. The

[PART SEVEN OF SECTION FIVE]
[All creation belongs to the people of God and so exists for their good]

[236] It seems to argue that God's goodness to them who are to be the eternal subjects of his goodness is the end of the creation, since the whole creation, in all its parts, is spoken of as THEIRS. 1 Corinthians 3:22, 23: "*All things are yours*, whether Paul, or Apollos, or Cephas, or the world, or life, or death, or things present, or things to come, *all are yours*." The terms are very universal, and both works of creation and providence are mentioned, and it is manifestly the design of the apostle to be understood of every work of God whatsoever. Now, how can we understand this any otherwise than that all things are for their benefit, and that God made and uses all for their good?

[PART EIGHT OF SECTION FIVE]
[All the works of providence are mercy for the people of God]

[237] All God's works, both of creation and providence, are represented as works of *goodness* or *mercy* to his people; as in the 136th Psalm. His wonderful works *in general*, verse 4: "To him who alone doth great wonders; for his mercy endureth for ever." The works of *creation* in all its parts, verses 5-9: "To him that by wisdom made the heavens; for his mercy endureth for ever. To him that stretched out the earth above the waters; for his mercy endureth for ever. To him that made great lights; for his mercy

---

sight of the wonderful power, the great and dreadful majesty and authority and the awful justice and holiness of God manifested in their punishment, will make them prize his favor and love exceedingly the more; and will excite a most exquisite love and thankfulness to him, that he chose them out from the rest to make them thus happy, that God did not make them such vessels of wrath, according to Romans 9:22-23." In addition, Edwards preached several messages on Revelation 18:20 ["Rejoice over her, thou heaven, and ye holy apostles and prophets; for God hath avenged you on her"] under the title "The End of the Wicked Contemplated by the Righteous: The Torments of the Wicked in Hell No Occasion of Grief to the Saints in Heaven," in: *The Works of Jonathan Edwards*, vol. 2 (Edinburgh: Banner of Truth Trust, 1974), pp. 207-212. His answer to the question why we are called on to love our enemies if we will not grieve over their destruction is: "[In hell] wicked men will be no longer capable subjects of mercy. The saints will know that it is the will of God [that] the wicked should be miserable to all eternity. It will therefore cease to be their duty any more to seek their salvation, or to be concerned about their misery. On the other hand, it will be their duty to rejoice in the will and glory of God. It is not our duty to be sorry that God hath executed just vengeance on the devils, concerning whom the will of God in their eternal state is already known to us" (p. 210).

endureth for ever. The sun to rule by day; for his mercy endureth for ever. The moon and stars to rule by night; for his mercy endureth for ever." And God's works of *providence* in the following part of the Psalm.

[PART NINE OF SECTION FIVE]
[The kingdom of God is prepared for the people of God]

[238] That expression in the blessed sentence pronounced on the righteous at the day of judgment, Matthew 25:34: "Inherit the kingdom *prepared for you* from the foundation of the world," seems to hold forth thus much, that the fruits of God's goodness to them was his end in creating the world and in his providential disposals; that God in all his works, in laying the foundation of the world and ever since the foundation of it, had been preparing this kingdom and glory for them.

[PART TEN OF SECTION FIVE]
*[The ultimate end of virtue among men
is that they do each other good]*

[239] Agreeable to this, the *good of men* is spoken of as an ultimate end of the *virtue of the moral* world, Romans 13:8, 9, 10. "He that loveth another hath fulfilled the law. For this, Thou shalt not commit adultery, Thou shalt not kill, &c. And if there be any other commandment, it is briefly comprehended in this saying, Thou shalt love thy neighbor as thyself. *Love worketh no ill to his neighbor; therefore love is the fulfilling of the law.*" Galatians 5:14: "All the law is fulfilled in one word, even in this, *Thou shalt love thy neighbor as thyself.*" James 2:8: "If ye fulfill the royal law, according to the Scripture, *Thou shalt love thy neighbor as thyself,* thou shalt do well."

[240] If the *good of the creature* be one end of God in all he does, and in all he requires moral agents to do; an end by which they should regulate all their conduct; these things may be easily explained; but otherwise, it seems difficult to be accounted for, that the Holy Ghost should thus express himself. The Scripture represents it to be the spirit of all true saints, to prefer the welfare of

God's people to their chief joy.[86] This was the spirit of Moses and the *prophets* of old: the good of God's church was an end by which they regulated all their conduct. And so it was with the *apostles*. 2 Corinthians 4:15: "For all things are *for your sakes.*" 2 Timothy 2:10: "I endured all things *for the elect's sake*, that they may also obtain the salvation which is in Christ Jesus, with eternal glory." And the Scriptures represent it, as though every Christian should, in all he does, be employed for the good of the church, as each particular member is employed for the good of the body: Romans 12:4, 5, &c.; Ephesians 4:15, 16; 1 Corinthians 12:12, 25, &c. To this end, the Scripture teaches us, the angels are continually employed, Hebrews 1:14.

SECTION SIX

WHEREIN IS CONSIDERED WHAT IS MEANT BY THE GLORY OF GOD AND THE NAME OF GOD IN SCRIPTURE, WHEN SPOKEN OF AS GOD'S END IN HIS WORKS

[241] Having thus considered what are spoken of in the Holy Scriptures as the *ends* which God had *ultimately* in view in the creation of the world, I now proceed particularly to inquire what they are, and how the terms are to be understood.

---

[86] Taken in isolation, this comment could lead us to think that Edwards meant that the "chief joy" of the virtuous and "the welfare of God's people" could really be at odds—as though we would have to choose between them. But this is emphatically not what he believes. He speaks sometimes with self-love in view which finds happiness in private, selfish pleasures, and sometimes with self-love which finds happiness in the welfare of others. The latter is not bad. For example in his sermon on 1 Corinthians 13:5 ["Love seeks not its own"], he says, "A man's love to his own happiness may be inordinate in placing that happiness in things which are confined to himself. In this respect the error is not so much in the degree of his love to himself as it is in the channel in which it flows. It is not in that degree in which he loves his own happiness, but in the placing his happiness. In this the man is limited and confined. Some, although they love their own happiness, do not place their happiness in their own confined good, or in that good which is limited to themselves, but more in the common good, in that which is the good of others as well as their own, in good to be enjoyed *in* others and to be enjoyed *by* others. A man's love of his own happiness when it runs in this channel is not what is called selfishness, but is quite opposite to it. But there are others who, in their love to their own happiness, place their happiness in good things which are confined and limited to themselves exclusive of others. And this is selfishness. This is the thing most directly intended by that self-love which the Scripture condemns. When it is said that charity seeketh not her own, we are to understand it of her own private good, good limited to herself" (Jonathan Edwards, *Charity and Its Fruits*, in: *Ethical Writings*, ed. by Paul Ramsey, p. 257-258). This would be confirmed by Biblical passages like 1 Thessalonians 2:19, "For who is our hope or joy or crown of exultation? Is it not even you, in the presence of our Lord Jesus at His coming?" (NASB). Psalm 16:3, "As for the saints who are in the earth, they are the majestic ones in whom is all my delight" (NASB). See footnotes 64 and 69.

[PART ONE OF SECTION SIX]
[What is meant in Scripture by the glory of God?]

[242] Let us begin with the phrase, the GLORY OF GOD—and here I might observe, that it is sometimes used to signify the second person in the Trinity; but it is not necessary, at this time, to prove it from particular passages of Scripture. Omitting this, I proceed to observe some things concerning the Hebrew word *kabod*,[87] which is most commonly used in the Old Testament where we have the word *glory* in the English Bible. The root it comes from, is either the verb, *kabad* which signifies *to be heavy*, or make heavy, or from the adjective *kaved*, which signifies *heavy* or weighty. These, as seems pretty manifest, are the primary signification of these words, though they have also other meanings, which seem to be derivative. The noun *kavod* signifies *gravity*, heaviness, *greatness*, and abundance. Of very many places it will be sufficient to specify a few: Proverbs 27:3; 2 Samuel 14:26; 1 Kings 12:11; Psalm 38:4; Isaiah 30:27. And as the weight of bodies arises from two things, *density* and *magnitude*; so we find the word used to signify *dense*, Exodus 19:16 (*'anan kaved, nubes gravis*, Vulgate: *densissima*) *a dense cloud*; and is very often used for *great*: Isaiah 32:2; Genesis 5:9; 1 Kings 10:2; 2 Kings 6:14 and 18:17; Isaiah 36:2 &c.

[243] The Hebrew word *kabod*, which is commonly translated *glory*, is used in such a manner as might be expected from this signification of the words from whence it comes. Sometimes it is used to signify what is *internal, inherent*, or in the *possession* of the person: and sometimes for *emanation, exhibition*, or *communication* of this internal glory: and sometimes for the *knowledge*, or *sense* of these, in those to whom the exhibition or communication is made; or an *expression* of this knowledge, sense, or effect. And here I would note that, agreeable to the use of this word in the Old Testament, is the Greek word *doxa* in the New. For as the word *kabod* is generally translated by the just mentioned Greek word *doxa* in the Septuagint; so it is apparent, that this word is designed to be used to signify the *same thing* in the New Testament with the

---

[87] I follow the Yale critical edition's (*Ethical Writings*, pp. 512 ff.) transliterations in the following Hebrew and Greek words rather than using the actual Hebrew and Greek letters which are in the Banner of Truth edition.

other in the Old. This might be abundantly proved, by comparing particular places of the Old Testament; but probably it will not be denied. I therefore proceed particularly to consider these words, with regard to their use in Scripture, in each of the fore-mentioned ways.

[DEFINITION ONE]
[Glory denotes what is internal]

A person's internal excellence or greatness is referred to as his glory

[244] The word *glory* denotes sometimes what is *internal*. When the word is used to signify what is within, or in the possession of the subject, it very commonly signifies *excellency*, dignity, or worthiness of regard. This, according to the Hebrew *idiom*, is, as it were, the *weight* of a thing, as that by which it is heavy; as to be *light* is to be worthless, without value, contemptible. Numbers 21:5: "This *light* bread." 1 Samuel 18:23: "Seemeth it a *light* thing." Judges 9:4: "*Light* persons," *i.e.* worthless, vain, vile persons. So Zephaniah 3:4. To set *light* by is to despise, 2 Samuel 19:43. Belshazzar's vileness in the sight of God, is represented by his being *Tekel*, weighed in the balances and found *light*,[88] Daniel 5:27. And as the weight of a thing arises from its *magnitude*, and its specific gravity conjunctly; so the word *glory* is very commonly used to signify the *excellency* of a person or a thing, as consisting either in *greatness*, or in *beauty*, or in both conjunctly; as will abundantly appear by considering the places referred to in the margin.[89]

Great possessions are sometimes called a person's glory

[245] Sometimes that internal, great and excellent good, which is called glory, is rather in *possession*, than inherent. Any one may

---

[88] *Tekel* by itself does not mean "light, but rather "weighed." Edwards is making his point from the reality of the scales and the lightness of the king in the balances which implies his lack of excellence in God's sight.

[89] Edwards's own footnote: Exodus 16:7 and 28:2, 40 and 3:8; Numbers 16:9; Deuteronomy 5:24 and 28:58; 2 Samuel 6:20; 1 Chronicles 16:24; Esther 1:4; Job 29:20; Psalm 19:1 and 45:13 and 63:3 and 66:3 and 67:6 and 87:3 and 102:16 and 145:5, 12, 13; Isaiah 4:2 and 10:18 and 16:40 and 35:21 and 40:5 and 60:13 and 62:2; Ezekiel 31:18; Habakkuk 2:14; Haggai 2:3, 9; Matthew 6:29 and 16:27; 24:30; Luke 9:31, 32; John 1:14 and 2:11 and 11:40; Romans 6:4; 1 Corinthians 2:8 and 15:40; 2 Corinthians 3:10; Ephesians 3:21; Colossians 1:11; 2 Thessalonians 1:9; Titus 2:13; 1 Peter 1:24; 2 Peter 1:17.

be called *heavy*, that possesses an abundance; and he that is empty and destitute, may be called *light*. Thus we find riches are sometimes called *glory*. Genesis 31:1: "And of that which was our fathers' hath he gotten *all this glory*." Esther 5:11: "Haman told them of the *glory of his riches*." Psalm 49:16, 17: "Be not afraid when one is made rich, when the *glory of his house* is increased. For when he dieth, he shall carry nothing away, his *glory* shall not descend after him." Nahum 2:9: "Take ye the spoil of silver, take the spoil of gold; for there is none end of the store and *glory* out of the pleasant furniture."

[246] And it is often put for a great height of prosperity, and fullness of good in general. Genesis 45:13: "You shall tell my father of *all my glory* in Egypt." Job 19:9: "He hath stripped me of *my glory*." Isaiah 10:3: "Where will you leave your glory." Verse 16: "Therefore shall the LORD of hosts send among his fat ones leanness, and under his *glory* shall he kindle a burning, like the burning of a fire." Isaiah 17:3, 4: "The kingdom shall cease from Damascus, and the remnant of Syria; they shall be as the *glory* of the children of Israel. And in that day, it shall come to pass, that the *glory* of Jacob shall be made thin, and the fatness of his flesh shall be made lean." Isaiah 21:16: "And all the *glory* of Kedar shall fail." Isaiah 61:6: "Ye shall eat the riches of the Gentiles, and in their *glory* shall ye boast yourselves." Chapter 66:11, 12: "That ye may milk out, and be delighted with the abundance of her *glory*. I will extend peace to her, like a river, and the glory of the Gentiles like a flowing stream." Hosea 9:11: "As for Ephraim, their *glory* shall fly away as a bird." Matthew 4:8: "Showeth him all the kingdoms of the world, and the *glory* of them." Luke 24:26: "Ought not Christ to have suffered these things, and to enter into his *glory*?" John 17:22: "And the *glory* which thou gavest me, have I given them." Romans 5:2: "And rejoice in hope of the *glory* of God." Chapter 8:18: "The sufferings of this present time, are not worthy to be compared with the *glory* which shall be revealed in us." (See also chapter 2:7, 10 and 3:23 and 9:23). 1 Corinthians 2:7: "The hidden wisdom which God ordained before the world, unto our *glory*." 2 Corinthians 4:17: "Worketh out for us a far more exceeding and eternal weight of *glory*." Ephesians 1:18: "And what the riches of the

glory of his inheritance in the saints." 1 Peter 4:13: "But rejoice, inasmuch as ye are made partakers of Christ's sufferings; that when his *glory* shall be revealed, ye may be glad also with exceeding joy." Chapter 1:8: "Ye rejoice, with joy unspeakable and full of *glory*."[90]

[DEFINITION TWO]
[Glory expresses exhibition or emanation]

Glory is also the outshining of the internal greatness or excellence

[247] The word *glory* is used in Scripture often to express the *exhibition, emanation,* or *communication* of the internal glory. Hence it often signifies an effulgence, or shining brightness, by an emanation of beams of light. Thus the brightness of the sun and moon and stars is called their *glory*, in 1 Corinthians 15:41. But in particular, the word is very often thus used, when applied to God and Christ, as in Ezekiel 1:28. "As the appearance of the bow that is in the cloud in the day of rain, so was the appearance of the brightness round about. This was the appearance of the likeness of the *glory* of the LORD." And chapter 10:4: "Then the *glory* of the Lord went up from the cherub, and stood over the threshold of the house, and the house was filled with the cloud, and the court was full of the brightness of the LORD's *glory*." Isaiah 6:1, 2, 3: "I saw the Lord sitting upon a throne, high and lifted up, and his train filled the temple. Above it stood the seraphim. And one cried to another and said, Holy, holy, holy is the LORD of hosts, the whole earth is full of his *glory*." Compared with John 12:41: "These things said Esaias,[91] when he saw his *glory* and spake of him." Ezekiel 43:2: "And behold the *glory* of the God of Israel came from the way of the east. And the earth *shined* with his *glory*." Isaiah 24:23: "Then the moon shall be confounded, and the sun ashamed, when the LORD of

---

[90] Edwards's own footnote: See also Colossians 1:27 and 3:4; 1 Thessalonians 2:12; 2 Thessalonians 2:14; 1 Timothy 3:16; 2 Timothy 2:10; Hebrews 2:10; 1 Peter 1:11,21 and 5:10; 2 Peter 1:3; Revelation 21:24, 26; Psalm 73:24 and 149:5; Isaiah 6:10.

[91] Esaias = Isaiah.

hosts shall reign in mount Zion, and in Jerusalem, and before his ancients *gloriously*." Isaiah 60:1, 2: "Arise, shine, for thy light is come, and the *glory* of the LORD is risen upon thee. For behold the darkness shall cover the earth, and gross darkness the people; but the LORD shall arise upon thee, and his *glory* shall be seen upon thee." Together with verse 19: "The sun shall be no more thy light by day, neither for brightness shall the moon give light unto thee: but the LORD shall be unto thee an everlasting light, and thy God thy *glory*."

[248] Luke 2:9: "The *glory* of the Lord shone round about them." Acts 22:11: "And when I could not see for the glory of that *light*." In 2 Corinthians 3:7: The shining of Moses's face is called *the glory of his countenance*. And to this Christ's glory is compared, verse 18: "But we all with open face, beholding as in a glass the *glory* of the Lord, are changed into the same image, *from glory to glory.*" And so chapter 4:4: "Lest the light of the *glorious* gospel of Christ, who is the image of God, should shine unto them." Verse 6: "For God, who commanded the light to shine out of darkness, hath shined in our hearts, to give the light of the knowledge of the *glory* of God in the face of Jesus Christ." Hebrews 1:3: "Who is the *brightness* of his *glory*." The apostle Peter, speaking of that emanation of exceeding brightness, from the bright cloud that overshadowed the disciples in the mount of transfiguration, and of the shining of Christ's face at that time, says, 2 Peter 1:17: "For he received from God the Father honor and *glory*, when there came such a voice to him from the *excellent glory*, This is my beloved Son, in whom I am well pleased." Revelation 18:1: "Another angel came down from heaven, having great power, *and the earth was lightened with his glory*." Revelation 21:11: "Having the *glory* of God, and her *light* was like unto a stone most precious, like a jasper stone, clear as crystal." Verse 23: "And the city had no need of the sun nor of the moon to shine in it; for the *glory* of God did lighten it." See the word for a *visible effulgence* or emanation of light in the places to be seen in the margin.[92]

---

[92] Edwards's own footnote: Exodus 16:12 and 24:16, 17, 23 and 40:34, 35; Leviticus 9:6, 23; Numbers 14:10 and 16:19; 1 Kings 8:11; 2 Chronicles 5:14 and 7:1, 2, 3; Isaiah 58:8; Ezekiel 3:23 and 8:4 and 9:3 and 10:18, 19 and 11:22, 23 and 43:4, 5 and 44:4; Acts 7:55; Revelation 15:8.

Glory sometimes refers to God's fullness of goodness and grace

[249] The word *glory*, as applied to God or Christ, sometimes evidently signifies the *communications* of God's *fullness*, and means much the same thing with God's abundant goodness and grace. So Ephesians 3:16: "That he would grant you, *according to the riches of his glory*, to be strengthened with might by his Spirit in the inner man." The expression, "According to the riches of his glory," is apparently equivalent to that in the same epistle, chapter 1:7: "According to the riches of his grace." And chapter 2:7: "The exceeding riches of his grace in his kindness towards us, through Christ Jesus." In like manner is the word *glory* used in Philippians 4:19, "But my God shall supply all your need, according to his *riches in glory*, by Christ Jesus." And Romans 9:23: "And that he might make known the *riches of his glory*, on the vessels of his mercy." In this and the foregoing verse, the apostle speaks of God's making known two things, his *great wrath*, and his *rich grace*. The former on the vessels of wrath, verse 22. The latter, which he calls *the riches of his glory*, on the vessels of mercy, verse 23. So when Moses says, "I beseech thee show me thy *glory*;" God granting his request, makes answer, "I will make all my *goodness* to pass before thee." Exodus 33:18, 19.[93]

[250] What we find in John 12:23-32 is worthy of particular notice in this place. The words and behavior of Christ, of which we have here an account, argue two things.

[251] That the happiness and salvation of men, was an end that Christ ultimately aimed at in his labors and sufferings. The very same things which were observed before, (chapter second, section third,) concerning God's *glory*, are in the same manner observable, concerning the salvation of men. Christ, in the near approach of the most extreme difficulties which attended his undertaking,

---

[93] Edwards's own footnote: Dr. Goodwin observes (Vol. I of his works, part 2d, page 166) that riches of grace are called *riches of glory* in Scripture. "The Scripture," says he, "speaks of riches of glory in Eph. 3:6. *That he would grant you according to the riches of his glory*; yet eminently *mercy* is there intended: for it is that which God bestows, and which the apostle there prayeth for. And he calls his *mercy* there his *glory*, as elsewhere he doth, as being the most eminent excellency in God. That in Rom. 9:22, 23. compared, is observable. In the 22d verse where the apostle speaks of God's making known the power of his wrath, saith he, *God willing to show his wrath, and make his power known*. But in verse 23d, when he comes to speak of mercy, he saith, *That he might make known the riches of his glory on the vessels of mercy*." [The reference is from *The Works of Thomas Goodwin* (London, 1681), vol. I. Pt. II, p. 166, from his sermon on Eph. 2:4-6.]

comforts himself in a certain prospect of obtaining the *glory of God*, as his great end. And at the same time, and exactly in the same manner, is the *salvation of men* mentioned, as the end of these great labors and sufferings, which satisfied his soul in the prospect of undergoing them. (Compare the 23rd and 24th verses; and also the 28th and 29th verses; verses 31 and 32.)

[252] The glory of God, and the emanations and fruits of his grace in man's salvation, are so spoken of by Christ on this occasion in just the same manner, that it would be quite unnatural to understand him as speaking of two distinct things. Such is the connection, that what he says of the latter, must most naturally be understood as exegetical [i.e., explanatory] of the former. He first speaks of his *own glory*, and *the glory of his Father*, as the great end that should be obtained by what he was about to suffer; and then explains and amplifies this, in what he expresses of the *salvation of men* that shall be obtained by it. Thus, in the 23rd verse, he says, "The hour is come that the Son of man should be glorified." And in what next follows, he evidently shows how he was to be glorified, or wherein his glory consisted: "Verily, verily, I say unto you, except a corn of wheat fall into the ground, and die, it abideth alone; but if it die, it bringeth forth much fruit." As *much fruit* is the *glory* of the seed, so is the multitude of redeemed ones, which should spring from his death, his glory.[94] So concerning the glory of his Father, in the 27th and following verses. "Now is my soul troubled, and what shall I say? Father, save me from this hour! But for this cause came I unto this hour. Father, *glorify thy name*. Then came there a voice from heaven, saying, *I have both glorified it,* and *will glorify it again*."

[253] In an assurance of this, which this voice declared, Christ was *greatly comforted*, and his soul even *exulted* under the view of his approaching sufferings. And what this glory was, in which Christ's soul was so comforted on this occasion, his own words plainly show. When the people said, it thundered; and others said, an angel spake to him; then Christ tells them what this voice meant, verses 30-32. "Jesus answered and said, This voice came

---

[94] Edwards's own footnote: Here may be remembered what was before observed of the church being so often spoken of as the glory and fullness of Christ.

not because of me, but for your sakes. Now is the judgment of this world; now shall the prince of this world be cast out. And I, if I be lifted up from the earth, will draw all men unto me." By this behavior and these speeches of our Redeemer, it appears, that the expressions of *divine grace*, in the sanctification and happiness of the redeemed, are especially that *glory* of his, and his Father, which was the *joy that was set before him*, for which he endured the cross, and despised the shame [Heb. 12:1-2]: and that this glory especially was the end of the travail of his soul, in obtaining which end he was satisfied. (Is. 53:10, 11).

[254] This is agreeable to what has been just observed, of God's glory being so often represented by an effulgence, or emanation, or communication of light, from a luminary or fountain of light. What can so naturally and aptly represent the emanation of the internal glory of God; or the flowing forth and abundant communication of that infinite fullness of good that is in God? Light is very often in Scripture put for comfort, joy, happiness, and for good in general.[95]

[DEFINITION THREE]
[Glory implies the view or knowledge of excellency]

God's glory is the honor accorded him by the creature

[255] Again, the word *glory*, as applied to God in Scripture, implies the *view* or *knowledge* of God's excellency. The exhibition of glory is to the *view* of beholders. The manifestation of glory, the emanation or effulgence of brightness, has relation to the *eye*. Light or brightness is a quality that has relation to the *sense* of seeing; we see the luminary by its light. And *knowledge* is often expressed in Scripture by light. The word *glory* very often in Scripture signifies, or implies, *honor*, as any one may soon see by casting his eye on a concordance.[96] But *honor* implies the *knowledge* of the dig-

---

[95] Edwards's own footnote: Isaiah 6:3—"Holy, holy, holy is the LORD of hosts, the whole earth is full of his *glory*." In the original, His glory is the fullness of the whole earth: which signifies much more than the words of the translation. God's glory, consisting especially in his holiness, is that, in the sight or communications of which man's fullness, i.e. his holiness and happiness, consists. By *God's glory* here, there seems to be respect to those effulgent beams that filled their temple: these beams signifying God's glory shining forth and communicated. This effulgence or communication, is the fullness of all intelligent creatures, who have no fullness of their own.

[96] Edwards's own footnote: See particularly Hebrews 3:3.

nity and excellency of him who hath the honor; and this is often more especially signified by the word *glory*, when applied to God. Numbers 14:21: "But as truly as I live, all the earth shall be filled with the *glory* of the LORD," *i.e.* all the inhabitants of the earth shall *see* the manifestations I will make of my perfect holiness and hatred of sin, and so of my infinite excellence. This appears by the context. So Ezekiel 39:21, 22, 23: "And I will set my glory among the heathen, and all the heathen *shall see* my judgment that I have executed, and my hand that I have laid upon them. So the house of Israel *shall know* that I am the LORD their God. And the heathen *shall know* that the house of Israel went into captivity for their iniquity." And it is manifest in many places, where we read of God glorifying himself, or of his being glorified, that one thing, directly intended, is *making known* his divine greatness and excellency.

[DEFINITION FOUR]
[Glory implies praise]

God's glory is the praise he receives from his creatures

[256] Again, *glory*, as the word is used in Scripture, often signifies or implies *praise*. This appears from what was observed before, that glory very often signifies *honor*, which is much the same thing with praise, *viz.* high esteem and the expression of it in words and actions. And it is manifest that the words *glory* and *praise*, are often used as equivalent expressions in Scripture. Psalm 50:23: "Whoso offereth *praise*, *glorifieth* me." Psalm 22:23: "Ye that fear the LORD, *praise* him; all ye seed of Israel, *glorify* him." Isaiah 42:8: "My *glory* I will not give unto another, nor my *praise* to graven images." Verse 12: "Let them give *glory* unto the LORD, and declare his *praise* in the islands." Isaiah 48:9-11: "For my *name's sake* will I defer mine anger; for my *praise* will I refrain for thee. For mine *own sake* will I do it; for I will not give my *glory* unto another." Jeremiah 13:11: "That they might be unto me for a people, and for a *name*, and for a *praise*, and for a *glory*." Ephesians 1:6: "To the *praise* of the *glory* of his grace." Verse 12: "To the *praise* of his *glory*." So verse 14. The phrase is apparently

equivalent to this, Philippians 1:11: "Which are by Jesus Christ unto the *praise* and *glory* of God." 2 Corinthians 4:15: "That the abundant grace might, through the *thanksgiving* of many, redound to the *glory of God.*"

[257] It is manifest the *praise of God*, as the phrase is used in Scripture, implies the high *esteem* and love of the heart, exalting thoughts of God, and complacence [i.e., satisfaction, delight] in his excellence and perfection. This is manifest to every one acquainted with the Scripture. However, if any need satisfaction, they may, among innumerable other places which might be mentioned, turn to those in the margin.[97]

[258] It also implies joy in God, or *rejoicing* in his perfections, as is manifest by Psalm 33:2. "*Rejoice* in the LORD, O ye righteous, for *praise* is comely for the upright." Other passages to the same purpose, see in the margin.[98] How often do we read of *singing praise*! But *singing* is commonly an expression of *joy*. It is called, making a *joyful noise*.[99] And as it is often used, it implies *gratitude* or *love* to God for his benefits to us.[100]

[PART TWO OF SECTION SIX]

[What is meant in Scripture by the name of God?]

[259] Having thus considered what is implied in the phrase, *the glory of God,* as we find it used in Scripture; I proceed to inquire what is meant by the NAME of God.

God's name and his glory often signify the same thing

[260] God's *name* and his *glory*, at least very often, signify the same thing in Scripture. As it has been observed concerning the glory of God, that it sometimes signifies the second person in the Trinity; the same might be shown of the *name* of God, if it were needful in this

---

[97] Edwards's own footnote: Psalm 145:1-12 and 34:1, 2, 3 and 44:8 and 21:14, 15 and 99:2, 3 and 107:21, 32 and 108:3, 4, 5 and 119:164 and 148:13 and 150:2; Revelation 19:1, 2, 3.

[98] Edwards's own footnote: Psalm 9:1, 2, 14 and 28:7 and 35:27, 28 and 42:4 and 63:5 and 67:3, 4, 5 and 71:22, 23 and 104:33, 34 and 106:47 and 135:3 and 147:1, 2, 5, 6; Acts 2:46, 47 and 3:8; Revelation 19:6, 7.

[99] Edwards's own footnote: Psalm 66:1, 2 and 96:4, 5.

[100] Edwards's own footnote: Psalm 30:12 and 35:18 and 63:3, 4 and 66:8, 9 and 71:6, 7, 8 and 79:13 and 98:4,5 and 100:4 and 107:21, 22 and 138:2. And many other places.

place. But that the name and glory of God are often equipollent [i.e., equivalent] expressions, is manifest by Exodus 33:18, 19. When Moses says, "I beseech thee, show me *thy glory*," and God grants his request, he says, "I will proclaim the *name* of the Lord before thee." Psalm 8:1: "O LORD, how excellent is thy *name* in all the earth! Who hast set thy *glory* above the heavens." Psalm 79:9: "Help us! O God of our salvation, for the *glory* of thy *name*; and deliver us, and purge away our sins for thy *name's* sake." Psalm 102:15: "So the heathen shall fear the *name* of the LORD; and all the kings of the earth thy *glory*." Psalm 148:13: "His *name* alone is excellent, and his *glory* is above the earth and heaven." Isaiah 48:9: "For my *name's* sake will I defer mine anger, and for my *praise* will I refrain for thee." Verse 11: "For mine own sake, even for mine own sake will I do it: for how should my *name* be polluted? And I will not give my *glory* unto another." Isaiah 59:19: "They shall fear the *name* of the LORD from the west, and his *glory* from the rising of the sun." Jeremiah 13:11: "That they might be unto me for a *name*, and for a *praise*, and for a *glory*." As *glory* often implies the *manifestation*, *publication*, and *knowledge* of excellency, and the *honor* that any one has in the world; so does *name*. Genesis 11:4: "Let us make us a *name*." Deuteronomy 26:19: "And to make thee high above all nations, in *praise*, in *name*, and in *honor*." [101]

God's name sometimes means the same as his praise

[261] So it is evident that by *name* is sometimes meant much the same thing as *praise*, by several places which have been just mentioned, (as Is. 48:9; Jer. 13:11; Deut. 26:19). And also by Jeremiah 33:9: "And it shall be unto me for a *name*, a *praise*, and an *honor*, before all the nations of the earth, which shall hear of all the good I do unto them." Zephaniah 3:20: "I will make you a *name* and a *praise* among all people of the earth."

God's name sometimes refers to the exhibition of his goodness

[262] And it seems that the expression or exhibition of God's *goodness* is especially called his *name*, in Exodus 33:19. "I will make

---

[101] Edwards's own footnote: See also 2 Samuel 7:9 and 8:13 and 23:18; Nehemiah 9:10; Job 30:8; Proverbs 22:1. Many other places import the same thing.

all my goodness pass before thee, and I will proclaim the *name* of the LORD before thee. And chapter 34:5, 6, 7: "And the LORD descended in the cloud, and stood with him there, and proclaimed the *name* of the LORD. And the LORD passed by before him, and proclaimed, The LORD, the LORD God, *gracious and merciful, long-suffering* and abundant in *goodness and truth*; keeping *mercy* for thousands," &c.

[263] And the same illustrious brightness and *effulgence* in the pillar of cloud that appeared in the wilderness, and dwelt above the mercy-seat in the tabernacle and temple, (or rather the spiritual, divine brightness and effulgence *represented* by it,) so often called *the glory of the LORD,* is also often called *the name of the LORD.* Because God's glory was to dwell in the tabernacle, therefore he promises, Exodus 29:43: "There will I meet with the children of Israel, and the tabernacle shall be sanctified by my *glory.*" And the temple was called *the house of God's glory,* Isaiah 60:7. In like manner, the *name* of God is said to dwell in the sanctuary. Thus we often read of the place that God chose, *to put his name there:* or, as it is in the Hebrew, *to cause his NAME* to inhabit there. So it is sometimes rendered by our translators, as Deuteronomy 12:11. "Then there shall be a place which the LORD your God shall choose *to cause his name to dwell there.*" And the temple is often spoken of as built *for God's name.* And in Psalm 74:7, the temple is called *the dwelling-place of God's name.* The mercy-seat in the temple was called the throne of God's name or glory, Jeremiah 14:21. "Do not abhor us, for thy *name's sake* do not disgrace the *throne of thy glory.*" Here God's *name* and his *glory* seem to be spoken of as the same.

SECTION SEVEN

SHOWING THAT THE ULTIMATE END OF THE CREATION OF THE WORLD IS BUT ONE, AND WHAT THAT ONE END IS

All that is an ultimate end of God in creation is included in "the glory of God"

[264] From what has been observed in the last section, it appears, if the whole of what is said relating to this affair be

duly weighed, and one part compared with another, we shall have reason to think that the design of the Spirit of God is not to represent God's ultimate end as *manifold*, but as ONE. For though it be signified by various names, yet they appear not to be names of *different* things, but various names involving each other in their meaning; either different names of the *same thing*, or names of several parts of *one whole*; or of the same whole viewed in *various lights* or in its *different respects* and relations. For it appears, that all that is ever spoken of in the Scripture as an ultimate end of God's works, is included in that one phrase, *the glory of God*; which is the name by which the ultimate end of God's works is most commonly called in Scripture; and seems most aptly to signify the thing.

The glory of God is the emanation of God's fullness

[265] The thing signified by that name, *the glory of God*, when spoken of as the supreme and ultimate[102] end of all God's works, is the emanation and true external expression of God's internal glory and fullness; meaning by his *fullness* what has already been explained; or, in other words, God's internal glory, in a true and just exhibition, or external existence of it. It is confessed, that there is a degree of obscurity in these definitions; but perhaps an obscurity which is unavoidable, through the imperfection of language to express things of so sublime a nature.[103] And therefore the thing may possibly be better understood by using a variety of expressions, by a particular consideration of it, as it were, by parts, than by any short definition.

---

[102] The terms "supreme" and "ultimate" correspond to "chief" and "last" as he interpreted them in his Introduction. "Supreme" or "chief" means highest or supreme as opposed to an inferior or less desired end. But "ultimate" or "last" means that the end in view is the one to which all others are subordinate means. The glory of God is the last or final end to which all things are a means. And it is also the best and most superior end of all the possible ultimate ends one could conceive of.

[103] It is very important, as we come to the end of this great treatise, that we let this repeated "confession" of a great theologian sink in. He has said before, at the end of Chapter One, Section Four, that there is "a degree of indistinctness and obscurity in the close consideration of such subjects and great imperfection in the expression we use concerning them, arising unavoidably from the infinite sublimity of the subject and the incomprehensibleness of those things that are divine" (see ¶ 124). We must be very careful to balance any given term or phrase or assertion in this treatise with the whole and, where possible, with what Edwards said in other places, so that we do not read too much, or too little, into some very provocative expressions.

The glory of God includes manifestations of his fullness to the creation and the creature's esteem and love and enjoyment of God's fullness

[266] It includes the *exercise* of God's perfections to produce a proper *effect*, in opposition to their lying eternally dormant and ineffectual: as his power being eternally without any act or fruit of that power; his wisdom eternally ineffectual in any wise production, or prudent disposal of any thing, &c. The *manifestation* of his internal glory to created understandings. The *communication* of the infinite fullness of God to the creature. The creature's high *esteem* of God, love to him, and complacence [i.e., satisfaction, delight] and joy in him; and the proper *exercises* and *expressions* of these.

[267] These, at first view, may appear to be entirely distinct things: but if we more closely consider the matter, they will all appear to be ONE thing, in a variety of views and relations. They are all but the *emanation of God's glory*; or the excellent brightness and fullness of the divinity *diffused, overflowing* and, as it were, *enlarged*; or in one word, *existing ad extra*.[104] God *exercising* his perfection to produce a proper *effect*, is not distinct from the emanation or *communication* of his *fullness*: for this is the effect, *viz.* his *fullness communicated*, and the producing of this effect is the communication of his fullness; and there is nothing in this effectual exerting of God's perfection, but the emanation of God's internal glory.

All God's internal glory is summed up in his understanding, virtue and happiness

[268] Now God's *internal* glory, is either in his understanding or will. The glory or fullness of his *understanding* is his knowledge. The internal glory and fullness of God, having its special seat in

---

[104] On the Latin phrase *ad extra* see footnote 27. Where Edwards speaks of the "divinity *diffused, overflowing* and, as it were *enlarged*, or in one word *existing ad extra*," at least three things are important to note, lest we construe him as a pantheist or see ourselves as God. 1) Note the crucial term "as it were," which cautions us that there is something very delicate and complex and easily misconstrued in this assertion. 2) Note that "divinity" overflowing may refer not to the extension of God's essence in his creation, but in some sense, overflowing of his glorious knowledge and love and joy that he has in himself. 3) Note what is said on this issue in numerous other places in the *Dissertation* that help us keep our balance in handling such a lofty theme. See the related footnotes mentioned in footnote 113.

his *will,* is his holiness and happiness.[105] The *whole* of God's *internal* good or glory, is in these three things, *viz.* his infinite *knowledge,* his infinite virtue or *holiness,* and his infinite joy and *happiness.* Indeed there are a great many attributes in God, according to our way of conceiving them: but all may be reduced to these; or to their degree, circumstances, and relations. We have no conception of God's *power,* different from the degree of these things, with a certain relation of them to effects.[106] God's *infinity* is not properly a distinct *kind* of good, but only expresses the *degree* of good there is in him. So God's *eternity* is not a distinct good; but is the duration of good. His *immutability* is still the same good, with a negation of change. So that, as I said, the *fullness* of the Godhead is the fullness of his *understanding,* consisting in his knowledge; and the fullness of his will consisting in his virtue and happiness.

God's external glory includes
the creatures knowing, loving, and rejoicing in God

[269] And therefore, the *external* glory of God consists in the *communication* of these. The communication of his knowledge is chiefly in giving the *knowledge of himself*: for this is the knowledge in which the fullness of God's understanding chiefly consists. And thus we see how the manifestation of God's glory to created

---

[105] Edwards sometimes distinguishes acts of the will and their more vigorous exercises. The latter he calls the affections, or, as we would say, the emotions (though not including the bodily effects). See footnotes 26, 107. That is what he is doing when he speaks of the holiness and happiness of God and of us, as acts of the will. *Holiness,* he says below, is love to God, and *happiness* is joy in God. But love to God is simply the broader term and refers to the esteem and regard that we are to have to God. When this is in vigorous exercise, as it should be, it is joy in God. Earlier in *The End for Which God Created the World,* he said that love to God included "complacence in" (¶ 257) God's perfections. This means "delight" in God's perfections. This is confirmed in his *Treatise on Grace,* where he says, "Divine love, as it has God for its object, may be thus described. 'Tis the soul's relish of the supreme excellency of the Divine nature, inclining the heart to God as the chief good" (*Treatise on Grace and Other Posthumously Published Writings,* ed. by Paul Helm, [Cambridge: James Clarke & Co. Ltd., 1971], p. 49). Thus holiness (love to God) and happiness (joy in God) are not two completely distinct responses to God. This is confirmed in other places, for example, Miscellany #448 (ed. by Thomas Schafer, p. 495), where he sums up the way we glorify God not with three, but only two responses: "God glorifies himself towards the creatures also two ways: (1) by appearing to them, being manifested to their understandings; (2) in communicating himself to their hearts, and in their rejoicing and delighting in, and enjoying the manifestations which he makes of himself."

[106] So he is saying that the *power* of God is not a properly distinct kind of good in God but is, for example, the virtue of God in unstoppable effectiveness. "Power" is simply the forcefulness of knowledge, virtue or happiness in accomplishing their ends. Similarly "eternality" is the extent of these three and "immutability" is the negation of change in these three. Etc.

understandings, and their seeing and knowing it, is not distinct from an emanation or communication of God's fullness, but clearly implied in it. Again, the communication of God's virtue or holiness, is principally in communicating the *love of himself*. And thus we see how, not only the creature's seeing and knowing God's excellence, but also supremely esteeming and loving him, belongs to the communication of *God's fullness*. And the communication of God's joy and happiness, consists chiefly in communicating to the creature that happiness and joy which consists in *rejoicing in God*, and in his glorious excellency; for in such joy God's own happiness does principally consist. And in these things, *knowing* God's excellency, *loving* God for it, and *rejoicing* in it, and in the *exercise* and *expression* of these, consists God's honor and praise; so that these are clearly implied in that glory of God, which consists in the *emanation* of his internal glory.

The glory of God is reflected mainly in man's two faculties: knowing and willing

[270] And though all these things, which seem to be so various, are signified by that *glory*, which the Scripture speaks of as the ultimate end of all God's works; yet it is manifest there is no greater, and no other variety in it, than in the internal and essential glory of God itself. God's internal glory is partly in his understanding, and partly in his will. And this internal glory, as seated in the will of God, implies both his holiness and his happiness: both are evidently God's glory, according to the use of the phrase. So that as God's external glory is only the emanation of his internal, this variety necessarily follows. And again, it hence appears that here is no other variety or distinction, but what necessarily arises from the distinct faculties of the creature, to which the communication is made, as created in the image of God: even as having these two faculties of understanding and will.[107] God communicates himself to the *understanding* of the

---

[107] See footnote 26 concerning the function of the will as the source of "decisions" *and* "affections." The affections (e.g., joy) are "the more vigorous and sensible exercises of the inclination and will of the soul." Thus there are not three faculties in man (understanding, will, and emotion), but only two (understanding and will). The emotions are the same as affections and the physical components of them (racing heart, sweaty hands, wobbly knees, etc.) are not properly part of the actings of the soul, but only the responses of the body, which Edwards calls "the motion of the blood and animal spirits" (*Religious Affections,* p. 96).

creature, in giving him the *knowledge* of his glory; and to the *will* of the creature, in giving him *holiness*, consisting primarily in the love of God: and in giving the creature *happiness*, chiefly consisting in *joy* in God.[108] These are the sum of that emanation of divine fullness called in Scripture, *the glory of God*. The first part of this glory is called *truth*, the latter, *grace*, John 1:14. "We beheld his *glory*, the glory of the only-begotten of the Father, full of *grace* and *truth*."

The glory of God is compared to the emanation of light from a luminary

[271] Thus we see that the great end of God's works, which is so variously expressed in Scripture, is indeed but ONE; and this *one* end is most properly and comprehensively called, THE GLORY OF GOD; by which name it is most commonly called in Scripture; and is fitly compared to an effulgence or emanation of light from a luminary. Light is the external expression, exhibition, and manifestation of the excellency of the luminary, of the sun for instance: It is the abundant, extensive emanation and communication of the fullness of the sun to innumerable beings that partake of it. It is by this that the sun itself is seen, and his glory beheld, and all other things are discovered: it is by a participation of this communication from the sun, that surrounding objects receive all their luster, beauty, and brightness. It is by this that all nature receives life, comfort, and joy. Light is abundantly used in Scripture to represent and signify these three things, knowledge, holiness, and happiness.[109]

The one end of all creation is God's internal glory existing in its emanation

[272] What has been said may be sufficient to show how those things, which are spoken of in Scripture as ultimate ends of God's

---

[108] As we have seen, joy in God is but love to God in more vigorous action. See footnote 105.

[109] Edwards's own footnote: It is used to signify *knowledge*, or manifestation and evidence by which knowledge is received. Psalm 19:8 and 119:105, 130; Proverbs 6:23; Isaiah 8:20 and 9:2 and 29:18; Daniel 5:11; Ephesians 5:13: "But all things that are reproved, are made manifest by the light; for whatsoever doth make manifest, is light," &c. It is used to signify *virtue*, or moral good. Job 25:5; Ecclesiastes 8:1; Isaiah 5:20 and 24:23 and 62:1; Ezekiel 28:7, 17; Daniel 2:31; 1 John 1:5, &c. And it is abundantly used to signify comfort, joy, and happiness. Esther 8:16; Job 18:8 and 22:28 and 29:3 and 30:26; Psalm 27:1 and 97:11 and 118:27 and 112:4; Isaiah 43:16 and 50:10 and 59:9; Jeremiah 13:16; Lamentations 3; Ezekiel 32:8; Amos 5:18; Micah 7:8, 9, &c.

works, though they may seem at first view to be distinct, are all plainly to be reduced to this *one* thing, *viz. God's internal glory or fullness existing in its emanation.* And though God, in seeking this end, seeks the creature's good; yet therein appears his supreme regard to himself.

The whole is of God, and in God, and to God; and he is the beginning, and the middle, and the end

[273] The emanation or communication of the divine fullness, consisting in the knowledge of God, love to him, and joy in him, has relation indeed both to *God* and the *creature*: but it has relation to God as its *fountain*, as the thing communicated is something of its internal fullness. The water in the stream is something of the fountain; and the beams of the sun are something of the sun.[110] And again, they have relation to God as their *object*: for the knowledge communicated, is the knowledge of God; and the love communicated, is the love of God; and the happiness communicated, is joy in God. In the creature's knowing, esteeming, loving, rejoicing in, and praising God, the glory of God is both *exhibited* and *acknowledged*; his fullness is *received* and *returned*. Here is both an *emanation* and *remanation*. The refulgence shines upon and into the creature, and is reflected back to the luminary. The beams of glory come from God, are something of God, and are refunded back again to their original. So that the whole is *of* God, and *in* God, and *to* God; and he is the beginning, and the middle, and the end.[111]

[274] And though it be true that God has respect to the *creature* in these things; yet his respect to himself, and to the creature, are not properly a double and divided respect. What has been said, (Chapter One, Sections 3 and 4) (¶¶ 57-124) may be sufficient to show this. Nevertheless, it may not be amiss here briefly to say a few things; though mostly implied in what has been said already.

[275] When God was about to create the world, he had respect to that *emanation of his glory*, which is *actually* the consequence

---

[110] On the question of the union of man and God see footnotes 38, 41-46, 104, 113, 115.

[111] These five preceding sentences are a beautiful summary of Edwards's message. This is the kind of writing that makes Edwards cross the line from philosopher to worshipper—and take us with him.

of the creation, both with regard to himself and the creature. He had regard to it as an *emanation* from himself, a *communication* of himself, and, as the *thing communicated*, in its nature *returned* to himself, as its final term. And he had regard to it also as the *emanation* was *to* the creature, and as the *thing communicated* was *in* the creature, as its subject.

Because God values his glory
he values the joy of creatures in that glory

[276] And God had regard to it in this manner, as he had a supreme regard to himself, and value for his own infinite, internal glory. It was this value for himself that caused him to value and seek that his internal glory should *flow forth* from himself. It was from his value for[112] his glorious perfections of wisdom, righteousness, &c. that he valued the proper *exercise* and effect of these perfections, in wise and righteous acts and effects. It was from his infinite value for his internal glory and fullness, that he valued the *thing itself* communicated, which is something of the same, extant in the creature. Thus, because he infinitely values his own glory, consisting in the knowledge of himself, love to himself, and complacence [i.e., satisfaction, delight] and joy in himself; he therefore valued the image, communication, or participation of these in the creature. And it is because he values himself, that he delights in the knowledge, and love, and joy of the creature; as being himself the object of this knowledge, love, and complacence [i.e., satisfaction, delight]. For it is the necessary consequence of true esteem and love, that we value others' esteem of the same object, and dislike the contrary. For the same reason, God approves of others' esteem and love of himself.

The key to uniting God's self-regard and his love for man
is to see that man's joy in God is an exaltation of God

[277] Thus it is easy to conceive how God should seek the good of the creature, consisting in the creature's knowledge and holiness, and even his happiness, from a supreme regard to *himself*; as his happiness arises from that which is an image and participation of God's own beauty; and consists in the creature's exercising a

---

[112] That is, "It was from his *valuing* his glorious perfections . . ."

supreme regard to God, and complacence [i.e., satisfaction, delight] in him; in beholding God's glory, in esteeming and loving it, and rejoicing in it, and in his exercising and testifying love and supreme respect to God: which is the same thing with the creature's exalting God as his chief good, and making him his supreme end.

God's respect to the creature's good, and his respect to himself, is not a divided respect

[278] And though the emanation of God's fullness, intended in the creation, is to the creature as its *object*; and though the creature is the *subject* of the fullness communicated, which is the creature's good; yet it does not necessarily follow, that even in so doing, God did not make *himself* his end. It comes to the same thing. God's respect to the creature's good, and his respect to himself, is not a divided respect; but both are united in one, as the happiness of the creature aimed at is happiness in union with himself. The creature is no further happy with this happiness which God makes his ultimate end, than he becomes one with God. The more happiness the greater union: when the happiness is perfect, the union is perfect.[113] And as the happiness will be increasing to eternity, the union will become more and more strict and perfect; nearer and more like to that between God the Father and the Son; who are so united, that their interest is perfectly one. If the happiness of the creature be considered in the whole of the creature's eternal duration, with all the infinity of its progress, and infinite increase of nearness and union to God; in this view, the creature must be looked upon as united to God in an infinite strictness.

Union with God by sharing the joy God has in himself will increase forever

[279] If God has respect to something in the creature, which he views as of everlasting duration, and as rising higher and higher

---

[113] The union is a sharing, more and more, for all eternity the very happiness that God has in himself. This is not a "strict" metaphysical, or essential union, but a real "strict" one nevertheless. It seems that Edwards guards himself from the charge of making the creature God in two ways: one is by stressing that the union is in the sharing of God's experience of God (knowing, loving, enjoying) rather than God's being God; and the other is by stressing that even this union will never be perfected to all eternity, but will be increasing forever. See related material at footnotes 38, 41-46, 104, 115.

through that infinite duration, and that not with constantly diminishing (but perhaps an increasing) celerity;[114] then he has respect
to it, as, in the whole, of infinite height; though there never will be
any particular time when it can be said already to have come to
such a height.

[280] Let the most perfect union with God be represented by
something at an infinite height above us; and the eternally increasing union of the saints with God, by something that is ascending
constantly towards that infinite height, moving upwards with a
given velocity; and that is to continue thus to move to all eternity.
God, who views the whole of this eternally increasing height, views
it as an infinite height. And if he has respect to it, and makes it his
end, as in the whole of it, he has respect to it as an infinite height,
though the time will never come when it can be said it has already
arrived at this infinite height.

[281] God aims at that which the motion or progression which
he causes, aims at, or tends to. If there be many things supposed
to be so made and appointed, that, by a constant eternal motion,
they all tend to a certain center; then it appears that he who made
them, and is the cause of their motion, aimed at that center; and
that term of their motion, to which they eternally tend, and are
eternally, as it were, striving after. And if God be this center, then
God aimed at himself. And herein it appears, that as he is the first
author of their being and motion, so he is the last end, the final
term, to which is their ultimate tendency and aim.

[282] We may judge of the end that the Creator aimed at, in
the being, nature, and tendency he gives the creature, by the mark
or term which they constantly aim at in their tendency and eternal
progress; though the time will never come, when it can be said it
is attained to, in the most absolutely perfect manner.

[283] But if strictness of union to God be viewed as thus infinitely exalted; then the creature must be regarded as nearly and
closely united to God. And viewed thus, their interest must be
viewed as one with God's interest; and so is not regarded properly
with a disjunct [i.e., disconnected] and separate, but an undivided
respect. And as to any difficulty of reconciling God's not making

---

[114] "Celerity" means rapidity or speed.

the creature his ultimate end, with a respect properly distinct from a respect to himself; with his benevolence and free grace, and the creature's obligation to gratitude, the reader must be referred to Chapter One, Section Four, Objection Four, where this objection has been considered and answered at large.

[284] If by reason of the strictness of the union of a man and his family,[115] their interest may be looked upon as one, how much more so is the interest of Christ and his church—whose first union in heaven is unspeakably more perfect and exalted, than that of an earthly father and his family—if they be considered with regard to their eternal and increasing union? Doubtless it may justly be esteemed so much one, that it may be sought, not with a distinct and separate, but an undivided respect. It is certain that what God aimed at in the creation of the world, was the good that would be the consequence of the creation, in the whole continuance of the thing created.

It will take an eternity of increasing joy to experience all the fullness of God

[285] It is no solid objection against God aiming at an infinitely perfect union of the creature with himself, that the particular time will never come when it can be said, the union is now infinitely perfect. God aims at satisfying justice in the eternal damnation of sinners; which will be satisfied by their damnation, considered no otherwise than with regard to its eternal duration. But yet there never will come that particular moment, when it can be said, that now justice is satisfied. But if this does not satisfy our modern freethinkers who do not like the talk about satisfying justice with an infinite punishment; I suppose it will not be denied by any, that God, in glorifying the saints in heaven with eternal felicity, aims to satisfy his infinite grace or benevolence, by the bestowment of a good infinitely valuable, because eternal: and yet there never will come the moment, when it can be said, that *now* this infinitely valuable good has been actually bestowed.

E N D

---

[115] This use of the word "strict" in reference between a man and his family should caution us not to interpret the "strict union" between God and his people as a divinization of man. See footnotes 42-46, 104, 113.

✳️ desiring**God**

Desiring God is a ministry that exists to spread a passion for the supremacy of God in all things for the joy of all peoples through Jesus Christ. We love to spread the truth that God is most glorified in us when we are most satisfied in him. John Piper receives no royalties from the books he writes—they are all reinvested into the ministry of Desiring God. It's all designed as part of our vision to spread this passion to others.

With that in mind, we invite you to visit the Desiring God website at desiringGod.org. You'll find twenty-five years' worth of free sermons by John Piper in manuscript, and hundreds in downloadable audio formats. In addition there are free articles and information about our upcoming conferences. An online store allows you to purchase audio albums, God-centered children's curricula, books and resources by Noël Piper, and over thirty books by John Piper. You can also find information about our radio ministry at desiringGodradio.org.

DG also has a whatever-you-can-afford policy, designed for individuals without discretionary funds. If you'd like more information about this policy, please contact us at the address or phone number below.

We exist to help you treasure Jesus Christ above all things. If we can serve you in any way, please let us know!

Desiring God
2601 East Franklin Avenue
Minneapolis, MN 55406-1103

Telephone: 1.888.346.4700
Fax: 612.338.4372
Email: mail@desiringGod.org
Web: desiringGod.org

SCRIPTURE INDEX

PERSON INDEX

SUBJECT INDEX